BEHIND THE STARE

BEHIND THE STARE

GEOFF PROCTOR

Published in the United States of America
Published by Deeds Publishing, Marietta, GA
www.deedspublishing.com

Library of Congress Cataloging-in-Publications Data is available upon request.
ISBN 978-1-937565-33-6

Books are available in quantity for promotional or premium use. For information, write Deeds Publishing, PO Box 682212, Marietta, GA 30068 or info@deedspublishing.com.

First Edition, 2012

10 9 8 7 6 5 4 3 2 1

DEDICATION

To Nadia, for your love, patience, and companionship.
To Atticus and Andriy, for your inspiration.
To Dad, Sue, and Annie for your encouragement.
To Martha (Mato), for your support.
To Mom and Uncle Marky, for your eternal presence.

CONTENTS

FOREWORD
BY SVEN NYS

Many years ago I met an individual with a tremendous passion for cyclocross. This individual was the national team coach for the United States Cyclocross team. He asked me for an interview about my lifestyle, diet, training, competitions, mental preparation, entourage, etc.

I immediately had a sense that Geoff was a person who himself had a lot of experience coaching young riders and carried that passion for cyclocross with him wherever he went. His thoughts about coaching our young cyclocross riders parallel mine and he had an immediate understanding of what I was talking about. It was a fantastic conversation in which I asked him some questions about cyclocross in the United States.

It was evident that we both had the same opinions about the future of our sport; we both had a strong desire for cyclocross to become an international sport with the larger challenge, the Olympics.

Throughout the years we have remained in contact and currently we both serve on the UCI cyclocross committee with the intention to grow the sport, not just in just in Belgium but also abroad because there is a real fear that we could lose cyclocross as a top sport.

As my career comes to a close I am preparing to enhance cyclocross in the future, make it more professional, coach young riders, provide mental support, teach love for the bike, how to make your hobby your profession and use your nutrition optimally.

There is a lot of work to be done in the future, and individuals like Geoff are of crucial importance to remain optimistic. To everyone who reads this book, I'd like to say that everything starts with passion, discovering the world through sport, feeling joy and sadness, day after day all year long thinking about your passion, feeling your body grow stronger, becoming world champion, dominating cyclocross for several years, managing defeat, pain, pressure, and finally passing these experiences on to the next generation. These are the things I lived through and still enjoy doing. I look forward to work on a lot of things with Geoff in the future. Cyclocross has grown tremendously in the past few years in the United States, and to bring these worlds together is wonderful.

The first steps have been made. The World Championship in Louisville is very important for our sport. Europe is coming to you and it will be an amazing event. It will increase the exposure of our sport.

In 2011 at the press conference in Koksijde, Belgium, I announced I would be racing my last World Championship because I feel that it will be difficult for me to become world champion again. I am a cyclist who is most successful when I can be consistent throughout the season with few ups and downs, and ride hard year round. However, as ambassador of an international sport I cannot be absent in Louisville and feel the need to help promote cyclocross in the United States. Therefore, I will be at the start of the World Championship in Louisville at 36 years of age, full of ambition to once again become world champion. With the support of the people in the United States, I will dig deep once more. [And] hopefully inspire a lot of young riders to take up cyclocross.

Geoff, I would like to congratulate you for the way you have always fought for the sport. Cyclocross in the U.S. can be proud of you because without all your hard work, we would only be practicing cyclocross in Belgium. That should never happen because this sport is too beautiful to disappear.

When I hang up my wheels in 2014, I hope to walk the same path you have and pass on the love of cyclocross to all the world.

See you in the field,
Sven Nys

Vele jaren geleden heb ik een persoon leren kennen uit de verenigde staten die zijn passie veldrijden was. Een persoon die op dat moment bondscoach was van het veldrijden in de States. Hij vroeg of hij een interview kon hebben over mijn leefwereld, voeding,training , wedstrijden , mentale begeleiding, entourage, enz…

Onmiddellijk had ik het gevoel dat Geoff een persoon was die zelf veel ervaring had met opleiding van jonge renners en de passie van het veldrijden echt met zich mee droeg overal waar hij kwam. Hij denkt op vlak van opleiding net het zelfde als ik, en snapte direct wat ik allemaal bedoelde, het werd een super fijn gesprek, waar ook ik soms vragen stelde over het veldrijden in de Vs.

Snel werd duidelijk dat we dezelfde mening hadden over de toekomst van onze sport. We wilden alle twee dat het veldrijden een internationale sport werd met als grote uitdaging de Olympische Spelen.

Nu zoveel jaren later zijn we contact blijven houden, en zitten we samen in de UCI veldrit commissie en hopen we nog steeds dat we onze sport groter kunnen maken, niet in Vlaanderen maar daar buiten, want de schrik om het veldrijden te verliezen zit er toch wel wat in.

Ondertussen zit ik aan het einde van mijn carreire en heb ik ook al stappen ondernomen om in de toekomst het veldrijden verder te proffessionaliseren,opleiding van jonge renners, mentale begeleiding, de liefde voor de fiets, van uw hobby uw beroep maken, je voeding optimaal benutten.

Er is in de toekomst nog zeer veel werk te doen en mensen zoals Geoff zijn van cruciaal belang om optimist te blijven.

Ik zou iedereen die dit boek leest graag meegeven dat alles begint met passie, de wereld verkennen via sport, vreugde en verdriet, hard werken, alle dagen van het jaar denken aan je passie, je lichaam sterker voelen worden, wereldkampioen worden, het veldrijden een aantal jaren kunnen domineren, kunnen omgaan met verlies, pijn, druk, en uiteindelijk al deze ervaring kunnen doorgeven aan de jongere generatie. Dit zijn de dingen die ik heb meegemaakt en nog steeds met heel veel plezier ervaar. Ik hoop dat ik in de toekomst nog veel dingen samen met Geoff kan doen, het veldrijden in de Vs is de laatste jaren

echt ongelofelijk gegroeid en de twee werelden bij elkaar brengen, dat zou schitterend zijn.

De eerste stappen zijn gezet, het wereldkampioenschap in

Louiville zijn super belangrijk voor onze sport. Europa komt naar jullie toe, en het zal een geweldig evenement worden, de uitstalling van onze sport zal er op vooruitgaan.

Ik heb vorig jaar gezegd aan de pers dat Koksijde mijn laatste wk zou zijn, omdat ik voel dat het voor mij moeilijker wordt om nog wereldkampioen te worden. Ik ben een renner die veel beter tot zijn recht komt over een volledig seizoen, regelmaat, geen pieken en dalen, hard fietsen en heel jaar door, dat is wat ik wil. Maar als ambassadeur van een internationale sport kan ik niet wegblijven en wil ik mijn sport mee promoten in de Vs. Daarom zal ik met veel ambitie toch proberen om nogmaals op mijn 36 wereldkampioen te worden. Met de steun van de mensen uit de Vs zal ik nogmaals het beste uit mezelf halen. En hopelijk weer zeer veel jongeren aanzetten om met veldrijden te starten.

Geoff ik wil je graag nog een ding zeggen, proficiat voor de manier waarop je altijd voor deze sport hebt gevochten, het veldrijden in de VS mag trots zijn op jou, want zonder al het harde werk zouden we in de toekomst enkel nog aan veldrijden doen in Vlaanderen en dat mag niet gebeuren, deze sport is te mooi om te laten verdwijnen.

Als ik stop in 2014 zal ik dezelfde weg bewandelen van jou, de liefde voor deze sport doorgeven aan de hele wereld.

See you in the feeld,

SVEN NYS

Sven Nys and author Geoff Proctor, Baal, (June 2012)

LOCATIONS

"He started nervously for the stoneblock for he could no longer quench the flame in his blood."

—James Joyce, A *Portrait of the Artist as a Young Man*

PROLOGUE

In the fall of 2007, I was awarded a one-year sabbatical from my position as a high school English teacher in Helena, Montana, to write a book about a passion in my life—the sport of cyclocross—and to fulfill a personal tenet I hold about my profession: teachers of writing should *walk the talk* and engage in the practice of writing themselves. Needless to say—now some five years later—I have a newfound respect for the demands I put on my students. Writing is hard work.

Equally hard has been capturing the story, in which I've not only been a fan, but also a competitor, a U.S. team coach, a manager, a technical director, a promoter, an official, and—now—a member of the International Cycling Union (UCI) Cyclocross Commission, a multi-national panel that oversees the development of the sport.

As complex as my involvement has become, there's no debating how it started. This story took root one unforgettable day many years ago—January 26, 1986—when I was teaching English in Portugal.

My journal reads:

It's late Sunday afternoon in my Lisbon apartment. I've been grading papers all day. I flick on my colossally decrepit barrio television. Foggy reception around the edges. Diffused grains of black and white. Specks of rain swell to tuber-like projections across the screen. Dark. Ominous.

Through the haze, indistinguishably muddied figures churn by bike through a cow pasture. RPM's under 50. A leader passes, laboring up some planked stairs, bike slung over his right shoulder, his free hand pushing down on his left knee for support.

And then—in an instant—the camera catches his empty stare.

Eyes of struggle. Sockets of strain.

They seem to fix on something beyond the camera.

Transcendent. Horse-like.

I'm glued.

I discover that this is the World Championship being telecast from Lembeek, Belgium. I see the snot of weather. And I witness the once-but-not-future king, Belgian rider Roland Liboton, with no answer. Four times wereldkampioen.

But, no more.

In that one frame, that one glimpse, I see something that ignites me. A flinting. The sparking of a quest.

Toward understanding? Toward epiphany?

Maybe. What I do know is that any answers are held in those eyes. In that numb stare. The stony gaze knows something I do not.

It starts here.

Man v. nature.

Man v. man.

Man v. himself.

In the Low Countries, they call it "riding in the field."

In the Low Countries, they call it "veldrijden."

Soon after, armed with a few pirated World Championship videos from the late 1980s—and fortified with *VeloNews* articles about European cyclocross and Simon Burney's classic book, *Cyclocross*—a few cycling buddies and I built our own 'cross courses in Montana and dreamed big.

I was in my late 20's at the time. As a latecomer, my ensuing results on an amateur cyclocross team in Europe, in national-level U.S. races, and as a three-time member of the U.S. World Championships team—in Italy, 1993; Belgium, 1994; and France, 1996—were modest at best. But through it all, I sensed that somehow my journey was tied up in that Lisbon apartment moment.

In 2002, I was appointed national team coach for American junior and under-23 riders at the World Championships. Taking place annually in late January somewhere in Europe, the "Worlds" serve as the competitive crescendo to the cyclocross season. In preparation, I began directing racing camps in Belgium to ready our nation's best young riders in their final push for the championships. This annual experience, the mud-in-your-face reality check known as EuroCrossCamp, has just completed its ninth season.

But I wasn't satisfied with only these sporadic stints at the sport's biggest races. I still had too many unanswered questions.

What is it about a sport, I wondered, that draws 35 million European television viewers? What brings 60,000 plus spectators to a booze-lathered frenzy, akin to the madness reserved in America for NASCAR, college football, and NFL playoffs? Who are these rock—no, dirt—stars? What's the real story behind the world's great riders—the number-one in the sport, Sven Nys; the down-home reality show celeb Bart Wellens; the hard-fighting American Jonathan Page; the calculating Erwin Vervecken; the wunderkind Lars Boom; and the dozens of others who endure the pain, mud, cold, and brutality of European cyclocross?

What are they like behind the scenes, at home, in quiet-happy-weak moments, or deep within their abstemious training regimens? How do they manage to ride, slog, climb and fly over the toughest 'cross circuits in the world? Through snow, ice, puddles, sand, pasture, cow and pig shit. On-road, off-road, on the bike, off the bike. Shouldering and running with the bike when it's too steep to ride. Hurdling obstacles at speed, running up stairs and vertiginous steeps. Dismounting as many as thirty times per race and remounting in fluid motion. Navigating smash-ups, off-cambers, hairpins, precipitous "death drops," to conquer the most intense hour in all of cycling. What inhuman resolve does it take to grind off every shred of energy to the point of dementia? Where—in the legs, the lungs, the mind, the heart—the hell does it come from?

Michel Wuyts, the venerable Belgian TV cycling commentator, once described it to me this way: "This sport has everything you could want. It lasts only one hour. When there are enough good riders, the battle is huge. And, to watch on television, it feels so good when you are on your couch, near a wood fire, warm, and watching the riders suffer and struggle against the elements of nature. It's fantastic."

Wuyts's words remind me of one sufferfest I experienced firsthand: the 1994 World Championships in the war-bunkered sand dunes of coastal Belgium.

Koksijde.

Even the venue's name sounds harsh to the ear. It's the sport's biggest stage. Wuyts calls the race, which I'm riding as a member of the undermanned American team. My first and lasting impression: astonishment at the speeds of the front guys as I'm lapped and pulled. At the halfway point, Dutch sensation Richard Groenendaal leads the brilliant Belgian Paul Herijgers—blasphemy for the partisan crowd. It takes another interminable fifteen minutes for Herijgers to lock in on his prey. Then, in one brazen swoop, Herijgers actually rides up alongside Groenendaal and nearly bearhugs the Dutchman with his right arm. Blue sleeve on orange shoulder. As if to say: "Valiant, dude, but not on my turf. It's over now."

And then there's Herijgers's last lap attack on the famous sanded incline, fellow Belgian Erwin Vervecken and Groenendaal in close pursuit. Fans—who during earlier laps only jumped in wild gesticulation—now literally kneel and spread-eagle on stomachs to pound fists into sand for Herijgers and Vervecken to bring it on home.

Veldrijden.

Veldriligion.

It's the first time the term occurs to me. The first instance where I truly witness this kind of sporting passion. Herijgers wins the victor's rainbow jersey—"*een absolute triomf*" for Belgium, Wuyts calls it. Groenendaal takes a close second and Vervecken settles for bronze. I head back to our team tent, physically crushed, but aglow with what I've seen. I weave in and out of the throngs. At one point, I'm forced to step over a sudsed-out zealot.

He's face down. Motionless in the sand.

I ask myself—what kind of athlete, what kind of sport, brings pilgrims *beyond* their knees?

In 2007, I set out to find the answer.

With the various hats I wear, I'd surely have better access to 'cross stars than most. I'd also be able to indulge in a related mission: my personal crusade to boost cyclocross to a rightful spot in the winter Olympics, since its non-Olympic status has relegated it to undeserved obscurity outside of Europe. Given the sport's huge popularity and historic importance abroad, Olympic exclusion suggests—no, screams—injustice.

The omission stems from a rule that all winter Olympic sports must take place on snow or ice. Cyclocross, with its September-to-February season, plays out on snow and ice, but also on dirt, grass, mud and sand, among other surfaces. In recent years, some people in cyclocross have argued that the sport should be included in the summer Olympics. But given the existing plethora of summer Olympic cycling disciplines—road, track, mountain bike, and BMX (added in 2008)—and considering the sport's heritage of adverse conditions and hundred-year fall/winter history, sentiments prevail that a winter slot represents cyclocross's best chance. And why not? The sport's simplicity, tradition, gravitas and objective scoring (with timed finishes instead of subjective judging) are at least as compelling as, say, the recently added ski cross.

It's a pity that it's not an Olympic sport yet, as Michel Wuyts told me. "You want to know what cyclocross can do to people?" he added. "I watch my daughter, in her third year studying psychology, very intelligent. She's always very quiet, very serious with her studies—but when she watches a cyclocross race, she loses her calm. First, she begins to shout, then she's jumping around, and by the end, she's standing on her chair, yelling at the TV. It's amazing. Truly crazy, really."

To understand the craziness.

This was the framework for my sabbatical year. I would follow and focus on the 2007-2008 European cyclocross season.

It would be full cyclocross immersion.

To find answers.

To what lies behind the stare.

Sven Nys (Oudenaarde 2007)

To the Pit

Photo: Tom Robertson

1: SONGBIRDS

Early July 2007. West Flanders. A windless morning sun. I ride in a reverent daze.

I'm near one of my winter cyclocross camp's trusted training grounds, the Ardooieveld, or Ardooie forest, where we ride in December's muck of leaves and frigid puddles. To get out of the wind, as it were.

But there's none of that inclemency or urgency now. It's July and I'm in Belgium doing some national team coaching on the road. I'm lost in the warmth of the moment, pedaling free, easy.

Abruptly, I'm shaken from my quixotic reverie by a row of cars parked down a side lane. What the hell? They weren't there yesterday. I slow. Nondescript Euro sedans line one side of the road. A row of maybe fifteen men sit on stools, some ten paces apart from each other. The men solemnly stare at little wooden boxes placed a meter in front of them. What the hell?

I soft pedal and circle, trying to conjure the meaning. Flandrian mecca? Ritual? Some sort of cobra ready to coil out of those little boxes? Should I ride up and query the lone figure making his authoritative rounds to each sitter, each box? Or maybe just stop and watch? The air is quiet and still.

Not wanting to disturb, I go for another lap, allowing my curiosity time to incubate. I come 'round again. Nothing's changed. Tall, yellowing corn stalks sway softly in the incipient sun.

Returning to the U.S.A. Team House in industrial Izegem—my home away from home—I can't contain my bafflement. I describe the scene to my most trusted camp soigneur, team caretaker Chris De Vos, aka "Fox," responsible for everything from massage and prepping race food to loading van luggage. He meets my questions with raucous laughter.

What I've witnessed, he tells me when he recovers, is the steeped Flemish tradition of *vinkenzetting*, or finch sitting, where the object is to have your prized songbird sing as many calls as it can within an hour. The owner of the winning bird gains financial glory—depending on the bets—as well as affirmation for dedication, preparation, and discipline.

I head for the showers, not sure what's more incongruous—the image of a bunch of older men genuflecting in front of little boxes aside some Flemish cornfield, or Fox's elaborate, provincially prideful explanation. But then again, I'm not surprised at my discovery. I've spent the better part of my adult life intrigued by another deeply European obsession where the competitor who finds a way to make his pedals sing the strongest in an hour goes home a champion. A sport that, when viewed from afar, across the cluttered landscape of modern sport, seems nothing more than insular and incomprehensible, yet when viewed from within is as rich and faceted as an Antwerp diamond. A sport that so best captures the essence of competition and athletic endeavor, it's hard to fathom why it isn't an obsession on the broadest scale.

***

I stand on the start line—mid-July 2007—at the Grand Prix Adolphe Thaon race in the tiny French-speaking hamlet of Bury, Belgium. I have eight American *nieuwelingen* (juniors aged 15 and 16) under my charge. It's their first Euro road race and their first time on the continent. They're understandably nervous, with nothing but foreign faces mingling outside the finish-line fencing. I feel a friendly nudge from the side.

"Hey."

It's Mario De Clercq, the three-time world cyclocross champion and former road racing pro.

"Long time no see," I respond warmly. It's been six months since we last crossed paths at the World Championships in Zeddam, Netherlands. I don't know Mario well, but I bump into him on a regular and friendly basis. The taut creases around his thin eyes and his silver-toothed grin suggest someone who's seen a few finish lines in his day.

We have a lot to talk about, starting with his son, Angelo, who's in the race, and Mario's natural inclination to help his son learn the trade; and moving on to his role as a trainer for top American 'crosser Jonathan Page and his new role directing Page's new pro team, Sunweb-Pro Job.

We do not talk about Mario's past doping controversy, dubbed "the Landuyt affair." Some things are better left unsaid.

Our amiable conversation cuts off. The race is starting.

Sixty kilometers later, with just over a lap to go, I've got two guys in the leading breakaway of four riders. The break has maybe a minute's lead on the peloton. I head out to look for a quiet section on the course to give encouragement and relay instructions for the finale. I position myself in a field about two kilometers from the finish line.

Another nudge.

It's Mario again. He's out of breath.

"The big guy in the blue and white, he's a good sprinter," he utters between breaths. Man, I think to myself. Even though Mario's own kid is in the race and he'd more than likely favor a Belgian win over one by my "foreign" American team, he's just given me a tip to help my guys reach the podium. Dumbfounded at his courtesy, I thank him and take my spot.

The break zooms by.

"You have to attack, guys. Don't wait for the sprint," I bark.

After they pass, I go into Euro Mission Mode—cutting through fields, jetting around buildings—to get to the finish line.

The winner, it turns out, is the big Belgian—seemingly too big to be 16 years old—by the name of Jonathan Breyne. The blue-and-white guy.

My guys, Jacob Rathe from Oregon and Cody Foster from Texas, take second place and fourth place, respectively. Chapeau.

Mario's son, Angelo, slumps disconsolately in the car, having had a bad race.

I extend my hand to Mario, thanking him for the heads-up, even if it didn't pan out for my riders this time. I tell him I hope to see him again.

"Don't worry," he says. "It's not such a big place, this world of cycling. We meet again."

He winks.

***

A few days later, the riders and I spend the afternoon-into-evening in nearby Diksmuide, taking in a must-see European cycling event, the ritualized showcase known as the post-Tour criterium. These two-hour races feature many of the recently finished Tour de France stars, as well as top cyclocross and mountain bike pros looking for some training.

After much pre-race pomp—with retired road racing heroes like the Lion of Flanders himself, Johan Museeuw, and other dignitaries riding on the decks of open convertibles for a lap-waving loop—the race gets going in fading, festive light.

As the riders depart, revered racing celebs Tom Boonen, Danilo Di Luca, and Frank Vandenbroucke (who would die in 2009 of a pulmonary embolism) garner the biggest cheers. But almost equally loud are the roars for Belgium's Bart Wellens, the 29-year-old extroverted cyclocross superstar from Vorselaar.

Bart's profile is understandably huge. He's been a television star for three seasons on the Belgian reality show *Wellens en Wee,* which chronicles his every move with his Fidea teammates, both on and off the bike. Foremost for me, Bart is a 'crossman among road racers.

For the road pros, post-Tour criteriums are a just dessert. A chance to milk their recent Grand Tour and spring classic performances. For Bart, criteriums are similarly about increasing his fan base, but they also represent a chance to work. To train. To prepare for the real season. The winter season.

Naturally, I watch him more than the others. Compact, efficient, born with a bike in his hand, as they say.

Around and around they go.

Gradually, as the laps pile on and the dense stone buildings cast longer shadows across the crowd-lined cobbled square, I feel disconnected. It's not like the crowd isn't having a good time. It's not like the riders aren't going fast. The course is pretty narrow and guys are attacking off the front. Maybe it's the choreographed nature of these events that has me out of sorts. Everyone knows these races are as fixed as a Disney script. Preset by organizers and riders to champion the best, most local rider, the races convey a certain sense of artifice that subverts the whole affair. It's sporting as entertainment rather than sporting in the Tennysonian sense of "nature, red in tooth and claw." I decide to try and find Bart after the race. Maybe he has an antidote for my ennui.

He's drenched with sweat and, as usual, in good spirits. I've been an acquaintance of Bart's since 2001, when Erwin Vervecken and I stopped by his house during a road ride. Now, we chat first about a constant topic for all cyclists: training. It's going well, he tells me. He's getting in 100 kilometers on the road in the mornings and another 80 to 100 kilometers in the evening during the criteriums.

"For the day, we can get maybe 250 K's for training, so the time on the bike is very good for us," he says.

"But where's the drama? Where's the fight?" I ask.

"I know, I know," he agrees. "In cyclocross, you have bad fields, you need to run, it's cold, it's raining. On the road, and especially in these criteriums, it's just one thing, just riding and going fast to the finish, and it's done. In the big road races, you can sit 180 kilometers in the wheel [behind the leaders] and if you're good, if you have a good sprint, okay—good condition, good team, and do nothing, then you have a nice victory. On the road, you can win if you're 95 percent.

"But in cyclocross, if you're bad, then you're not the winner," he says. "In cyclocross, it's honest, the best guy wins mostly. In the beginning of the 'cross season, when the races are fast, you can maybe stay in the group of five or six guys, but you can still never win if you're not 100 percent."

I like the honest part. The best guy wins mostly. Sure, the occasional cyclocross race is thrown, bought, sold, but in my experience, Bart speaks mostly the truth.

Mostly the truth.

I love the Belgian idiom for that. *Het achterste van zijn tong niet laten zien*: literally, "not speaking with the end of your tongue." Americans might call it cunning. Either way, Bart's got it and he knows how to use it.

I round up my guys and, tired—it's almost midnight—we drive back to Izegem. On the way, we recap the race. Stijn Devolder clad in the black-yellow-red Belgian road champion's jersey, recent Tour sprint winner Boonen in commemorative green, and Giro d'Italia champion Di Luca adorned in the *maglia rosa*—fancy that—all podium. On the top step: West Flanders local boy Devolder from St. Lodewijk-Deerlijk. All according to plan. Belgian tricolor flanked by green to one side, pink to the other.

Not a speck of mud to be seen.

Ardooie, West Flanders

Chris De Vos aka "Fox"   Photo: Matthew J. Clark

2: SVEN THE CANIBAAL

"Blessed are those

Whose blood and judgment are so well commeddled

That they are not a pipe for Fortune's finger

To sound what stop she please."

—Shakespeare, *Hamlet*

EARLY AUGUST 2007

Slivers of sun angle through rowed pine trees on a quiet road. The trees crown a canopied ridge with verdant meadows sloping off in both directions. Wisps of condensation dance off the warming pavement. Down the shady ridge side, mourning doves woo-woo and, faintly, a lone rooster crows. Somewhere on the sunny side, a farmer's tractor revs and a carpenter's hammer pounds home. Another day begins. Another tranquil country lane bathes in the ease and flow of Belgian summer. Another pastoral *helling* wakes to the sun. I'm here, parked, and walking along the top of one of the most storied promenades of pavement in international cyclocross, the midpoint of the home parcours of the greatest 'cross rider ever, Sven Nys.

I have a few minutes to kill before I meet up with the 31-year-old from Baal. I've chosen this meeting spot not just to get a sense of what it's like to train here, not just to get a cultural feel for this small hamlet in the heart of provincial Vlaams-Brabant, not just to compare summer laziness with the winter craziness I experience when I'm here as national cyclocross coach. And not just to spend another moment on the hillock where I've greeted the past five New Years during Sven's hometown race, which happens every January 1.

I'm also here because somehow I sense—as a competitor and coach—that my twenty-plus-year quest is turning a corner. For decades, I've been searching for the secret to the sport and the reason it's hooked me so hard—a search for the secret to all sports, perhaps. And now I'm turning toward ... what? A merging of all the evaluation, planning, implementation? A converging of the endless hours of examination, experience, and practice?

Maybe.

But they're here—those answers. Somewhere. In the air. In the dirt. In the stairs.

Stairs?

Nearing the top of the stand of trees, the summer landscape seems surreal. No 15,000 people. No massive aluminum bridged flyover. No frenetic mechanics chuffing bikes back and forth to the hoses. No mud.

I've lost my winter bearings.

Can I even find those stairs?

But, then, after a short walk, led on by some sort of ancestral homing instinct all 'crossers seem to possess, I spy—well—there they are. A neglected set of steps, maybe ten meters left of the main driveway to a private home, devoid of any sort of well-beaten path or seeming destination, grass growing through knot-holed weathered planks embedded in rust-colored earth. The kind of nondescript stairs you might find in a city park leading up or down to some playground equipment or picnic area. From where do they come, to where do they go?

***

In many ways, a set of cyclocross stairs is a central and fitting metaphor. For the 'cross rider, stairs only go in one direction—up. For the most part, any time 'crossers are going down, they're on the bike. And to see a 'cross rider running up is to know—immediately—that this pursuit is something different, something remarkable. Bikes are made to be ridden, not carried. And here is a sport that combines riding a bike through every condition imaginable and running with it slung over a shoulder when the going gets too steep, too muddy, too arduous to ride. For good measure, it's also a sport obsessed, beyond the literal, to the figurative concept of moving up. Up the rankings, up the salary scale, up the team hierarchy, up the public opinion polls, up the ladder.

In many ways, this set of 'cross stairs is also a fitting metaphor for Sven Nys, the world's number one. A dominator in every sense of the word—from his series titles to his World Cup wins—Sven, by all accounts, is the best of his generation and all the others. Ten years in the orange colors of the Rabobank team, and now at the brink of essentially owning the ladder. To read his autobiography, to spend time with him, to watch him race is to witness ascendancy. Apotheosis.

I turn away from the stairs, reminding myself to ask Sven about them. Within seconds—the rooster quiet now—Sven greets me. We jump in our cars, and I struggle to tail his black custom paint-jobbed Nissan Pathfinder through narrow farm roads down to his house. Despite having exchanged greetings with him for five years running and visited with him at countless races and in the occasional stark but obligatory post-race anti-doping chamber, I've never spent time with him where all great athletes are most comfortable—in their own home.

We arrive. Brick-red roof tiles that look like half-shelled flower pots, tight green canopied grass around the back, a mixture of glass and earth-toned brick: the Residentie Family Nys seems characteristic of many in Flemish-speaking Belgium. From its well-pruned trees and blooming hyacinths to its cool marble floors and understated interior decor, the home is a proud showcase of the legendary Flemish work ethic. Sven's wife, Isabelle—chief supporter, caregiver, cook, handler of all paperwork and emails—joins us in their bright, simple living room. Their 5-year-old son, Thibau, plays outside with a friend.

We sit on white leather couches facing a giant flat screen television. Sven's glass-framed 2005 rainbow jersey from St. Wendel, Germany refracts the glinting sun.

To get to know Sven is to begin to understand the meaning of the word "consummate." With every turn of phrase, every data point of analysis, every anecdote, he exudes fastidiousness, implacability. As down-to-earth as he is, as friendly as his bluish gray eyes can be, you can cut the aura with a hatchet.

Clad in a casual navy Rabobank T-shirt, Sven converses freely.

For three hours.

*****

How do you do it? That's what I'd like to ask, but don't. Sven winds up answering anyway, via a completely different question. A question about the infamous tree move.

It's my all-time favorite cyclocross moment, a brazen bid to win the 2002 World Championships in Zolder, Belgium. Some 60,000 people, the largest audience ever to witness a 'cross race, teem the circuit in and around the Formula One racetrack. It's my first year as U.S. Cyclocross coach and I'm at course-side, yelling in my radio to alert our mechanics in the pit about how our guys are doing. But I can't cut through the noise.

It's pandemoniously loud.

So I just watch. And a familiar scenario plays out. Three Belgians—Sven, Mario De Clercq, and Tom Vanoppen—punish each other, lap after lap. It will take something special for Sven to avoid a sprint against the superior speed of De Clercq, I realize. I watch on the JumboTron as De Clercq and Vanoppen exchange words to begin the last lap.

They're planning something—I can feel it. Sven's gonna get the flick. No matter that they're all from the same country, that they're all going to podium. At this level, on this stage, it's pure dog.

Half a lap to go, on the upper part of the course, and I can't hear myself think. Then, in the filtered din of cigarette smoke and etiolated Belgian light, I see something strange.

Sven is sprinting Mario for the right to be first down a small hill that leads to the course's only run-up. As Mario leads to the last corner before the descent, I piece it together. Sven's only chance to outgun Mario is to be first to the descent so he can have an unobstructed shot at the run-up. But Sven is too far behind. There's no way he can do it.

What happens next is pure genius.

Sven drifts to the right and moves forward on the bars to suck up a pine-needled bump on a heretofore unseen outside line *through* a couple of trees. It's a line too dangerous to consider, the speed unconscionable. But swooping around the corner, *around the tree*, neck in neck, left foot unclipped to somehow tripod his railing speed, Sven overtakes Mario.

"When I saw Sven go between the trees on the side of the course to pass Mario, I started to cry," Isabelle says.

"I still think it was my most beautiful moment of my career," Sven picks up. "I was first down the climb. First into the uphill and I rode the whole climb. I got the gap I needed. Even though it didn't work—Mario was very strong in the sprint—it showed what I can do, what I will do, to win. That I can use my head, and that I can use my heart to give it everything."

The move looked spontaneous, but wasn't, Sven says. "I put a special 26 cog on for that climb, for just that moment." Mario prevailed. "But I was not disappointed with that race because I did everything that I can to win."

So there it is. The first whiff of what I'm questing for. The nascent crossing of some threshold, a keystone turned upwards. When all things are considered, when everything is factored in and tallied—the training, the personnel, the psychology, the implementation—there is indeed an extra dimension that only a few athletes in the world possess. A sixth sense. An inner chamber to the competitive soul that makes the difference.

Sven moves on to talk about the externals. His support team is paramount, he says. In the tradition of Lance Armstrong (and cycling in general), Sven tells me he firmly believes in surrounding himself with helpers. With his energetic narration, you can feel the strength he draws from his support staff, his entourage—each member a crucial cog in the process.

Key to the crew is Paul Van Den Bosch, Sven's coach and trainer, who designs all of Sven's training plans and works directly with him during training in the nearby woods. Conveniently, Paul lives 10 km away in Lichtaart, as do a large number of other people supporting Sven and his career.

Fons Wouters, Sven's chief mechanic, takes care of every equipment need, from gluing on hundreds of tires to cleaning Sven's bikes after a training ride in the rain. He works for free.

Gert Leinders, the team doctor, talks to Sven every two months about his training and discusses how he is going; he also watches over Sven's health by checking Sven's iron levels about seven times per season to make sure his counts are normal.

Psychologist Danny Weyns sees Sven for ten to fifteen two-hour sessions per season, offering him soothing music, talks, and occasional massages. He also attends most of the races and works with Sven if he sees the cyclist getting tired.

Rudy De Bie, Belgian National Cyclocross and Mountain Bike coach, advises Sven about hotels, mountain bike racing schedules during the spring and summer, and race selection. An out-of-the-limelight type of guy, but an important voice, Rudy spends 300 days a year traveling, to meet the demands of being the figurehead for Belgian off-road cycling.

Willy Bogaert, the team physiotherapist, gives Sven a massage every Monday to flush his legs from the hard racing, and again every Friday to help him recover from the hard week of training.

Omer Van Noten, 64, a life-long running coach and an advisor to Sven since 2004, trains Sven with running drills.

Guy "Biste" (pronounced "beasty") Verbist—the Rabobank Continental team's soigneur—is Sven's masseuse at all of his races and training camps.

Jerome Galicia, Sven's uncle and current motor-pacing driver, was also Sven's first coach. Sven feels it's very important not to have parents coach their children, to reduce the risk that young riders focus on cycling all day. Jerome served as Sven's coach for the first 11 years of his career.

Francois Nys, Sven's father, drives Sven to all the races and arranges hotel reservations and other logistics. Sven's mother—Vera—is his number-one supporter.

Sven points out that while he does pay some of his staff, a guy like Fons, his mechanic, still happily works for free. There's more appearance money and prize money in the sport these days, so not as many people work for love and glory. Most riders have their own campers, their own power-washers to clean the bikes after the races, and their own paid staffers. But the ancestral past of cyclocross, where supporters contribute to the cause, is still very much alive. A big component in the sport's survival is free help from family and friends.

And the riders need all the help they can get. From an equipment and mechanical standpoint, cyclocross is the most labor-intensive of any cycling discipline. Racers need a pit crew during the race to wash, fix, and ferry bikes to and from pit hoses. Often, fathers, mothers, sisters, brothers, uncles, aunts, and friends all chip in.

I experienced this myself when I raced for a small amateur 'cross team in Switzerland in the early '90s. The cover photo from the local Swiss newspaper *Tages-Anzeiger*, December 23, 1991, shows our team's host-family father doubling as a mechanic, clenching one of our Guerciotti's hub-deep in a swollen river. His ostensible task was to get it clean before the next lap. But the diluvial torrent rendered his job secondary to simply clutching the bike. For dear life. The headline: "Die Lust am Bad im Schlamm."

Desire in the Bath of Mud.

***

Sven tells me he's in the midst of the front-load phase of his training, sticking religiously to the theory that if he has the form to start the season winning, then the other, bigger victories will follow. August 2007 is no different; his training is going smoothly, clinically.

The only hitch has been his lingering Olympic dream. Since cyclocross is not an Olympic sport, Sven's only chance to compete in the 2008 games in Beijing is to make the Belgian Olympic mountain bike team. But recent testing—involving atmospheric simulation in a hypoxic chamber to see how he reacts to hot weather—shows he doesn't perform well in the kind of heat expected for Beijing. Since then, he's apparently scrapped any Olympic hopes.

I let this thread lie. Is it possible that Sven is actually taking himself out of the game?

I ask him about training, honoring his apparent wish to change the subject. This particular week, he says he's training for 25 hours. Four of the seven days involve two sessions per day. Sven boots up his laptop to show me his regimen.

As he does, two notions occur to me. First, there are no secrets here. All the data is available. Freely exchanged. Second, training, training, training defines Sven Nys. To hear him speak about it is to understand what psychologist Mihaly Csikszentmihalyi calls the flow state. An absorption so complete that nothing else seems to matter. Contrary to what we might believe, the best moments in our lives are not passive or receptive, but active, Csikszentmihalyi writes. In an optimal experience, an activity is so enjoyable that time and distraction disappear.

In this moment for Sven, time and distraction truly vanish. His training is quite literally what he eats and breathes.

His PC chimes. Out come the spreadsheets. The pie charts. No power files just yet, so he's not looking at wattage outputs like "functional threshold power," a measure of average power over the course of a hard training session. He says it's not easy to switch over to power recording after compiling ten years of heart rate data, but he wants to work with a power meter in the near future.

"When it comes to improving your fitness, even the slightest percentage points make a difference. And any improvement is good mentally, for the results, for everything," he says. "When you're standing still, it's finished."

Tilting the computer in my direction, he begins to narrate his week. Isabelle drifts in and out, answering doorbells, telephones. Every few minutes or so, I spy their son Thibau ripping around the periphery of the yard on a mini 'cross bike. Lap after lap.

"Monday morning is my first running training of the week," Sven says. "In the past, I only would run with my bike for 50 meters, 100 meters, but now, for the past three to four years with Omer"—his running coach—"I do running training for one hour in the woods. We have a little running course and Omer is there with the chrono urging me on. Always moving. Running up. Running down.

"In the beginning, I would get really sore, but now, it's like how I built up my engine on the road in those early years—I can do it now so strongly."

The daily training includes explosions—full tilt uphill running sprints—and running uphill at various speeds. "We go to the course and Omer says 'Okay, you do a warm-up and then this next lap, you do the three climbs as explosions, then two to three laps easy, and then one lap full on, about three to four minutes.'"

At this point in the season he does this workout two or three times a week, and mixes in running drills on a football field for recuperation.

"It's dangerous to do too much running because it hurts your speed on the bike, but I do it year-round because that's what you need to be a good 'crossman: sprint uphill, then jump on the bike, then off, then again running—explosion. I'm not one who can run for 80 percent of the circuit like in the Belgian Championship last year in Hamme-Zogge, but I'm a good runner when it's all about bursts of running."

I scan the data from that Monday: "On the road bike behind the motorbike"—aka the moto—"for 80 km: 2:11:00; average heart rate 133 beats per minute (bpm); maximum 180," the chart says.

"Just the normal *souplesse*"—literally, suppleness—"training behind the moto," Sven narrates, referring to rides at high rpm's to create a supple feeling in the legs.

On Tuesday he did endurance training—*duurtraining*. "And again emphasizing souplesse, with a heart range of 101-to-130 for 4:08," Sven says.

On Wednesday morning he trained on his 'cross bike with Paul in the woods. "One-and-a-half hours hard training. Interval laps. Warming up with five explosions." Then four laps at 85 percent of maximum heart rate, then three laps at 90 percent, two laps at 95 percent, and one lap à bloc—in the range of 175 bpm average and 195 maximum heart rate.

By the afternoon, he's behind the moto again for two hours of speed training.

"To do it, really hard training, in the woods, you must have a fresh mind. And when Paul is there, yelling 'Come on,' and you're trying to beat your best lap time, it's motivating. Having Paul there means everything. It's much easier to push."

"Thursday," he continues, "I train for five hours endurance with, you see, an average of 134 and a maximum of 183. Very good."

And today?

"Today, after our interview, I go for two hours on the road easy." By evening, he'll compete in a special derny race consisting of heats and finals where each rider has a moto driver to draft behind.

"Finally, tomorrow, Saturday, another two hours in the morning and then in the evening, the post-Tour criterium in the Netherlands and then Sunday a rest day with an easy run for 30 minutes."

"Hard week?" I ask.

His voice seems to fill the room. "My training now is totally different than eight or ten years ago. With my running, my 'cross training, my mountain bike training and, of course, my road training, my altitude work, it's much more varied. And my engine, I have built it up all of these years, so now I can do so many things with it."

"You see here?" He points to another chart that shows altitude blocks—periods when he sleeps in an altitude chamber, a tent-like device that replicates oxygen levels at high altitudes. In so doing, a rider increases his number of oxygen-carrying red blood cells, or hematocrit (the number and size of the red blood cells), so that oxygen is processed more efficiently to help increase endurance. Sven sleeps at altitude before big races, adjusting the elevation up or down depending on how hard he trains.

"If it's a recuperation week, I sleep at 3,000 meters (9,800 feet). If it's a heavy week, with heart rates of 180-plus, then 3,000 meters is too high—I can't recuperate. So for the hard trainings I sleep at 2,600 meters (8,500 feet)."

"You're sleeping now at altitude?" I ask.

"Yes, and some training in the hypoxic chamber."

"Training and sleeping?"

"I'm entering a period where I want to be good—Ireland, the world mountain bike championships, and the first 'cross in Erpe-Mere," he explains. "And then I will do another altitude block in the beginning of October to be ready for the first Superprestige race in Ruddervoorde, the first GVA"—Gazet Van Antwerpen series race—"and the first World Cups."

All this talk about sleep brings an unexpected question. "You want to see our bedroom?" Isabelle says, and beckons.

I mull. An encroachment? An imposition? A violation?

Up past a brimming glass trophy case, Isabelle and Sven provide escort. It doesn't get much more inner sanctum than this.

The bedroom atmosphere approximates 2,400 meters, Sven says. "You feel the high?"

My eardrums feel like tin.

"When I'm going up the stairs fast and come in here, I feel it," Sven says.

I ask him about expense, and Sven says he bought the unit eight years ago for 20,000 euros, or about $20,600. It's saved him from traveling to St. Moritz for August altitude training exposure, as the Fidea team—the most well supported team in Europe—does it.

His natural hematocrit level is 42. "Not very high," he reports.

"When I train really hard"—he motions his hand downward and gives a descending whistle sound—"it goes down. But sleeping in the altitude room, it stays at the same level. In the winter, when I'm racing a lot, I need it to stay at the same level."

"And Isabelle? Where does she sleep?"

"She sleeps too, with me. But she sometimes gets tired from it and takes a nap during the day."

"The sacrifice…" My voice trails off and I'm left in my own thoughts. People don't see the sacrifice. The sacrifice of someone who lives, whose family lives, for a sport.

"Of course," Sven confirms.

Not only would Sven not have it any other way but, more to the point, he can't imagine it any other way.

He has the titles to show for it. In 2004-2005, 25 victories, including cyclocross's Grand Slam—winning the GVA, Superprestige, and World Cup overall titles, plus the Belgian Championship and the World Championship. In 2005-2006, he took the Belgian Championship, and overall titles in the Superprestige, GVA and World Cup. 27 wins in all. Last season, 30 victories along with overall titles in the World Cup, SuperPrestige, and GVA. This upcoming season, he hopes to win still more.

We head back downstairs.

"In my mind, I am 21, not 31," he says. "That's important. When I'm 35, I'll take it year by year. Then I will evaluate: Am I good in my mind, is the condition still good? Because what I do, every second, every day of my life, is cycling."

Some riders win only three or four races a year, he explains. When you win more than 20 races a year, it's all consuming. "It's so mentally heavy to do what I do, a whole year, every day. Even in my three-week break in March"—he and fellow 'cross pro Sven Vantourenout take their families to the Dominican Republic for a vacation—"I still think about my sport, still going for easy running training."

"I don't know, when I reach 35, if I can still do it. If I'm on a level not so high as now, then I stop. It's 100 percent or nothing."

He reconsiders. "Victories are not the most important things," he says. "The most important thing for me is to learn something new every day and to learn each day something about my body. Then the results come by themselves. The results are for the winter. The summer is for your mind, for the pure enjoyment of riding your bike.

"And when I miss a day on the bike, I feel myself sick."

***

I let his remark about the relative unimportance of victories slide. It's obviously a deflection. It's also a contradiction voiced by all top sportsmen. Their drive to win is extraordinarily well developed: it's what makes them successful. But athletes these days are also supposed to pretend they don't love winning "too much." The public wants sports stars to be conquering heroes who are not only supremely talented and dedicated but are also self-effacing, a blend of Michael Jordan and Mother Teresa. Losing is not acceptable, either.

For Sven, two incidents serve as telling examples of the complexity of trying to win with grace.

The first is the well-chronicled incident at the 2000 World Championships in St. Michielgestel, Netherlands, where Sven had to weigh loyalty to his native Belgium against support for his Dutch-based trade team, Rabobank. Poignantly, in cycling, riders always race a World Championship in their national team's uniform, and victory for the country is seen as a source of inimitable pride. By contrast, riders wage every other race during the season in the kit, or uniform, of their team's sponsor (read: the team that pays the rider's salary).

Sven's predicament at the 2000 Worlds was whether to chase down an off-the-front Richard Groenendaal—a Rabobank trade teammate of Sven's, but also a rival Dutch national team member. Groenendaal attacked early in the race and built up a sizable lead. Also in the chasing group, but without the baggage of being Groenendaal's trade teammate, was Mario De Clercq, Sven's countryman. In the end, Mario chased and Sven sat on, riding in Mario's draft. They never caught Groenendaal, and the Dutchman became world champion. The media held nothing back. The newspapers labeled Sven a traitor: a rider who put his Dutch sponsor ahead of his own country.

The final result? Admonition from the masses which eventually melted, but Sven's alleged secessionist tactics still rankle to this day, for the Flemish hard-core nationalists, fans, and press alike.

Fast forward to the final World Cup of 2004 in Pijnakker, Netherlands. Sven has won three of the season's five World Cups and only needs to finish sixth or better to earn the overall series title. Rabobank teammate Richard Groenendaal, ever the master at calculating his own chances, privately knows he's close to the overall title as well. The two men talk before the race and ostensibly agree.

Richard will take the race, Sven gets the overall.

But Lady Fortune plays her hand.

Richard gets off the front again and Sven's legs are bad.

This time, Sven argues for a different aligning of the elements. He urges the playing of the national team card: everyone joining together to help him win. Sven's Belgian countrymen—Bart Wellens, Erwin Vervecken, Tom Vanoppen, Wesley Van Der Linden—say no deal.

"Normally, I shouldn't lose the race, but because of double points, my overall lead is not enough," Sven tells me. "My condition isn't so good and by the last lap, we're all together chasing Groenendaal. I ask the guys for help. No reaction. The only guy to help is Sven Vantourenhout. I never forget that. In the sprint, I have nothing. Richard wins; I come seventh."

Sven sits up. His words become more deliberate.

"That's the day it all changed for me. That day and race permanently on my brain. Pijnakker, February 15, 2004."

Sven declares it his watershed, both to me and in his 2006 book, the autobiography *Ik, Sven Nys*. Meeting everyone else's expectations, playing the dutiful teammate, being defined by others bedamned.

Cyclocross's cannibaal—the cannibal from Baal—is born.

***

It's time for the interview to end. I need to go back to Izegem, and then back to the U.S. It's August. The Flandrian fever for *veldrijden* is beginning to rise. The stories are about to unfold. Just as they have for the past one hundred years in this cycling-mad corner of the world.

Thibau's bike, a Colnago, is quiet now. It's lunchtime. Sven sees me to the door.

"Hey, Sven, what about those stairs?" I remember to ask.

"What stairs?"

"You know, the ones on your parcours. Just past the paved asphalt section on the ridge, just past the rows of trees?"

"Oh, yes. The stairs," he says.

Laughter. He's on to me and where I'm going with my question.

"Years ago, we constructed the stairs because the *reglement*"—the International Cycling Union (UCI) regulation—"says you can only have one place for [planked] obstacles. We already have the set of hurdles near the beer tent. So we thought, 'Okay. We make the stairs, and they become not an official but rather, a natural obstacle.'"

"They're considered a natural obstacle and therefore legal under the rules?"

"Yes, natural. That's why we did it. So I can jump two times in one lap. One time over the hurdles by the beer tent and one time on the stairs.

"And each year," Sven winks, "we go out two or three weeks before, and they're all grown over with grass, and before the race we raise up the planks, make the stairs a little bit higher."

***

I slide into the Team U.S.A. Saab, pop on Euro-homey-time-warp Radio Donna and pin it out of Baal toward the E314, direction Leuven. Bouncin' to Beyoncé.

Baal-Tremulo is also home to up-and-coming Belgian 'cross talent Niels Albert. Cyclocross's biggest stars—Bart Wellens, Erwin Vervecken, Richard Groenendaal, and the Dutch Lars Boom—are all within 30 clicks to the north and east.

Somehow, I have the vague sense that I've spent the morning in the antechamber of the Great Pyramid with pharaoh Sven dispensing girdie stones of knowledge. For sure, one thing is clear: I'm in the valley of kings.

Sven and Thibau, Baal, (August 2007)

Sven and Rudy De Bie, (Igorre 2007)   PHOTOPRESS.BE

Sven and Isabelle

The Stairs, Baal   Photo: Tom Robertson

3: AMERICAN ABROAD

For me, suffering has two meanings:

suffering can be negative.

If you try to suffer for its own sake,

that's bad. That's unhealthy.

There's something wrong in your head.

But when you talk about suffering

that you must get through

and that you can survive through enormous effort.

That is something else.

That is positive, good, and beautiful.

Beautiful because you can think of courage, stamina, loyalty,

the willingness to make sacrifices, modesty, love.

From this perspective, the suffering during training,

during sporting competitions,

while doing one's job which all require great effort,

is the same as religious suffering.

It is love.

It is beautiful.

—*Hell on Wheels*, Team Telekom film

EARLY AUGUST, 2007

Jonathan Page knows suffering. The good kind. The positive kind. Perhaps more than any other top 'crossman. I have sensed this all the years I've known him. How else to explain his pugnacity?

It's a windy mid-summer day as I zip past the most famed cobbled climbs in Belgian road cycling history—the Patersberg, the Oude Kwaremont, the Koppenberg—to arrive in the city of Oudenaarde's twisty narrow streets. Just past the Tour of Flanders museum, I get real-time directions from Jonathan by cell phone.

A few quick turns past the strikingly gothic town hall and I'm at Jonathan's newly purchased row house across from the soccer complex. Good place for running training, I think to myself. Pulling up, I see Jonathan nestling baby Milo in the sling. Jonathan's wife, Cori, a former road and cyclocross racer, and two-year-old daughter, Emma, poke their heads around the red brick entryway. Big family grins, customary for the Page family, greet me. As the first and only American ever to be offered a professional cyclocross contract from a European team, Sunweb-Pro Job, effective July 1, Jonathan is enjoying life. The suffering can wait. The suffering has been worth it.

To know how far Jonathan has come is to understand how precarious his place is in the world of professional cyclocross. And to learn his story is to begin to understand how athletic suffering is, in essence, love.

First impressions of Jonathan "J.P." Page go a long way. Brick-solid, sturdily-muscled, low center of gravity. None of the emaciated, gaunt look that you see in road climbing specialists. Assertive eyes that could just as soon kill you as look at you. And what you see is what you get. Not many pros meet you with a baby around their neck. Right away, if you know anything about Euro cycling mores, you realize that Jonathan's core connection with family runs against the old-school cycling grain.

Devotion to kids? Women's work. Bad for the legs, the old guard says. Behind the scenes, the 'cross world isn't exactly a bastion of feminism.

"It's enough to make you go crazy," Jonathan says.

Cori offers to get some coffee as Jonathan and I sit down in a well-lit living room looking out over their narrow plotted back yard, small shed, and the backs of neighboring row houses.

"According to some people, I should be doing nothing but training, racing, eating, sleeping, and sitting on the sofa. But I don't think I would be better if I did that. I would feel so bad about missing out on my kids' lives and everything else, that I would go nuts," he says.

"It would cause me more stress to sit on the sofa and not be present for my family. I like to mow the lawn, play with my kids, and have coffees on the square with my wife."

Does he ever feel like he's living out a soap opera? Does the fishbowl ever get to be too much?

"Yes! It makes me laugh. Everyone is always telling us to our faces and talking behind our backs about what we should be doing to suit my 'cross racing. But you know what? It's not just about me. If my wife and kids aren't happy, I'm not happy, and I'm not going to perform as good. So what if I take my daughter for a bike ride? Why the hell not? Who are they to judge? Besides, I know who's been there for me all along."

If he did more training, he might win more races, he allows. "But would it mean I am happy? Because that's what matters to me most."

Jonathan proudly shows me what they've done with the house. Refurbished hardwood floors, a skylight in the roof. Modest by a top pro's standards, but just fine for the Pages. They've been in Europe for nearly seven years. It's been a long, long road.

J.P. grew up the youngest of four kids in a divorced household, splitting time between parents in Connecticut and rural New Hampshire. With no great inclination toward school and a love for biking at an early age, he devoted himself to racing, and joined the New England-based Hot Tubes team as a teenager. There he came under the tutelage of team manager Toby Stanton and New England fixtures like Frank McCormack, and he enjoyed a scintillating spell in the junior ranks, winning multiple national titles on the road and in cyclocross.

As with so many pros, he did a lot of soul-searching during his espoir years, ages 19 to 22. In between putting in strong rides, he delivered pizzas and did landscaping. He worked at Keystone ski resort in Colorado. He washed dishes at a fish restaurant in San Diego.

Ultimately, in 2000, he dedicated himself to Euro 'cross, and a new script began. It called for long, slow development and perseverance.

As we head down to the basement to see his trove of bikes and new team kit, I mention my first impression of him—at the 1994 U.S. Cyclocross Nationals at North Sea-Tac, on a course by the airport outside Seattle. As planes roared overhead, I watched kid J.P. take the junior crown, his second win of the season after snagging the junior road title that summer. A few hours later, he finished fourth in the elite race, the category reserved for the best and strongest pros.

"Man, that seems like ancient history," he says, as we step over clothing boxes. Those were hard times, he adds. "From my good juniors years on through starting to live in Europe, it's been rough."

At one point while training and racing, he and Cori cleaned houses for a living or worked at big chain stores taking inventory.

"The inventory job was good because we could pick our own hours. We'd go into a Walmart and have to scan a product and then inventory their stock on that item. We'd often work in the early morning, say from 4:30-ish to noon, and then train and then work again at night or overnight. Cori was racing then, too. A lot of times we slept in our car so we could save money driving from job to job. We'd drive to one night job and if it was close to the next morning's job, we'd just sleep there."

Maybe it's fitting he's made his home in Oudenaarde, literally "old field," I realize as Jonathan talks. The town, now referred to as the pearl of the Flemish Ardennes, was once "the city of the nobles." Dedication to Euro 'cross is a pretty noble path.

Europe, meanwhile, hasn't been a cakewalk for Jonathan, either. "It has been incredibly hard over here … I won't sugarcoat it," he told *The Ride* magazine in 2004. "I have magical days on the bike and those are what keep me coming back for more."

His first stint in Europe began in 2000 with a few months in Germany, followed by three months in Switzerland during the 2001-2002 season. The next season, from November through January, he began planting Belgian 'cross seeds—learning the courses, registering impressions of the level and style of racing. In the process, he returned to the States and claimed his first National Championship jersey in the December 2002 Napa, California quagmire—torrential showers pounded the course, which wound around choice wine vineyards and caused heavy erosion and damage.

By this time, I had gotten to know Jonathan better and saw that I might be able to help him find a sponsor for the next year. At the World Championships in Monopoli, Italy, in late January 2003, I introduced him to Paolo and Alessandro Guerciotti, the renowned Italian frame-builder and his son. Paolo sponsored the amateur cyclocross team I'd raced for a decade earlier. Jonathan's meeting with the Guerciottis, and their subsequent agreement, resulted in his first full 'cross season in Europe, from October to February 2003-2004.

While the contract was really only a foot in the door, providing clothing, bikes, and travel money, it was a start.

The first season, Jonathan survived with Cori in an apartment that didn't have hot water for two months. "Then we got a decent place above a factory where the only problem was sharing space with two office workers and an alarm that got set off accidentally at night. Then we moved to a house with a real psycho for a landlord. We found out the husband of this crazy landlord had hanged himself in the garden shed after finding his wife sleeping with someone else in the house."

Life on the bike wasn't much easier. Top cyclocross riders (unlike top-level road racers) earn hefty appearance fees called "start money," in addition to their salaried contracts. Low-ranked riders aren't so lucky.

"Getting start money was a major hurdle," Jonathan says. His longtime friend and mechanic, Franky Van Haesebroucke, once fought with race organizers for two hours to get Jonathan 25 euros—all of $26.

The advancements came so incrementally it was difficult to see progress.

"Most of all, it was a challenge because I was not accepted in the field," he says. "Nearly every race, someone yelled a profanity at me. It was a real breakthrough to begin to be accepted. To be moving up."

But, as with everything in Jonathan's view, "It's been what it's been." He stayed positive. He kept fighting. And in December 2003 he won his second straight elite National Championship in monsoon-ish Portland, Oregon, grabbing headlines in *VeloNews*.

In October 2004 he was on his first Euro podium, placing third in the cornfields of Ardooie, just north of Izegem. In December 2004 he claimed his third straight national elite National Championship in the clay bath of Portland.

Remarkable achievements—but not real-deal status. For me, Jonathan takes that prized label in a lead-up race to his first (and to date only) Euro victory, in Pétange, Luxembourg, on New Year's Day 2006.

***

It's a particularly epic period of cyclocross racing—deep December 2005. Weeks of ashen gray sky. Sheets of rain. I'm in my third consecutive Christmas in Belgium chasing dreams of developing future American cyclocross success as director of EuroCrossCamp III.

On a blustery Thursday, I go to the windswept dunes of coastal Middelkerke, just east of the port city of Ostend, to watch a race. A small race during the *kerstperiode*—literally Christmas period—but an opportunity, nonetheless. Beachfront apartment cheeks rise high above polder puddles. Their stature does little to blunt the cold North Sea wind. These summer vacation monstrosities suggest something almost sardonic. They hold promise of seasonally distant warmth and hospitality, but in December you face only gale.

Jonathan has had a tough go of it over the previous two weeks. He suffered food poisoning prior to the U.S. Nationals in Providence, Rhode Island, and returned to Europe for the first time in three years without the stars-and-stripes jersey for being U.S. national champion. A listless ride in the World Cup in Hofstade, Belgium, three days before does little to lift his morale.

Nonetheless, here, in Middelkerke, Jonathan fights his way into the lead group.

Conditions are leaden. Sven Nys, Sven Vantourenhout, Swiss pro Christian Heule, even longtime Swiss pro Thomas Frischknecht are racing.

Disaster strikes.

Somehow, a piece of random rebar flicks upright, and—on Jonathan's downstroke—pierces his shoe hard enough to impale his foot. Unable to feel his feet due to the cold, his adrenaline surging, he yanks the piece out of his shoe, not realizing that it has actually stabbed through his arch.

Through the shoe.

Through the insole.

Deep into his foot.

He cops a brilliant third place but his podium appearance is overshadowed by a sock rapidly filling with blood. A hasty trip to the doctor ensues.

"First, the doctor has to cut away the fat that's hanging from the inside of my arch," Jonathan says. "He doesn't want to put me on antibiotics right away in case I don't need them. Just a tetanus shot. Then when I return the next morning, I'm in so much pain. My leg is swollen and red from infection."

What really bothers him is this: He has to sit out the World Cup in Hooglede that day, despite trying to make an insole and cut a shoe that would let him race again as soon as possible. "I tested each design on the trainer while I watched the race on TV," he says.

Two days after the impaling, Jonathan forgoes the bigger race in Baal and heads to Luxembourg.

Bike. Check.

Insole. Check.

Hole in foot. Check.

"I was kind of nervous because the doctor said that it was not smart to go, and I could hardly walk on my foot. I had to try to limit the amount of running I did, so in the first laps, I struggled to pedal through the muddy sections that were faster to run. At first I was nowhere near winning. Third, at best. But slowly the leaders got tired. I was good in the downhill section and I started to run some sections to see if I could catch up."

He could. And did.

And won.

***

We pile in the Page family minivan that doubles as the motor-pacing car and head to the town square for a sandwich. Ham-and-cheese baguettes, Cori nursing Milo, Jonathan tending to Emma's choices for a post-lunch pastry. Our conversation ranges from basic expat miscellanea to key psychological dashboard indicators for an athlete striving to make the top echelon.

Cori laments the Belgies' lack of good coffeehouses, à la Starbucks.

"How come Belgium can't do malls, either?" Jonathan chimes in. "With shit weather, a mall would be nice once in awhile."

His conversation veers to travel—"Self-declared rule: one-week limit away from home"—and to Cori's surprise appearance at the recent Tour de Liège, flaunting the Sunweb rules.

"The team says no to spouses for camps and stage races. They couldn't believe her temerity—to find a place on her own, locate the stages without a GPS," Jonathan says.

Jonathan tells me he's been given the cold shoulder by organizers of the GVA series this season. Evidently, they've never forgiven him for missing one of the series races a few years ago in order to go home and race in the U.S. National Championships. Fortunately, he's signed a contract with the other big Belgian series, the Superprestige, for this season.

A year ago, he'd almost given up on racing in Europe —"our bags were packed, no money, no sponsors"—when he won a silver medal at the January 2007 World Cyclocross Championships in Hooglede-Gits. Jonathan's door-blowing second-place ride in Hooglede constituted one of his grandest achievements, at a race filled with more drama—and spectators—than any in years. On race day, Jonathan was the man of the moment, exercising cardinal 'cross rule number one: always stay near the front.

First Bart Wellens, then Sven Nys tasted asphalt after Bart collided with a floating pylon bumped by a forerunning television moto. Sinkholes and wayward ruts claimed other big names.

And still, Jonathan was there. At the front. In the biggest upset in the history of the sport.

"An American?" the Belgians whispered late in the race.

This visit is the first chance I've had to ask Jonathan about it.

"Going into it, I knew this was the time," he recaps the race for me. "I felt quite calm on the start line. I changed gloves from short finger to long finger with two minutes to go. I knew it was imperative to have a good start." Coming from the sixth row, this wouldn't be easy.

"But I noticed right away, I was riding cleaner than most others and I was picking up more spots than I had anticipated. Next thing, I saw Wellens and Nys picking themselves up off the ground as I rode by. I was thinking, 'What the hell?' Then Groenendaal was off at one point and it was just a blur. I moved through so many riders that I had no idea where I was. Coming into the pit, I asked Franky about my placing. 'You're winning the fucking bike race!'" he yelled at me.

"I kept riding hard, trying to calculate who was missing, who I hadn't passed yet. Like counting cards in Vegas. Then I just tried to keep calm and always keep in an advantageous position. This was it. No thoughts of saluting the crowd, I focused only on trying to win the bike race."

Leader Erwin Vervecken was his main concern. So was a line he picked near the finish. "I hit a rut before the dip and got thrown off line to the left side and—boom—I was like, 'oh shit, oh shit.' Three bad pedal strokes in slow motion and Erwin got the gap.

"But just before the last little hill, the last half-lap, I put in an attack. Vervecken, remember, is two-time world champion. I didn't care. It was the best moment.

"I had tears at the finish line," he says. "Hugging and kissing Cori with her big belly"—Milo was yet to be born. "People telling me it was the most exciting bike race they'd ever seen. To beat all the odds and finish second—that was the payoff.

"To gamble everything and have it pay off—that was the sweetest taste of success."

The ride also brought the pro contract with Sunweb. "My Hooglede ride saved everything," he says.

The Pages are excited about the upcoming regular paychecks from Sunweb, something that will boost their stability. Hearing them, one can see the depth of Jonathan's emphasis on home life, an admirable and necessary strength. But to pair it with the game he's playing—professional European cyclocross—is to get at a deeper truth. Beyond the course conditions, terrain challenges and the brute speed of Euro racing—beyond the language barriers, the cultural differences, the difficult logistics—the biggest obstacle to the expat cycling life is isolation.

The Euro bike-racing scene has chewed up many a well-intentioned rider. Laurence Malone, Clark Natwick, Paul Curley, Jonathan Vaughn, Tom Clark, Tom Hayles, Don Myrah, Jed Fox, Dale Knapp, Tim Johnson and many others have all strived to break into the territory. But Jonathan Page, far and away, has come closest to the summit. Jonathan is the American 'crosser who seems to have the best ability to euro-cope.

For Jonathan, his family, friends, and success are conjoined weapons. One cannot come without the others. Unfortunately, the same familial fortress that brings Jonathan indispensable strength also presents a few barriers to outsiders—the American press, his fellow competitors, perhaps even to himself—in the form of stubborn defensiveness. I see it as national team coach: his wanting to arrange things his way at a given World Championship in terms of lodging or travel; the tension between him and the other U.S. riders he seldom races against; his sensitivity to slights or negativity in the media (a part of life for any star). But in each case I end with utmost respect for Jonathan and his methods, for one simple reason. Bottom line: No American has more international 'cross starts.

Inimitability precludes argument.

***

Despite reportedly signing with Sunweb for 54,000 euros, or about $55,000—despite the fresh Ridley bikes in the basement, the crisp, manic yellow Sunweb kit, the poster-pasted camper van—despite all the outward appearances of having arrived, there seems to be, still, a hint of angst in Jonathan's demeanor.

First, there's the burden of travel. Jonathan is sandwiching his first road races with Sunweb between two blocks of U.S. racing. It goes like this for the summer and fall:

Fly.

Nature Valley, June. Fitchburg, early July.

Fly.

Tour de Liège in the Ardennes.

Family time and training in Switzerland.

Fly.

U.S. criteriums, August.

Fly.

Belgian team obligations.

Fly.

Mid-September 'crosses in Michigan and Vegas.

Fly.

Begin Euro 'cross season.

Beyond the travel insanity, there's another prickly undercurrent. It's only mid-summer, yet—

His team's website is already reporting—

Jonathan Page's every move.

He's happy with Sunweb, Jonathan says. "But the reverse side is that I now have to get used to dealing with all the stress and pressure to get good results every weekend. It's been a hard adjustment honestly, but I think I'm getting over it and concentrating on what I need to do … which is race my bike."

It's not like he doesn't know how to overcome the odds, he says. "But the closer I get to the top or having a chance at the top, the more people don't like me, and the more people talk badly of me." He pauses. "I've learned to take people's doubts and bad words for me and turn them into fuel for my fire. I let the doubters swirl around in my head during hard training rides."

World Championships Podium, Hooglede (January 2007) PHOTOPRESS.BE

Jonathan Page, (Roubaix 2008)   PHOTOPRESS.BE

4: CONTRASTS WITH SVEN

A week or so after seeing Jonathan, I touch base again with Sven. The difference is striking. Sven's routine is well-oiled, smooth, humming. He's in his element.

We first speak of Sven's start contracts. They're mostly finished, negotiated by his manager. The big race arrangements—the GVA and Superprestige series—are set; all that remains to be signed are his contracts for the smaller, individual races, like the season opener in Erpe-Mere and the stand-alone Belgian classic in Overijse.

Sven, the boss of 'cross, has no trouble earning start money. With his marquee status and his *palmares*, race organizers are only too happy to pay him top euro for his presence, or 6,000 euro per race for the 2007-2008 season. Supporters by the busload come to watch their man Sven, and organizers reason that since each of these fans pays a 10- to 15-euro entry fee, the investment in Sven pays off. Reigning world champion Erwin Vervecken will earn the same. Current Belgian champion and ex-world champion Bart Wellens will command slightly less.

The UCI World Cup series—encompassing eight to ten races per season in four to five European countries each season—pays start money to the top fifty riders in the overall UCI ranking. But, curiously, big stars receive less start money for World Cup races than for the big Belgian series races, the Superprestige and GVA Series. On the other hand, the World Cup offers crucial UCI ranking points, which ultimately determine ever-so-important start positions at the races. It also delivers a handsome, season-ending prize list. As a result, almost all riders aspire to be a part of the World Cup, as well as one or both of the big Belgian series.

It's an uneasy relationship for the UCI. As governing body, the UCI wants its series to be the biggest and best, but the commercial power and tradition of the sport in Belgium still holds sway.

Sven Nys, Bart Wellens, Erwin Vervecken. These are the riders everyone wants to see. The top of the pyramid.

Sven is the hottest of the hot. Organizers don't forget that in his Grand Slam season of 2004-2005 he won 88 percent of the time, finishing off the podium just five times out of forty-one races.

As the podium pyramid widens, the fruits of the labor diminish. Rising stars Niels Albert and Lars Boom get 2,500 euros per race for the 2007-2008 season. On the basis of his silver medal at the World Championships in Hooglede-Gits, Jonathan Page makes in the neighborhood of 1,250 euros per race.

The message is anything but chimerical. A rider's worth is as black and white stark as his name on the most recent *uitslag, rangeliste, resultat*. You're only as good as your last race.

Sobering.

Cold.

Hard.

Blue sky?

No such animal in Euro 'cross.

***

Sven's objectives against this backdrop are unwavering.

"I start every season the same. To be the best rider of the season."

There are still several weeks left before racing begins, and he wants it to start with a bang. "For me, it's very important to start the season with a victory. Then I know I have had a really good way of training, that the whole summer I trained really good, and it makes me strong in my mind.

"I realize that I'm very lucky to be an athlete out training on my bike," he adds. "That's what I mostly think about when I start a training. That I have luck, my health. For an athlete like myself, it's most important that I have everything positive: my family, my sense of self. Morale is so important to an athlete. When everything is running good, then I can get good results. If there's a negative with me or with my family, or something else, then I can't concentrate on the training, and the racing and the morale goes downhill."

The altitude dials are idle for now; the Tour of Ireland comes in a week, and then it's game-on in Scotland for the world mountain bike championships. Once again, Sven's goals at the mountain bike World Championships are concrete: from a start position of 50th, the position he's assigned based on his ranking points for the race, he feels he can place in the top 16. The Sven template—of well-engineered workloads, of scripted precision, of skimming off the margins—should proceed without a hitch.

Photo: Tom Robertson

5: ERWIN AND BART, PEDAL TO PEDAL

MID-AUGUST 2007

Three-time and current world professional cyclocross champion Erwin Vervecken's voice sounds hollow. Skyping through my computer, I'm reaching the Belgian master to ask about the build-up to the 'cross season for his Fidea team. As it turns out, the summer's training has been a mixed bag.

Fidea is the best-organized and best-supported cyclocross squad in the world, with a budget of over one million euros per year. Its traditional May training camp in Mallorca and spring Belgian road races in May and June have gone according to plan. But rain dampened a late June training camp in the French Vosges region, and at the Belgian road championships in Ronse, the team's other superstar, Bart Wellens, had an adverse reaction to a bee sting, forcing his withdrawal from a July trip to the Tour of Quinghai Lake in China.

Now, at the annual August training camp (this year back in St. Moritz), the wind and rain are lashing. The training, thus far, inconsistent. With five professional world titles between them—Bart's in 2003 and 2004, Erwin's in 2001, 2006, and 2007—Erwin and Bart know too well that summer is the time for World Championship seeds to be sown.

Erwin arrives about five days after the start of the camp, preferring not to be away from his wife and infant twins for the almost three-week training block at altitude. Bart plugs away from the get-go, anxious to make up for missing the China trip.

I've been friends with Erwin since 2001, when we were introduced through a mutual friend. I ask him first about his family, and if he might come to the U.S. to race in the early season, as he did in 2001 and 2003. (I helped orchestrate his trips on those two occasions for races in Gloucester, Massachusetts, and the Seattle-Portland area.) The melody in Erwin's excellent English returns. His soon-to-be one-year-olds are thriving, he says, and a quick get-away with his wife to Egypt in early August has him fresh for the long climbs—the Maloja, the Julier, the Stelvio of the Swiss-Italian Alps. He hopes maybe a deal can be reached to bring him to CrossVegas, the biggest 'cross race in America, or maybe to an East Coast race in September. I tell him I'll see what I can do.

We move on to talk of the new bikes, of how maybe the past two summer training camps in Tuscany are the way to go in terms of decent weather, of how the team is a bit jumpy with so many big guns.

Fidea, sponsored by a Belgian insurance company, holds the distinction of being—unequivocally—the most talent-deep and complexly webbed team on the circuit. It not only boasts Erwin and Bart, but also includes two-time espoir world champ Zdenek Stybar; fellow Czech on-the-mend-from-injury Petr Dlask; new precocious addition and fellow Belgian Klaas Vantornout; and a slew of younger guys: Jempy Drucker, Kevin Pauwels, Tom Meeusen, Quentin Bertholet, and Vincent Baestaens. Adding to the intrigue are Danny de Bie, the congenial director and ex-world champ, who's responsible for keeping everyone happy; and Hans Van Kasteren, the head of affairs, volatile chief, and "George Steinbrenner" of pro cyclocross. Top it off with the fact that virtually every Fidea rider has his own father as a chief mechanic, and the whole reactor looks ready to go nuclear.

Erwin doesn't talk about the team dynamics. Like most elite 'cross athletes, he's more eager to discuss immediate concerns—Swiss altitude training, for example. It's crucial that it goes well, he says, his voice a bit weary.

It's been nothing but a day at the salt mines. While fans, supporters, cyclotourists, masters racers, and perhaps even the general public might romanticize pro bike racing—or the life of any pro athlete—the reality isn't pretty. "Training is work. It's not supposed to be fun," as top nordic skier Ivan Babikov once put it. "Winning is fun. That's why you train."

For Erwin, for Bart, it goes like this: Rise 0730, easy jog 2 km in 5 C (41 degree) darkness. Muesli, bread, jam, coffee. Ride in full weather gear—booties, thermals, hats—climbing past Pontresina ski stations on up the Val Bernina. Climb 15 k at 7.5 percent. Reach Passo del Bernina, 2,328 meters. Continue up over the Forcola di Livigno on the Swiss-Italian border, climb higher. Summit Piz la Stretta at 2,476 meters, or 8,123 feet.

Ride on.

Down into Livigno, along the grey Lago del Gallo, through the frigid border tunnel back into Switzerland and the slow grind to and through the town of Zernez.

Glacial.

Then nothing but squall in buckets the last 30 K.

Marrow-cold.

Then glorious shower. Massage.

Put the afternoon to bed.

Root fatigue.

But it's more than that. For every naked-eye meter of measured August effort in this massif, there's an equal casting of the mind's eye, down past the sweeping Trentino Alto Adige, across the graped, timbered and industried Dolomite foothills, to the Venetian suburb of Treviso in late January.

That is what *this* is all for.

The 2008 World Cyclocross Championships.

Erwin and Bart together, pedal for pedal.

On this day, they cannot see—at times only meters above them—the rarified, cloud-enshrouded summits of the Ober Engadine.

But they can see, acutely—five months and 200 kilometers away—the white graveled finish line in Treviso.

***

The relationship between Bart and Erwin, something to marvel at and ponder, is winning scrutiny in new venues, including the publishing world. Erwin has just sent me the book by the encyclopedic Philippe Maertens entitled *Wellens en Weetjes: Met Het Fidea-Team Door Het Veld* ("with the Fidea team in the field"). After years of almost zero books about cyclocross, Belgian publishers Borgerhoff-Lamberigts in 2006 also released the Sven Nys autobiography. (And in 2008, Borgerhoff-Lamberigts will publish Bart Wellens's autobiography *Open Boek*.)

Considering the three years of the *Wellens en Wee* TV drama, the extension to print media seems natural. But how will Maertens portray the uneasy relationship between two of the sport's biggest stars *and* teammates?

Predictably, as it turns out. Bart exudes pure fun and outgoingness, flamboyance, and extroversion. Erwin comes across as I know him, more calculating and worldly. Both feed off each other in a mutually competitive relationship.

The TV and book titles, meanwhile, demonstrate the Belgian fabric of the sport. *Wellens en Wee* comes from the Dutch expression *wel en wee*, meaning the good and the bad about things. *Wel* is everything going the right way, the happinesses; *wee* means the sorrows, problems, troubles. The incorporation of Bart's last name adds further layers of meaning, a stroke of fortunate phrasing and testament to his household-name status.

The book title *Wellens en Weetjes* plays it a step further. *Een weetje* is a little fact, a small detail. In other words, the good, the bad, and everything you'd want to know in between.

***

The stories in *Wellens en Weetjes* let me glimpse events I've seen and written about myself, like a highlights reel through a different lens. My first view of Erwin's magnetism comes at the 1994 World Championships, when he finishes third after the chase in the sand. Even more indelible is what takes place in the frigid cold of Poprad, Slovakia during the 1999 Worlds, and in the icy slop of the 2001

Worlds in Tabor, Czech Republic. Both races illuminate the slippery slope of teamwork in modern cyclocross.

Erwin is the man of the moment in each race's high voltage chase, but in Poprad, personal rivalry burns even hotter. It's no surprise that in *Wellens en Weetjes*, the Poprad chapter is titled *Fratricide*.

Despite the long travel, the despair of spending the pre-race week on the rollers due to the weather, the actual -20 C (-4 F) race day temperatures, the awkward single barrier just before the biggest climb, the ridiculously glass-slick off-cambers, frozen woodchips, and wooden legs, Erwin is there in Poprad, gunning for the win. After riding shotgun in support of victor and Belgian teammate Mario De Clercq in Middelfart, Denmark, in 1998, he's done with sacrifice. In the Poprad race, with four laps to go, Erwin has 15 seconds on Mario and Dutchman Adri van der Poel.

It's glory moment.

But, in *the* most heartwrenching catch-and-release stories in World Championship cyclocross, Mario won't back down. Not even for his loyal-in-the-past countryman, Erwin.

With three laps to go, Adri is 11 seconds behind; Mario is 18 seconds down.

With two to go: Adri is still 14 seconds behind, and Mario is 23 back.

With one to go: Adri is 9 behind; Mario 13.

Last lap: Erwin bobbles twice trying to ride the last big climb. Then he dabs a late-race sweeper.

Incredibly, Mario swoops up and through Erwin in the final turns.

Mario niftily pockets a second world title.

Erwin hurls his right arm forward in disgust. Plundered.

During the post-race interviews, Mario hints that nothing could have stopped him from chasing Erwin down.

Erwin is quoted in *Wellens en Weetjes*: "Well then, he's a bigger *klootzak*"— asshole—"than I thought."

Erwin shivers on the second step of the Poprad podium, 8 seconds and an arctic gulf apart from Mario.

If defeat is palpable, it is so on this day.

No words for the awards ceremony.

No feeling at all.

Numb as steppe.

Two years later, 2001, Erwin is back at his resilient best, in front in Tabor. The conditions are Eastern bloc, with slushy spray freezing fingers and jaws. Again Erwin is at the sharp point of the arrow. Homeboy Czech Petr Dlask is there, but the real threat is who else?

Mario De Clercq.

After battling for most of the race, the three funnel into the final, staired run-up. Erwin is in front. Mario on his shoulder. Petr, in third position, crawling up Mario's ass.

They dismount.

The moment is small—as monumental sporting moments tend to be—and the gesture is exceedingly fine-spun.

Petr makes to pass. Mario sees Erwin two steps, no more, ahead of him.

Erwin is the strongest. Mario senses it. Has sensed it the entire race.

Ever so slightly sideways, Mario makes a beleaguered flick with his bike, obstructing Petr's pass. Inherent meaning: If there is no way I can win, I will help my country win.

Aflush with muddied face, Erwin shines a toothy smile against a backdrop of circa-communist highrise apartments. Mario takes second.

Fast-forward to 2007, six years later, and Erwin, 35, is a huge star—a rider who bridges the toe-clipped, traditional era with the sport's current moneyed modernity, a world of carbon and campers.

To describe Erwin—a friend for almost a decade—I try to search for consistencies, metaphors, anecdotes. The task seems like paring away so much peach that little fruit remains. But an old coach once told me that the rider who knows his limits is the rider most to be feared. This, I realize, fits Erwin like a tightly stretched Dugast. The Erwin approach? Ride in the front group for as long as you can, then put them away in the sprint. Hang with them on the climbs and in the technical sections, and put the hammer down where there's a running section. Ride to your strengths. Never put science, fads, or gadgets ahead of traditional training methods, mental strength, morale. That's Erwin.

Your hematocrit, VO2 max, fiber twitch? They are what they are. Work with what you've got.

Show me a believer in boundlessness, or cycling by the scientific numbers, Erwin seems to say, and I'll show you a fool.

***

Where Sven and Bart fly entourage, Erwin goes coach-less. No advisors dictate what he does. No one hands him diagrams for the day's training. For Erwin, having a training plan and not being able to follow it is more stressful than training on instinct. He doesn't use the latest high-tech devices. He still hasn't invested in an altitude tent, and travels to glacial training camps instead.

It's all about feel, all about what works, what's working.

"For one month after 'cross season, I stop completely without bike or any physical training at all," he describes his training routine to me in a series of emails. "Then I begin training season for six weeks before my first race on the road. I don't do any mountain biking anymore because it's not good for cyclocross. This period I start with one hour every two days for the first week, going up to every day, two to three hours in the second week, and ending in the last week with trips up to 200 km, with in between days of one to two hours."

From May to July, he does lots of stage races and training hours. "Three to four stage races of 4-6 days; 600-1,000 km per week. It's better to do a day of 200 km followed by two to three days just two hours very slowly than to do every day big kilos. When I feel tired, I take a week and maybe 8 hours training and then start again.

"The beginning of August, I take two weeks rest. Then I start to build again with a lot of kilometers at our training camps, and on the 10th of September, I start to take my 'cross bike in the woods for technical training and running.

"During the 'cross season," he continues, "I only train on the 'cross bike once during the week and by December, I stop with the 'cross workouts altogether because I'm racing so much."

He goes by feel, backing off when his body tells him to. He doesn't even use a Polar, a device that measures heart rate.

"The best thing to do a week before a big race is to do the same things you do during the year, except maybe the last two days, slow down a bit. If you feel better on Sunday's race than on Saturday's, then you didn't train with enough intensity during the week."

And for gearing?

"I race all the time with a 13-25 gearing and a 39-48 on the front," he writes. "But I never use my 39 in a race. If my legs are good, I always like to push big gears."

Curiously, the un-science of Erwin's physical preparation doesn't seem to match his exacting qualities outside of cycling. He is multilingual, he has an accounting degree and does website design, and he's completing his first level (initiation) for his Belgian cycling coaching credential—all of which suggest a methodical side and bring significant dimension to his resume. Throw in his love of travel, his supportive wife Liesbeth and their children, and he's got more brewing than your average bike racer.

Erwin has another role, too. Along with Richard Groenendaal, he serves as the senior member of the pro 'cross world, which makes him a diplomat of sorts. He hasn't yet won the type of fan base that Sven Nys claims. He doesn't have Bart's popularity or the promise of Lars Boom and Niels Albert. But Erwin can never be counted out in any competition if he's racing well. In the meantime, he represents the riders' collective voice on the UCI Cyclocross Commission, the board that determines the future and development of the sport. He continues to be one of the few riders to actually follow through with the sport's globalization efforts, continually racing abroad. At the end of the day, he exudes a certain ethos, a certain way of conducting himself, that harkens back to cyclocross's humble past.

And—oh, yeah—he's the only current guy with three rainbow shirts in his closet.

Bart Wellens, (Middelkerke 2007) PHOTOPRESS.BE

Erwin Vervecken, (Koksijde 2007)

PHOTOPRESS.BE

6: FOLLOW THE MONEY

With a few exceptions, the American cyclocross season has always culminated with U.S. National Championships sometime in December, six weeks before the World Championships in late January, with no races in between. For the top riders aspiring to strong performances at the World Championships, this gap in the racing schedule presents a problem: how to gain and hold form with no racing for six weeks and then compete in the biggest 'cross race in the world.

After facing this dilemma myself, as a U.S.A. Worlds team member in 1993, 1994, and 1996, I spent time researching the prospect of some sort of European race camp for this crucial period.

The idea was not a new one. In 1974, a group of five Americans (Californians Laurence Malone, Fritz Liedl, Chuck Canepa, Tyger Johnson, and Jeff Saunders, led by American cyclocross pioneer Eckhard Rieger), spent the better part of a month based in Switzerland racing and training for the 1975 World Championships in Melchnau, Switzerland. There had also been many previous efforts by Americans to race cyclocross in Europe, both individually and in groups—most notably by Paul Curley in the late 1980s and by a 1997 group including Dale Knapp and Craig Undem. But the sport still lacked a euro-bridge, a way for Americans to stay on top of their game and get experience abroad.

With that as a backdrop, I enthusiastically accepted an internship in 2003 with U.S.A. Cycling (U.S.A.C), working under Noel Dejonckheere, the Under-23 national team director. A Belgian who raced professionally in the 1970s, Noel had built strong American ties via his role as director with top American team Motorola in the early 1990s. While helping him that summer, I began working on a program that I would launch the following December: the annual EuroCrossCamp for American riders, offering an intensive European cyclocross racing experience. The inaugural camp was a success: in the first year, twelve riders—including names like Jeremy Powers, Jackson Stewart, Carmen D'Aluisio, and Gina Hall—came with me to Izegem, Belgium, where they competed in seven races in twelve days.

By 2007, when I was looking forward to directing CrossCamp's fifth season, both the level of rider and the knowledge base had risen significantly. American results at the World Cyclocross Championships had improved dramatically, and EuroCrossCamp attendees like Powers, Danny Summerhill, Bjorn Selander, Ryan Trebon, and Barry Wicks were finding significant 'cross pollination—interdisciplinary success— on the road and mountain bike circuits.

This is precisely what Swiss national champion Christian Heule wants to discuss when he contacts me in late August 2007. He and galactic mountain bike and cyclocross icon Thomas "Frischy" Frischknecht both organize big Swiss 'cross races at the end of December. While the halcyon days of Swiss cyclocross are long gone—the Swiss appetite for the sport has faded, while Belgians still lust for it—both countries are doing their best to build back up to the legendary days of *radquer,* as the Swiss call it. They're hoping to entice me to bring my sixteen-rider-strong camp to Christian's hometown race in Switzerland, the Badiquer Schmerikon on December 30, and to Frischy's Fluuger Quer race in Dubendorf, Switzerland, on January 2. With a free hotel stay, some start money and spectator numbers in the 3,000-to-4,000 range, I have to admit the change of scenery would be good for my riders' *esprit.*

Seems like a no-brainer. Except for one critical component to Euro 'cross.

Loyalty.

Over the nearly five years of running the camp, I've built up considerable loyalty with the Belgian race organizers at the Superprestige leg in Diegem and the GVA stop in Baal. These Belgian events, which we normally attend, are in direct conflict with the Swiss races. In addition, I've cultivated a relationship with the youthful Belgian manager Gert Matthys and his father's contract company—one of the oldest in Euro 'cross—with whom I negotiate start money. There's one thing you learn pretty quickly in Euro 'cross: honor your contacts. The camp has forged a relationship with the Belgian races. I'm not about to jump ship just yet.

Christian understands I can't accept his offer. He knows this loyalty game more than most. As a foreign rider he has to fight for every franc, just like us. This off-season, he undertook the rather unsavory task of switching managers from Matthys to ProContract.be, a competing contract company managed by none other than Fidea team boss Hans Van Kasteren and his daughter, Nancy. These two entities manage almost all professional Euro 'cross start contracts in Belgium. Van Kasteren takes care of Fidea riders and a select group of others, now including Christian. Matthys oversees most of the non-Belgian riders like the Czechs and Americans.

Few images of European 'cross stand out as vividly for me as the first time I went to collect start money as manager of the American team at a Christmas race in 2003. At the time, Gert's father, Eric, is handling affairs. My riders are at some nameless soccer complex, shivering under feeble water spigots not up to the muddied task. I pass them and duck my head under bleachers, make my way through a web of doors and hallways. Dim light. A rider stands next to a door, waiting. It's Petr Dlask, I think. His English and my Czech don't get us far. The door opens. Out comes another Czech rider, Vaclav Jezek.

Okay, I see. We do this one by one. Riders go in alone, come out with money.

Soon it's my turn. I enter. A small man huddles over a card table. No one else around.

A list of riders and teams. A sealed envelope. A space on the list for each signature.

He signs.

I sign.

The envelope exchanges hands.

We shake.

Not a word spoken.

For some reason I feel like Jason Bourne.

Photo: Tom Robertson

7: VOLKSPORT

September arrives with my own concerted cyclocross training efforts. I still race when I can, but the training is what keeps me feeling healthy when I'm grading endless essays. High country leaves yellow in golden sun. The earth dry and fast under tire pressure run high. In my head, words shuffle and reshuffle trying to get the mix right. Phrases frame thoughts. The good ones resonate.

I have a 'cross training circuit near my house in Helena, Montana, encircling a small lake, encompassed by stands of ponderosa pine and meadows. I pound out laps and sift cerebral grains. I believe my own practice of the sport helps me as a coach, advocate, writer.

Belgium seems a million miles away. But not.

To ride cyclocross is to suffer. To watch cyclocross racing is to watch suffering. When the two meet, a transaction between viewer and do-er transpires. A lifting up for both. And that, I suddenly understand, is cyclocross's heart, its essence—as *volk* sport.

The races on Belgian TV? "They brought color to my disconsolate winter days," Paul Van den Bosch, Sven's trainer, says about watching as a child.

In Belgium, the sport is literally within touch. Supporters can touch their favorite stars, watch them warm up on the rollers, study them out on the parcours, shout encouragement—in their ears—when they're racing.

Sven puts it another way: "The supporters go by bus," he tells me. "The whole time, they're talking about who's gonna win today. For one day or one weekend, they can forget their jobs. It's the highlight of their week. Sometimes they win, sometimes they lose, but every time they go, it's satisfaction. When you come to a cyclocross race it might be raining, but the sun is always shining."

Why this connection? And why is it so exceedingly and specifically strong in Flanders? The history tells some of the story.

Flanders for most of its early years was poor and played doormat to the French-speaking Wallonia industries of coal and steel. Flemish was the language and farming was the way of life. People with power were French-speakers, the bourgeoisie; they drove cars and kept their hands clean. A shift came in the 1900s when Flanders became the center of Belgian textile successes. Spoken Flemish became a point of national pride. Flemish, by virtue of the fact that nearly every cyclocross race was held in Flandrian farming fields, also became the volk language of cyclocross—the *volk*-speak of the *volk* sport.

Albert Van Damme, great compatriot and foil to seven-time world champion Eric De Vlaeminck, used to work his flower fields east of Ghent by week, then till the same earth by weekend. Commentator Michel Wuyts confirms that Flemish organizers in the 1960s sought out the deepest fields of heavy mud, resonating with the German sense of *arbeiten*.

Work. Struggle. Toil.

The 1980s 'cross icon Roland Liboton reflected this image in every way, Michel tells me. He describes what it was like to hear Liboton in a race—bike on shoulder—pass by. "I could hear him arrive. And it was not a man that was running. It was more the gallop of a horse."

The arduousness of the sport was matched in Belgium by the treacheries of winter. The months are dark and nasty as North Sea winds swoop and spit. Finally, add in the Belgian role of the bicycle as the beloved EUV (earthen utility vehicle) and its exalted status as SAV (sport achievement vehicle), and you begin to understand the recipe for cyclocross's huge success.

Of all cycling disciplines, it still dwells closest to the plebian. Even in all its beer-tented, JumboTron'd splendor, the sport isn't over the top. Modern cyclocross is just this side of extreme. Inside—not outside—the parameter of what's do-able on a bicycle. Within the scope and fathom of the hoi polloi. As American 'cross legend Laurence Malone once wrote, "Cyclocross entails all the movement and aerobics any bicycle commuter knows. It, as they say, is just like real life."

On the bike, off the bike, over the curb, through the slop—get where you want to go. The *volk* way.

But the *volk* need adrenaline, something to cut through the slog of winter. The cyclocross race season, perfectly timed, stretches from September to February, the most sun-starved days.

During the *kerstperiode*, the December blitzkrieg of the biggest cyclocross races on the planet, it's only light for some six hours a day. Our team's race departures—from Izegem in West Flanders—are always dark. Our returns—just as dim. It's bleak time.

When it's race day at EuroCrossCamp, the team members feel it, and sleep. On the road trips to the races, most of my passengers—many of them U.S. national cyclocross team members—have their eyes closed before they can even switch their iPods on.

Not me. I'm driving. I have to be on it.

And not because we're late. Not because the rain might be sideways or the slush hydroplane-able.

No, I have to watch out, as I drive, for kids going to school. For the postman delivering mail. For folks going to the bakery or the factory. In the dark.

On their bikes.

On any given weekend, in any given province across Flanders, from September to February, there's a cyclocross race.

These same schoolchildren, errand-goers, factory workers will be there.

For one talismanic hour, mundanity is thrust aside and supporters and competitors merge. The cyclist rides for himself and his public. The supporter—no matter what denomination—breaks from the humdrum and froths to vicarious lather.

Even he—for brief moments—believes he can fly.

Diegem   Photo: Tom Robertson

Diegem   Photo: Tom Robertson

8: RYAN'S HOPE

EARLY SEPTEMBER, 2007

Ryan Trebon, arguably the best cyclocross pro among those predominantly based in America, has chosen a much more conservative build-up to his 'cross season than Sven or most of the other top men. Finishing the mountain bike season with a ninth place in Aspen on August 11, the rider taller than a Flemish cornstalk has done only one criterium and a few Thursday night training races in his newly adopted hometown of Bend, Oregon.

Of course, Ryan has always been a guy who likes a more American approach—train more, race less. Working closely with Jim Lehman, his coach of five years, he likes a preparation with a healthy dose of threshold workouts—four by 15 minutes, five by 20 minutes—mostly on the flats, where he finds the wattage different than when doing the same workouts on a climb. Never hard enough that he can't do another day, back to back. Overall, he likes to put in 20-to-25 hours a week as part of a progressive training block, with a four-day rotation: a medium day, then two hard days with intervals, followed by a long day, and then a rest day.

The motivation, he tells me, has been good.

"Your legs hurt," he says, "but after you've done these workouts long enough, you realize the benefit out of it. That's the easy part for me. I know it works. And you have to do it.

"'Cross is so hard on your body, your arms, your back. Getting the body ready to be abused like that for an hour is the hardest part for me. Mountain biking is hard, but it's sustained. 'Cross is like that too, but you're still doing these really hard explosive accelerations."

Having known Ryan since 2003, and having spoken with him frequently throughout this August and September, I try to help him solidify his race program, both for the big U.S. races—the U.S. Grand Prix of Cyclocross (USGP)—and for his prospects for some headline Belgian races.

As someone who believes in his talent—he's a two-time USGP champion, national champion in 2006, has a few top tens in World Cups, a 15th at the 2005 Worlds in St. Wendel—and someone intimately aware of his weaknesses (his physical fragility and tendency to lose morale when things aren't going well), I do what I can to help him. American pros have a lot on their plates.

First, there are the vicissitudes of life—buying a house, moving into a house you might occupy only a few months per year, getting all your equipment together, arranging your travel. All perfectly ordinary demands, but for a pro cyclist, also perfectly distracting.

A second distraction is the lean support level for the country's best 'crossers. These guys, Page and Trebon, handle—by themselves—a blinkingly large amount of life's minutiae in addition to their workloads on the bike. The constant moving creates real problems. Not only are American pro riders not necessarily living near where they grew up, where their families are, where the support is, but they're also trying to make it in Europe, an ocean away.

Back in the summer of 2001, before meeting his future wife, Erwin told me he wouldn't consider marrying a girl from more than 40 kilometers away from his home. When Erwin married Liesbeth (who, indeed, is from a small village 25 km away) and needed to buy a house, his father was nearby, and helped him organize and build it. Put another way, here's a little-known fact: many Euro pros still have their laundry done—by their mothers.

For Ryan, the process of buying a house in Bend means relying on realtors and bankers. He could get more money, and perhaps win more fame, if he followed Jonathan's lead and moved overseas. That's what I want to see him do. But it's not what he wants.

For the past few seasons, Ryan has dabbled on both sides of the Atlantic much as Jonathan did in his early years, launching forays and getting decent start money in the Belgian races, then returning home for the easier, bigger point returns in the U.S. All summer, I've encouraged him to take the next step.

In Euro 'cross, there are stand-alone races, and then there are the series races. To be offered a Belgian series contract—to be listed as one of the series' regular riders—not only guarantees you decent start money for up to ten of the biggest races in the world, but it also comes with a huge morale-boosting pat on the back from the organizers. As if to say, "Hey, we want you, we believe in you."

On the phone for much of August with my Belgian contract manager, I succeed in getting Ryan to this critical juncture. The Superprestige wants Ryan in its pool of twenty-five paid-to-appear riders.

But Ryan opts out.

He appreciates the offer, but he doesn't want to be pinned down, doesn't want to have to race when he feels he can't give his best effort. He wants to remain more flexible. In short, for better or worse, he wants things on his own terms.

With a quiet August and September spent training, and with two close second-places to Swiss rider Christian Heule in the two season-opening West Coast UCI races in the States, things seem to be on track for Ryan.

I'm not in a position to argue.

Ryan Trebon, (Ruddervoorde 2007)

9: VEGAS LIGHTS

SEPTEMBER, 2007

Vegas is about as far from *volk* as you can get. I'm arriving here for the annual CrossVegas race because this is where the industry is, where I can talk to riders and sponsors as the National Junior and Under 23 coach and the director of EuroCrossCamp. The event promises to be electric: elite men's to start at 9 p.m. under the klieg lights on a desert track.

The best of the U.S. men and women, as well as Christian Heule and U.S.-based Italian Davide Frattini—and Elvis— will create the buzz.

CrossVegas promoters Brook Watts and Chris Grealish, longtime acquaintances of mine, have done an excellent job of getting everyone who's anyone to attend this early season race, which falls on the Wednesday night of Interbike trade show week. Interbike, the largest bicycle tradeshow in North America, started way back in 1982 in Las Vegas and provides the perfect forum for people to check out the adrenaline rush of nighttime cyclocross racing.

The afternoon is afizz on the trade show floor. The riders are everywhere: signing posters, standing at booths, mingling. Tim Johnson, America's first espoir 'cross Worlds medalist in 1999, tells me he's going back to his 'cross roots by taking on a more Euro-based race program after the U.S. Nationals in December. The last time he extended his cyclocross season by racing in Europe was in 2002.

Twin towers Ryan Trebon and Barry Wicks, both EuroCrossCamp veterans, look ever casual as they sign autographs and joke around with a sizeable throng of supporters at the booth for Kona, their sponsor.

Loyal 'cross supporters Clif Bar and Crank Brothers enjoy packed booths manned by business reps who offer free energy bars and stylish pedaling demonstrations.

At the Ridley bikes expo, I catch up with one of our best espoirs, Wisconsinite Bjorn Selander. As with many of our top young 'crossers, I've spent some great times with Bjorn in Europe, at Worlds and at three EuroCrossCamps (2004-2006). His ride in the 2006 Zeddam Junior Worlds—in with a shout for a medal with a lap to go, and finishing with a still-amazing seventh place—will always rank high on my goosebump-o-meter.

I also chat with fellow National Cyclocross Team coach Marc Gullickson over at the Hutchinson booth, and talk with Julian Absalon, there signing posters. The last time I saw Julian was at the Hofstade World Cup the previous December, where he showed up for a little start money and posed as demon to Sven and Bart.

"You gonna be in Hofstade again, Julian?" I ask.

"Non. Pas cette année. Mais, quelle ambiance à Hofstade! Incroyable, les spectateurs!"

'Ah, oui. C'est le cyclocross, mon ami."

"Oui, c'est vrai."

Sooner than I realize, it's time to head to the Desert Breeze Soccer Complex, six miles into glaring sun and strip-plugged traffic. Upon arrival, I immediately check out the course. Some serious heavy grass riding mixed with some fast sidewalks. It's gonna be brutal.

Then I'm back in the team parking area sharing a makeshift dinner with Colorado 5280 team director Ben Turner, and giving a hand to a kid I've spent the past two Christmases and the World Championships with, reigning junior cyclocross silver medalist Danny Summerhill.

I'm beat.

Between bites of savory burrito, I watch an approaching white taxi, which doesn't seem to know where to stop. Through dusky light I see bodies and luggage in the rear seat. I realize it's Jonathan Page with family in tow. Bikes, bags, wheels begin to tumble out, and the cabbie waits to be paid. Things look a bit disorganized. I offer my help.

"You here with anyone?" I ask.

"Lots of family. Cori's side."

"Mechanic? You have anyone to pit for you?"

"It's dry, right?"

"Yeah."

"Probably won't need to change bikes."

"You want me to pit for you?"

"You're busy."

"You want me to pit for you?"

"Yeah, that'd be great."

We unload, get situated, and Jonathan kits up to reconnoiter the circuit. I thumb and forefinger his Dugast Typhoon tires.

"What pressure you want?"

"The tires are good. The pressure's good."

"Okay. Get out there and fight."

He spins off toward the bright lights of the course.

Soon it's dark on the 85-degree desert. The moon rises. A prodigious orange disc.

It's show time.

***

All the big American guns are mixing it up on the grass, including Ryan Trebon, Barry Wicks, Tim Johnson, and Jeremy Powers. Also out to play under the lights are Swiss champ Christian Heule, privateer Jon Baker (getting ready to sell his house and move his family to Belgium), and Italian pro Davide Frattini. Not to be overlooked, and ready to push some watts, are roadie 'crosser Chris Jones and Canadian mountain biker/cyclocross hard-man Geoff Kabush.

From the pit, with my view of the barrier-strewn run-up, I can see and hear the crowd throttling the lead group with noise. The rest of the ninety-two-rider field seems mired in the concrete-like grass. Some riders resort to fetching dollar bills tossed onto the track by doting fans.

The Offering, Vegas-style.

In Belgium they pitch only empty beer cups.

Because it is indeed a dry race, my work in the pit is light. All I have to do is be ready in case Jonathan punctures and keep an eye on him for any mechanical problems.

Down to the wire, Christian miscalculates the slight jog on the grassed finish and Ryan Trebon takes the win. Jeremy Powers pips Barry Wicks for third and Jonathan follows in for fifth.

I catch the victorious Ryan on my way back to the cars. It's been an all-systems-go race for him. Give him the right environment and he is very difficult to beat. With his long-legged power, he can burn off riders just by laying down the watts.

"Nice job," I congratulate him.

"Yeah, now if I could just put down one attack like that in a big race in Europe."

Back at the parking lot, I tidy up Jonathan's wheels and second bike, his wife standing by. I peel off the Sunweb thermal jacket Jonathan has given me, honoring the custom of the mechanic wearing the same kit as his rider for added visibility in the pit. The jacket smells of European laundry soap.

It's midnight. My circadian cyclocross rhythms are stuck on TILT.

Jonathan spins in, his hair soaked. Before turning to his family, he towels off, gets on some dry clothes. His eyes seem glazed, his expression grave. He says something and I can't make it out. I shoot him a puzzled look.

"Geoff, I'm just not good."

"Your form?"

"Yes, I'm just not good."

"Hang in there."

For Jonathan, it's on to the Seattle clinic and then home to Belgium to start the season. The American swing has helped his UCI ranking, but things don't seem to sit well.

Desert solitaire.

This joint's played.

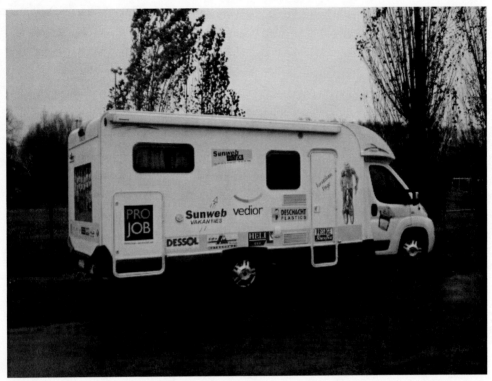

Back in Belgium, Jonathan's camper awaits.

10: VIEW FROM ABOVE

SEPTEMBER 20, 2007

After a 2 a.m. only-in-Vegas dinner on the strip and a fitful fear-and-loathing few hours of sleep on a hotel pull-out couch mattress, I catch a wee-hour flight back to Montana. It's been an exhausting 24 hours. But before I give in to sleep, I try to put some perspective on this day in the life, in the desert and beyond.

First, Americans are catching on. An estimated crowd of 5,000 came to Vegas, forging cyclocross's new frontier.

Second, I know via the Internet that things are gaining momentum in Europe, nine time zones to the east.

Sven has been testing his legs in the last of many, many strategically planned road races—the 185-K Omloop van het Houtland in Lichtervelde, Belgium.

Erwin's revamped website is up and the new Fidea trading cards and posters are arriving for his inspection. Thousands will be handed out to adoring fans throughout the season. His legs are good for his upcoming race trip to America.

Bart's prep continues, along with plans for a fundraising fashion show in Herentals. The catwalk beckons.

And a different kind of story is wafting in, as well. Something I had forgotten about. Several riders mentioned it to me in passing during the Vegas blur. Only now—as my head begins to bob somewhere over Nevada—does it pester me. For some reason, William Butler Yeats's famous poem *The Second Coming* comes to mind.

"Surely some revelation is at hand …

… a vast image out of Spiritus Mundi

Troubles my sight: somewhere …

A shape with lion body and the head of a man …

Is moving …"

The news I'd heard earlier is from the streets of west Stuttgart, Germany. Eleven a.m. local time, a 21-year-old Dutchman averages 46.86 kph to win the U23 (under 23) World Time Trial. He dons his third career rainbow jersey, after winning the junior cyclocross 2003 title in Monopoli, Italy and the January 2007 Under 23 (U23) cyclocross crown in Hooglede, Belgium.

He likens the brutal effort of time trials to the arduous exertion of cyclocross. He explains that the key to his time-trial win lies in the weeks leading up to Stuttgart, when he ups his motor-pacing sessions to three times per week from his customary one: 100 to 120 kilometers at 50 kph behind the moto. Driven by his dad.

He says he'd like to add a fourth rainbow jersey later in the winter, to become elite cyclocross world champion.

His name is Lars Boom.

The cyclocross world already knows the name Lars Boom, but his ride on this day is of the shot-heard-'round-the-world variety.

Laying down the smack.

Laying down the law.

With (Yeats again) "a gaze as blank and pitiless as the sun."

***

I'm reminded, suddenly, of Lance Armstrong, but not for the obvious reasons. In 2007, Armstrong's Tour de France victories are enjoying a robust afterlife; his quest for cancer solutions continues to inspire. But when it comes to American cycling, there's another contribution he's made that gets far less coverage: his attention to training programs.

Today, thanks in large part to Armstrong, the opportunities for personalized cycling coaching in America are as ubiquitous as graffiti in a Brussels train station. Armstrong's work with Chris Carmichael of Carmichael Training Systems popularized this coach-athlete team approach, and now virtually every top cyclist is mentioned in the same breath as his trainer.

With the plethora of new training devices—power meters, altitude tents, hypoxic chambers—added to old standbys like heart rate monitors, periodization and coaching columns—physical preparation has become pointedly sophisticated, even for the six-hour-a-week master racer warrior.

In America, queries to syndicated coaches—online, in the cycling press, and in coaching journals—run along the lines of, "At 14 hours a week for the past four weeks (TSS: 1040, 630, 710, 1000), do I need to take some recovery rides because my power and HR are down and Perceived Exertion is way up?"

Performance supplement spending is through the roof. Fifteen-year-old American juniors are sleeping in $20,000 altitude tents and taking portable tents with them to warm-weather training camps.

Regardless of this sophistication, the most underrated master key in the process is one you still can't buy.

Motivation.

No matter how dialed, bioluminescent, clairvoyant a program is, you still have to execute. The best-laid plans are just good intentions.

After the novelty of downloading and analyzing yesterday's power data wears off, you still have to get out the door. And you have to hurt when no one's watching.

Stars like Sven don't seem to have problems with this. When the 1990s Belgian National Team Coach Eric De Vlaeminck demanded that his juniors wrap 1.5-kilo packets of lead to their top tubes and carry extra packets in their back pockets, Sven got out the electrical tape. When De Vlaeminck honked his car horn during sprint training to signal that it was time to jump, Sven jammed on the pedals.

"*Er zijn er die luisteren en de zullen er komen*" was De Vlaeminck's motto: "Those who take my advice and are mindful of it will make it."

When Rabobank teammate Adri van der Poel made a toast to teetotaler Sven on Sven's 23rd birthday in 2000—the same day they had ridden a 270-kilometer stage of the Tour of Sweden (still, to date, the longest ride of Sven's career)—Sven drank only a half-glass. This is a guy who, without a hint of complaint, says, "When I'm 40, I'll have my first full glass of wine." This is a guy who, in ten years as a pro, has used the excuse 'I don't feel like it' to miss exactly zero days of training. This is a guy who has a sign on a nondescript wall next to his massage table that reads:

Mensen zijn niet gemaakt voor een gemakkelijk leven.

Mensen willen een boeiend leven.

En een gemakkelijk leven is nooit boeiend.

People are not made for an easy life.

People wish for a wonderful life.

But an easy life is never wonderful.

For Lars Boom, if vanquishment is his goal, Sven is the guy to chase.

Lars Boom

11: REIGN IN SPAIN

OCTOBER 8, 2007

It's Monday evening in Mallorca, Spain, and Sven places his evening phone call to trainer Paul Van Den Bosch back in Belgium. He's nearing the end of a ten-day block of speed, endurance, and intensity training on the climbs of his favorite warm Mediterranean training ground. He phones Paul to both inform and affirm. There's an ease to his voice, and for good reason.

His legs are good enough after the day's three-hour endurance ride to do the next day's final five-hour interval session encompassing 150 to 200 kilometers. To wit: six climbs incorporating ten ten-minute intervals, mixing high heart rates (160-180) with climbing recovery (130-150) and engine maintenance.

His legs are good after a week of alternating four- and five-hour days that include forty-minute runs with ten 50-meter explosions, for a total of twenty-six hours of training for the first week in October.

And his legs are good after a weekend detour: a Saturday afternoon flight to Amsterdam and on up to Gieten for the Sunday morning Hondsrug Classic UCI mountain bike race.

Which he wins. In a sprint. After 54 kilometers in 1:44.24.

On a cyclocross bike.

All of this he relates to me when I call him a few days later, just before he heads into the first important cyclocross races of the 2007 season, which will either confirm or deny him the assurance that his preparation has been perfect.

"So you have a date with destiny this weekend," I say.

"Yes," he tells me. "It's the same as the last few years. I put in so much work that I have confidence I will be good in the first big 'crosses all the way through to the last big races in February."

"And your rivals?" Some of them seem to be panicking a bit, I mention.

I can almost see him nodding in agreement. "At the beginning of the season, many riders say, 'Holy shit, I'm not so good'—and so they're gonna train harder, but that's wrong. The hardest training is finished now. You can't say, 'Oh I'll be good in a month,' or whatever. Now you must show the world you are good."

Sven ticks off the races ahead: Dottignies on Saturday, the first Superprestige in Ruddervoorde on Sunday. Then, the next weekend, a small race in Lebbeke, followed by the first World Cup, in Kalmthout. "Normally I am really good there," he says.

I weigh his words, remembering Kalmthout last year, when he was pushed by the Frenchman Francis (I call him "the Mosquito") Mourey.

"Weren't you worried last year about Mourey?" I ask.

"Never. That race, that day, I knew during the whole race that I could win."

There are times, as in this particular early October phase, when Sven's preparation, his confidence, seem—well—inhuman. Clinical. Robotic.

Deus ex machina. Sven—the God. Sven—the machine.

For comparison's sake, take Erwin's previous week. His focus has been broader, more humanistic.

Priority one—his racing. Priority two—his financial stake. Priority three—inextricably woven between the first two—his role as an ambassador. If the sport is to globalize, Erwin's thinking goes, then the best pros need to take their craft beyond the fields of Flanders. And that means travel to the U.S., in this instance a flight from Brussels to the U.S. to race in two early season UCI 'crosses in Southampton, New York.

Noble, but risky. Transatlantic flight, different atmosphere, difficult conditions, inherent pressure to dominate. In one of the pre-race news stories, there's even a misquote portraying Erwin as a hothead who says he's "gonna crush the Americans." In the end, he only wins one out of two. Mechanical troubles, heat, high speeds—"all not what I hoped," he writes in his web journal. "My objective to come away with two weekend wins—unsuccessful."

For the top U.S. riders—Ryan Trebon, Barry Wicks, Jeremy Powers, Tim Johnson—it's not easy competing in Europe. Apparently it's not always easy for Europeans to compete stateside, either. For the Americans, there's some schadenfreude in the tables being turned for once.

For Erwin, there's the long flight back to Belgium, the self-questioning about his condition.

For Sven—no such trouble.

Sporza commentator Michel Wuyts writes about Sven's infamous Mallorca training block for the Dutch publication *Wieler Magazine*. The title: "Als alleen perfectie loont."

All rewards go to perfection.

The phrase has another meaning, too. In Dutch, the tense is not conditional. It's not the hypothetical "if only perfection guaranteed reward." It's "perfection guarantees reward."

It's a given. If you're Sven.

His public is left with a weird sensation: Smitten with respect, reverent—hagiographic, even—but simultaneously suspicious that there must be some hidden stress fracture. Sportsmen can't be this much larger than life. Can they?

Ruddervoorde 2007

PHOTOPRESS.BE

12: THE DOPE

It's nothing new to say the culture of doping has changed fandom. We constantly have our guard up. Road cycling, track and field, Nordic skiing, baseball—the sports world is littered with examples of heroes exposed as cheaters. As with all unrelenting bad news, we internalize a shield to soften the blows.

But it's not like that—not yet, for me—with cyclocross. Sure, top 'cross has its cases—Luca Bramati (2000), Jan Ramsauer (2002), Maxime Lefebvre (2003 and 2006), Martin Zlamalik (2005), and Ben Berden (2004-2005).

Berden, cyclocross's most recent doping confessor, has been trying to make a comeback after a 15-month ban and hefty 60,000 euro fine. In December 2004, Berden tested positive for EPO (erythropoietin, a performance-enhancing hormone) while he was third in the UCI rankings. He admitted to the offense but protested the length of the ban and said he was being unfairly punished for having told the truth.

Similar revelations had come in 2003 regarding the legendary Mario De Clercq, the three-time world cyclocross champion and future trainer for Jonathan Page's Sunweb-Pro Job team.

After investigators visited De Clercq's house in April 2003, a diary was found with references to EPO and the banned blood booster Aranesp, both considered to be illegal doping products. De Clercq, who retired the following year at the age of 38, maintained that the diary notes were made for research reasons. The alleged incident also involved three other riders, including former Belgian racing star Johan Museeuw, who admitted in 2007 that he'd taken performance-enhancing drugs in the last year of his career. [A Belgian court in 2008 found Museeuw, De Clercq, and the two other cyclists guilty of possessing EPO and Aranesp, giving each man a ten-month suspended jail sentence and a

2,500-euro fine. Veterinarian José Landuyt, the supplier, received a one-year suspended sentence and was fined the same amount.]

But, from what I've personally seen—in a decade of being in the international 'cross trenches—I truly believe doping is not a common practice, particularly given the nature of the sport and the stars' altogether human performances. First, the events themselves are only one hour, rather than the five and six hours required for a spring classic or a stage of the Tour de France. Second, with the exception of the *kerstperiode*, most riders race two times per week rather than in multi-day stage races or three-week Grand Tours, so inhuman endurance is not so much a part of the sport's DNA.

Erwin has told me on several occasions that he doesn't believe it's a sport for widespread doping. He admits he doesn't truly know what others do or have done to enhance their performances, but says, "Look at my career. I raced at a top level for almost fourteen seasons. In 1994, I was third in the World Championships, and now, 2007, I wear the rainbow jersey again. Look at Sven, he's been one of the best, if not the best, for the last ten years. That consistency shows talent, not doping."

Over the years, some observers have questioned, say, how a rider like Sven can maintain his domination without doping. For his entire career, Sven has adamantly denied using any performance enhancers. When we talked about the subject earlier in the summer in reference to the daily doping controversies during the Tour de France, Sven simply said, "I don't believe in road racing anymore." But it's clear to me that he does believe in cyclocross racing. The fact that Sven chooses to end his autobiography by looking into the eyes of his son avowing purity on this issue is reassuring. "I convey the same values to my son as my father imparted on me. I can still look everyone right in the eyes and I want to keep it this way."

It goes without saying that all the top pro 'cross riders today must submit to in-competition testing for banned substances and out-of-competition testing as well. For instance, Sven's steady tally of victories means he's tested at least twenty times per season after a competition, and at least five times out-of-competition per year. That's over 250 tests in the last 10 years. And, for pro cyclocross as a whole, there have been no broad scandals to date—nothing approaching the magnitude of the busts in road racing, which have tainted the sport for years.

Certainly, as the history shows, there is doping in cyclocross. And in road racing, fans know all about cases where riders pass the tests, yet are caught via methods like the UCI's biological passport program, which tracks riders' blood values throughout their careers. It's possible that the same kind of under-the-radar doping has been tainting cyclocross, but evidence of team doping or systemic illegal enhancement doesn't seem to be there.

I may be naïve and ultimately proven wrong. I admit that. At the same time, with all of the allegations, trials, denials, mistrials, confessions, and comebacks in road racing (and to some extent in cyclocross), the whole shitteree has become so mind-numbing that it almost ceases to interest me.

Joseph Conrad's *Heart of Darkness*—one of the most difficult books I teach—comes to mind. Conrad's story about Kurtz, an ivory trader in Africa, challenges readers not only to grasp the "horror" of Kurtz's dark *hamartia*, but also to gauge the believability of the novel's main narrator, Marlow, who is relating the tale of Kurtz many years after meeting him in the jungle. On the question of doping, I sometimes feel like Marlow. I've heard murky stories from the "jungle" of cyclocross during my racing days back in the 1990s, but without solid evidence, the stories are only speculation.

Sports scientists call doping a "dilemma"—a quandary for anti-doping officials in which dopers are one step ahead of the law, using increasingly sophisticated methods to boost their performance by means that can't yet be detected. Sports ethicists speak of "moral equivocation," in which athletes—after they're caught—will always attempt to justify why something they know is wrong is nevertheless allowable for them. They turn black into gray. Because it's necessary to win. Because they need the money to get their families out of dire circumstances. Because it's so pervasive. Because it's their body, and they have a right to tamper with their body if they choose to.

Former American road racer and sprinter extraordinaire Davis Phinney drew the following comparison: "In America, we come from puritanical roots. We look at the doping questions in more absolute terms. In Europe, the viewpoint is different," he told *VeloNews* in 2007.

Phinney described the European point of view this way: "You're sent out to chop down a tree and you're given three tools—your hands, a hatchet, and a chainsaw. The choices represent the ethical spectrum," he said. "The purist would use his hands, no matter how long it took. Others would choose the hatchet as the middle ground. But a lot of people would see no problem in using the chainsaw. *As long as no one asks how you got the tree, it's all good.* But what has come to light, so much more in the last decade, is that it's not okay to use the chainsaw."

In the end, if there's any doubt about why doping is such a problem, perhaps only one thing needs to be said: Follow the money.

The millions of dollars, the contracts, the endorsements, the corporate profits, depend on athletes who capture the imagination with superhuman feats. Feats that most humans can't do without drugs.

At this point, the abuse of performance boosters in road racing is so well documented that mustering surprise is the superhuman feat. Suffice it to say that fans are left with an elevator-plunge of disillusionment. As sports writer Jeremy Whittle puts it in his disquieting 2008 book *Bad Blood*: "The essence of doping is cheating and the essence of cheating is defeatism … And living and working in an environment where those values are the currency of everyday relationships, kills you a little. It colors your belief and taints your faith in human nature."

José Luis Barrios, a Spanish doctor who worked with the U.S. Postal cycling team in 2002, put it this way at a December 2001 conference in Spain: "Races like the Tour are too aggressive. They are killing cyclists," writes Alasdair Fotheringham in the April 2002 issue of *Cycle Sport*. "What we have to do is limit the physical damage to the body as far as we can. A Pyrenean stage [of the Tour de France] is more harmful to a cyclist than the therapeutic use of certain banned substances."

Maybe so, but my response—as a coach, rider, teacher, and father is this: At the end of the day, the "absolute" perspective which Phinney speaks of, as in *zero tolerance*, is all we've got.

Call it what you will—puritanical, overly simplistic, too black and white—but nothing in the world is worth compromising when it comes to one's personal code of ethics. If you have to cheat just to do your job, then go do something else.

Finally, crucially and affirmingly, it is fundamental to acknowledge that the human mind and body—when in sync—are capable of supreme accomplishments, allowing athletes to discover something they never knew they had, something they never believed possible.

I am an optimist. This is the enhancement I—most and only—want to know.

***

What makes an athlete excel, aside from natural-born talent and hard work?

Sports medicine experts have their own theories about how certain riders succeed, or crack, as the case might be. One theory about Sven, for example, is that he produces too much adrenaline in the big races, particularly in the World Championships. Some riders don't produce enough of the stress hormone during the build-up races, and their performances suffer. Others produce too much adrenaline when the stress is greatest, and ultimately get tired and lose energy due to the override. Sven's crash on the last lap of the 2006 Worlds in Zeddam might be an example of this—he rode with winning confidence for most of the race, only to fall to pieces. Still, two espoir and one elite world champ cyclocross tunics on his wall make the premise hard to believe.

Another theory involves psyching oneself out: getting so concerned about what rivals are doing—how they're training, what they're saying in the press—that it hurts an athlete's own performance.

In the European media, at least, the attacks and counter-attacks are pervasive. If Niels Albert says one thing, Sven offers up counterspin. And the Belgian sportswriters hang like piranhas on every word.

To one-up a rival on the playing field is one way to exert strength. To do it in the press reinforces the blow. It's an even bigger whammy if the flack comes at you from all directions—in the press, in the races, from your rivals, and from your own teammates or manager. Consider, if you're Erwin, the exchange during a televised panel discussion that included Sven, his teammate, and his manager, Hans Van Kasteren, recounted in a November 2007 Belgian *Cycle Sprint* article.

Sven: "I want to ask you something Hans. The organizers at Erpe-Mere"—the first 'cross of the season—"wanted both Bart and me, which meant they couldn't pay start money for Erwin. You threatened that if Erwin couldn't start, then the whole Fidea team would not start."

Hans Van Kasteren: "Well, that's the way it is in Belgium. I have already told Erwin he has to establish himself differently. I told him he is not Nys or Wellens. If he doesn't like it, I told him, don't race. How popular is Erwin? Not like Bart and Sven. Erwin attracts a totally different public, an invisible public. He has many fans, but they don't express themselves by coming by the busload to the races."

George Orwell put it this way: "Serious sport has nothing to do with fair play. It is bound up with hatred, jealousy, boastfulness, disregard of all rules and sadistic pleasure in witnessing violence. In other words, it is war minus the shooting."

Maybe Sven struggled with this side to the sport in his earlier years, but after a decade at the top, he seems to take it all in stride.

If there's any fraying in Sven's apparent seamlessness, I sense it's in his love of structure and order. At the core of all modern sports is the obsession to get it right. No one wants to be seen as a mistake-maker. And in Sven, there is a seemingly maniacal pursuit of control. From training plans and counseling sessions to mechanical matters and press posturing, Sven literally pours himself into calculation. This type of "life by forecast," as writer Richard Ford labels it in his brilliant short story *Charity*, helps feed a man's delusion that he can "avoid the big calamities."

But some things can't be controlled. The slowing, sinking leak. The once-frozen, now thawing rut. The once-pliant, now glazed ice corner.

The head slap—broadside—from a rowdy fan. The beer douse on a late lap. The one-too-many supporter's double-cheeked greeting kiss, insidiously attacking the immune system.

The only thing a rider can always control is his own sense of internal calamity. That it's possible to ward off despair or a senseless failure with endless exertion and training. Then, if things do go south, well, you've done all you can. All you could ever do. There's no fault, blame, or victimization. Sven's attempts to forge total control offer a safety valve, a coping device when the world rests on his shoulders. By leaving nothing to chance, he leaves everything to fate.

Maybe his weakness is not an inability to accept lack of control over the exterior world; maybe it's an incapacity to recognize something within himself that can't be controlled. Exactly what, I don't know, but it has something to do with the symbiotic dance between will and chance.

Choreographed.

Calibrated.

But never fully in our command.

"Our thoughts are ours, their ends none of our own," the Player King says in Hamlet.

This is where it all gets interesting.

Photo: Tom Robertson

Photo: Tom Robertson

13: TOUGH TIMES

"They said that it was no accident of circumstance that a man be born in a certain country and not some other and they said the weathers and seasons that form a land form also the inner fortunes of men in their generations and are passed on to their children and are not so easily come by otherwise."

— Cormac McCarthy, *All the Pretty Horses*

Hard. To call a cyclist that word is to offer the highest compliment. To call the sport that word is to offer an understatement.

The highlights of road racing throughout history portray near-insane perseverance and nails-for-breakfast resolve.

Road cycling legend Bernard Hinault? Oh, yeah. Liege—snowstorm—1980.

Englishman Sean Yates' toughest hour? Gent-Wevelgem—1989.

Five-time Tour de France winner and greatest cyclist in history Eddy Merckx? Wherever. Whenever.

How much press did Andy Hampsten's 1988 Gavia epic through a snowstorm receive on its recent 20th anniversary passage? It is still the stuff of myth and legend.

Root canal cold.

Why does *Bike* magazine choose Thomas Frischknecht's muddied mug for a famous cover photo?

The essence of hard.

American football fans love their gridiron for the same reasons. January 12, 2008. Green Bay Packers vs. Seattle Seahawks. Divisional playoff wrencher. The game opens with a 13.2 Nielsen rating, but once a near-blinding blizzard hits, the rating soars to 18.7—28.2 million viewers.

When it comes to epic toughness in cyclocross, the Maertens book, *Wellens en Weetjes*, offers a good starting point. A section entitled "Shiver" lists some of the hardest 'cross races of recent times, including Tabor Worlds 2001, St. Wendel World Cup 2003, Hooglede-Gits World Cup 2005 and Hoogerheide World Cup 2007. For good measure, I'll throw in Poprad Worlds 1999.

We're talking the gutsiest, harshest conditions. Full-on triage. For spectators, mechanics, and soigneurs alike. But most of all for the riders.

Feet? Blocks of wood.

Bodies? Cubes of pain.

Since Maertens's book is about the Fidea kingpins, he naturally mentions Bart's troubles with the damp cold and Erwin's incredible ability to perform well when nature chooses adversity. Rightfully so: Erwin's record in the abovementioned epics: 2nd. 1st. 23rd. 2nd. 3rd.-

Going beyond the scope of the Fidea team, it's also worth mentioning the hardest guy in these hardest races. Sven Nys: 6th. 4th. 1st. 1st. 1st.

I'll never forget meeting Sven in the anti-doping room after the Hooglede World Cup 2005, where I was serving as U.S. National Team coach. I don't remember being more cold and tired from working a race. The pell-mell of the false start—running from pit to start, start to pit, pit to start for restart, back to pit—and the infinite bike changes rendered by the cold muddy conditions. No hands left. No feeling at all.

One of my riders, the ever-considerate American cyclocross stalwart and Portland bike shop owner Erik Tonkin, waits to be tested—a urine test in this instance. The minutes in the tight anti-doping quarters seem to take forever as UCI officials test other riders first. Sven is in the middle of seven races in eleven days. He takes the delay with grace. We talk of the previous day's snow, today's heavy race, the false start, Erwin's key last lap crash, Bart's stop to put on a vest during the race, the brutal mud and frigidity, Sven's overcoming, his winning.

Sven gives a huge sigh and pulls his blue-and-white fleece hat closer around his head. In his exhale, I can hear a thousand-and-one training sessions. Then he tells me that winning and recovering from races like this are crucially related to the resiliency built up during those 25-hour summer weeks.

Build the resistance.

Otherwise ...

The man with the hammer will come.

The man with the hammer plays no favorites.

Keep him from the door.

Don't let him in.

Then Sven turns to the others in the room with that likeable Euro-English tendency of using the present tense to describe a past action:

"Today we really earn it," he says.

But Europeans aren't the only tough guys. The hardest races reflect well on Yankee pluck, as well. Some of America's greatest rides have happened under the nastiest conditions. Maybe it's because we have to come from so far away, overcome so many odds, put up with so much shit, just to toe a World Championship start line. Maybe we simply don't want to squander the opportunity. It might never come again. Maybe we're angry. Or stubborn.

A catalogue of the hardest includes:

1978 Worlds, Echano, Spain—Thirteen days of preceding rain create a nightmarish circuit six inches deep with mud; breaking from tradition, the amateurs race after the pros, making the Basque mountain goat perches-to-plunges particularly sketchy. After spending five weeks racing in Switzerland prior to the Worlds, Laurence Malone maintains a top-20 for much of the amateur championship race, eventually finishing 29th.

1979 Worlds, Saccolongo, Italy—Only 50 percent of the circuit is rideable due to bog-like conditions; 45 percent of that 50 percent is pavement; lap times hover at around 15 minutes; the San Francisco Bay Area's Joe Ryan opts for the keen strategy of riding only the paved sections and shouldering his bike for the remaining swamps; he runs for minutes at a time and scores an incredible 16th place in the amateur race. Italian Paolo Guerciotti calls the pro race the hardest in his twelve-year career.

1980 Worlds, Wetzikon, Switzerland—Crazy-slick snow-packed off-cambers are the norm on the "old" Wetzikon course, a back-in-the-day staple on the Superprestige circuit; Swiss superstars Peter Frischknecht and Albert Zweifel stack it into snowbanks like small children in the pro race while in the amateur race, 26-year-old Malone is on track to finish 18th. But on the second of his three crashes, Malone loses his hairnet helmet. The race jury eventually DQ's the five-time U.S. champion, citing "failure to safeguard his head." He takes it with good humor, citing amnesia as the reason he kept going. (When I talk to him years later, he still doesn't recall his disqualification.) It's Malone's fifth and, sadly, final Worlds appearance, leaving fans wondering what he might have been able to achieve with better support.

1986 Worlds, Lembeek, Belgium—This is the event that transports me into the cyclocross world back in that Lisbon apartment; only 35 percent of the quagmire circuit can be taken on the bike; U.S. Coach Milos Linhart quips to *VeloNews*, "This isn't cyclocross, this is a cross-country run." Paul Curley, Massachusetts fireplug and American cyclocross pioneer in Europe, slogs his way through the Belgian mud and heavy snowstorm to finish his best-ever Worlds, coming in 33rd in a field of 45 amateurs. Curley describes the race: "Oh, so many guys quit and it was such a mudbog. Even riding the downhills was nasty. There were snowflurries and my hands were completely frozen due to how wet it was. Just brutal." But Linhart, quoted in *VeloNews*, underscores a point I still harp on today: "Everybody is trying to have a good road season, and they try to make progress in the winter using the gym. The gym is boring. You can have the same quality training using cyclocross, and it's more fun."

1987 Worlds, Mladá Boleslav, Czechoslovakia—With race time temps around -2 degrees Celsius and frozen mud texturing the circuit, it's a see-your-breath icebox. Slivovice—a particularly strong plum brandy—flows freely among the 40,000 weekend spectators who make the pilgrimage to the spiritual home of Czech cyclocross, abutting the giant Skoda car plant. Paul Curley is again best American in the amateur race, maneuvering the snow-banked circuit to a respectable 36th after his third winter of European racing based in Steinmaur, outside of Zurich. "My placing was okay, but my time down, 4:45 from the winner, was pretty good. In those days, that was one of the better deficits to the winner for an American rider," Curley says.

1988 Worlds, Hagendorf, Switzerland—With the rain and snow as brutal as Lembeek two years before, the vertiginous circuit, endemic to Swiss cyclocross, is an absolute grinder. Riders can't get any traction on the slippery-planked run-up, let alone on the muddy in-filled steps. A former cross-country runner, Czech Karel Camdra, goes on to win the amateur race. An early crash forces Californian Don Myrah to come from way back, but he perseveres to finish 26th in his first Worlds. Fellow Californian Clark Natwick makes his sixth and last start at a world championship, finishing 46th. (He later becomes an instrumental U.S. National Cyclocross coach in the 1990s.) In one of the best cyclocross photos I've ever seen and perhaps one of the only cyclocross photos ever to run in *Sports Illustrated* (by Bruno Bade of Presse Sports in the December 26, 1988 issue), the tongue-wagging Frenchman Marc Madiot strides mano-a-muddy-mano with Swiss rider Albert Zweifel in the pro race. (Fraying and yellowing, the photo graces my classroom wall. When my students whine, I point to the photo and smile. "You want to talk about hard?" I say to them. "Let me tell you a little something about hard.")

1999 Worlds, Poprad, Slovakia—Tim Johnson gives the U.S. its first World Championship cyclocross medal—a bronze—in the Under 23 race, and Matt Kelly comes out of his Wisconsin basement to go two better and capture gold in the junior race. When it comes to miserable conditions, Poprad is probably the granddaddy. Tim picks up the story:

"Traction was the name of the game. The course had a solid six inches of fresh snow atop a base of sheer ice when we arrived, and a few inches of fresh stuff fell on Wednesday and Thursday, before the Saturday race. Our pre-ride on Friday gave us a chance to spend some time on course and see where the lines might be. As we arrived, a group of Slovak infantrymen were busy shoveling the start/finish straight. For the thickest sections of ice and snow, they were pouring diesel fuel down and then lighting it. It was shocking, but it worked well. The pavement was clean and ready for the weekend."

2001 Worlds Tabor, Czech Republic—Six-time Worlds competitor (and current U.S. National Mountain Bike and Cyclocross Director Marc Gullickson) describes his race which, at the time, was the best American elite world's performance—13th place. "The ground's cold, still frozen under the thawing top layer, maybe 40 degrees. Guys like Groenendaal show up to the line with thin white cotton gloves. The second the race starts, I'm saturated with freezing cold water and on an early big sweeper turn, I crash. I'm on my ass, sliding across the course. Probably a couple spots from last place at that point. But luckily, everyone starts to freeze to the bone during the second half of the race. I just start passing riders left and right. Ann Knapp"—who finished fourth in the morning's women's championship—"is on the side screaming at me. I can't feel the shifters despite some good neoprene gloves. If it's another lap, maybe I'm a few places higher, but I'm just convulsing at the finish. It's survival, pure and simple."

Throw into the mix the travel, the cultural-physical-emotional battles—then add elemental adversity—and at races like these you're suggesting something close to soul.

2007, Hoogerheide, Netherlands—It's the World Cup in late January, the race made famous on YouTube with bodies flying left and right like a cheap B war movie. Hail and rain bring core body temps dangerously low. Guys who start well—Bart, Richard Groenendaal, Klaas Vantornout, Sven Vantourenhout—all pack it in early with the World Championships just a week away.

Hardhead Sven out-duels Erwin. My hands become so frozen, I can barely pass up bikes in the pit. Jonathan churns in the top five for most of the race but is overcome and fades in the last two laps. Ryan rides what he sees as his best-ever Euro race, steadily moving up and almost catching Jonathan. Both finish with their tanks well below empty in 9th and 10th place.

All Ryan remembers is his head freezing—perma ice cream headache—and beelining to any familiar face he can find after he crosses the line to try to warm up.

The guys are so cold they can't make it to the showers. They can't even make it to the car. They can't even undress.

The hypothermia of Hoogerheide reminds me of a race where it all seems to fall into place, two years previous. It's the 2005 World Championships in St. Wendel, Germany—cold, snow-packed and flurrying. Another one of those moments when you question the sanity of trying to ride a bike up and down nature's white carpet. As coach, I always try to find a quiet place on the circuit to shout encouragement, give splits. From my spot, I can see the trickiest descent with plastic-covered hay bails lining the run-out and then a flat spot before the course charges up one of the many short climbs. In the elite race, where we've rarely had even one guy up front, this time we have two—Jonathan and Ryan—in the top fifteen. The motivation to be the highest placing American has them chasing each other around to finish 14th and 15th, respectively.

Walking back to the van that day in a town as steeped in history as any other small European village, I get a familiar feeling. It happens after every European cyclocross race. The afternoon haze makes everything look tired and old. I feel a million Euro cook-fires in my bones and the church steeples glow orange. Is this how the town's namesake, the ascetic Saint Wendelin, felt when he secretly left home in the 7th century to make a pilgrimage to Rome? A man exploring the verisimilitudes of the secular and the sacrosanct? A herdsman. An eremite. I feel I've just been a part of something that's been going on, around these streets, over these hills, in these fields, forever.

PHOTOPRESS.BE

14: A LITTLE PATCH
OF GROUND

OCTOBER 20, 2007

I touch down—from Helena, Salt Lake City, JFK—to Brussels for the first World Cup in Kalmthout. As an experienced trans-Atlantic traveler, I'm normally good for the cardinal rule of staying awake on European arrival day, but this time I'm so tired I have to ask junior road coach and soigneur Erly Beeuwsaert to drive back to Izegem from the Saturday evening manager's team meeting. I haven't seen Erly since the summer, so we compare notes on our young U.S. guys and the cyclocross season so far.

Sven is crushing, we both agree. He wins easily in Dottignies (Mouscron), notably the only big 'cross race in French-speaking Belgium. Our two best guys hit the ground running, with Ryan taking 7th and Jonathan 9th. Next day in balmy Ruddervoorde, Sven takes his tenth Superprestige in a row. Jonathan out-sprints Ryan for 18th. Midweek, in Ardooie, Jonathan comes in 8th with Ryan a distant 29th.

Today, in Lebbeke, Sven finishes a conservative 3rd. Jonathan again rides respectably for 12th; fresh off the plane from Colorado, Jonathan Baker rides to 19th.

The next day the World Cup morning comes early as we return north of Antwerp to near the Dutch border. This area—more wooded, less industrial—seems more prim than the Izegem countryside of west Flanders.

With only one junior, two women and three elite men competing for the U.S.—most with their own mechanics—I have time to make some pre-race rounds. First stop, tire tycoon Richard Nieuwhuis, for a small order of tubular tires. First impressions of Richard, peddling his wares out of the back of a gray Dutch national team van, remind me of Professor Marvel and his wagon awaiting Dorothy on the Kansas plain. It's a modest affair marked by kindheartedness (his), and wild activity (all the riders want these tires). Richard sells Dugast, the most sought-after threads in cyclocross history. His factory back in the Netherlands churns out over 400 tires a week, and 75 percent of his tires tread Pro Tour teams. Rumor has it that for the famous "Hell of the North" road classic Paris-Roubaix, Richard's company produces some 1,200 tires. For just one race!

Separate bunches of tires hang from inside the van with riders' names like "Simunek" and "Heule" labeled on the casing strips.

"Hey Richard, the Pipistrellos, you have any for me?" I ask.

"I've got your order here, but no Pipis."

"No?"

"Well, let me see," he says, sliding his blue Rabobank fleece hat up on his forehead.

"Okay, here we have an order for a Swiss rider who can't make it. I can switch a few of these out for you."

"Bedankt, my man."

It occurs to me that Pipis is an odd name for a tire. "Where'd you get the name?" I ask him.

"Well, you know we have the Rhino for Rhinoceros, with the big hooked tread. We wanted another animal. Pipistrello is Italian for bat"—the flying variety, he means. "The whitish-gray color of the tire fits with the animal perfectly."

"Very sexy, Richard. You want to know the connotation of pipis in English?"

"No dirty jokes today. I'm too busy."

Laughter.

The big-name rider rigs are parked inside a huge garage. What started as a practical means to a shower and relative travel comfort several years ago has become a form of strut-one's-stuff ostentation. While Sven and Bart have self-contained, massive campers, Erwin takes things over the top this year with an actual semi-rig plastered with his likeness, in addition to his big camper.

I climb aboard and find him reading the paper in a crisp white thermal jacket with rainbow stripes. He fills me in on his trip to the U.S., his frustrating results, his concerns.

Next, I catch Sven outside his camper. Most of the rigs come with loud colors, but Sven's is sleek gray, emblazoned with his logo. It's the same logo Isabelle is making famous with her thriving leisure clothing line, named after her husband. The large blocky S—for Sven—is underscored by an N—in the concise shape of a cyclocross hurdle, and overscored by a shallow arc—to suggest the grace with which Sven flies over planked obstacles, either jumping or running. Young Thibau gives me a smile from inside the camper. Mechanics scurry about and constant pen-thrusting autograph-seekers ask to pose with the world's number one.

Niels "The Prince" Albert is not a happy man when I run into him outside the changing rooms. The 22-year-old has just learned that the Belgian Federation expects him in Switzerland November 4 for the European U23 Championships in Hittnau. If he acts accordingly, he will miss a key leg of the Superprestige series in Hamme Zogge, not to mention a chunk of change.

"What are you going to do?" I ask.

"If I have to go to Hittnau … that's a lot of money I lose."

I do some quick math. He's right.

He stands to lose start money—plus prize money—plus overall Superprestige series prize money. Assuming he were to have a good result in Hamme-Zogge, he could be out 8,000 to 14,000 euros by season's end if he misses doing even one round of a Superprestige.

"Sorry, man," I tell him.

Next, a visit to Jonathan's camper. His mechanic busily prepares for the day. Mario De Clercq helps as well. As I approach, Mario extends his hand with an I-told-you-it's-a-small-world grin.

I study Mario's face, the lines on his forehead, the compact way he clenches his teeth. His silent, stoic nature.

What lies behind the face of a three-time world cyclocross champion? A son who used to climb the stairs past his father's cyclocross medals four, five times a day—dreaming. A kid who, at 16, rode 20 km every day to and from his factory job—dreaming. A rider who retired in late 2004 at almost 39 years of age before his doping sentence in the Landuyt affair took effect. A man whose father always told him, "We descend from ordinary people, and that is something we must always remember."

Jonathan, with his usual determination, goes about getting ready, but he tells me the Sunweb team vibe has gotten dicey since Vegas. He's had two good European races out of four, but his manager is putting the pressure on, saying in news stories that he wants more. "We expect Jonathan to become a regular top-ten finisher," Sunweb's manager, Jurgen Mettepenningen, tells Cyclingnews.com. "There has to be a healthy ambition since this is top-level sport, so you have to deal with the pressure."

Jonathan appears more stressed than usual. Now I know why.

The Kalmthout circuit is nothing special, really. But it's a fast track—especially this year with dry grass and dirt—and it's an extremely circuitous route. Running almost like single-track due to its tight lines, the course definitely favors a good start and riding from the front.

Katie Compton, our country's greatest female cyclocross performer, sets the tone with a brilliant ride, dueling the entire race with Dutch veteran Daphny van den Brand. The rest of the opposition rides in the next provincial postal code. Daphny gets the better of Katie this day with a cagey, late-race attack. Daphny, perennial favorite, is clearly on some good form. Sharing some pit time with Katie's husband and mechanic (an old Montana acquaintance of mine, Mark Legg), we talk about tire pressure, race schedules, and the state of women's racing in the U.S. and Europe.

We continue to be struck by the differences. In Europe, the competitive level is certainly higher; it's where Katie needs to be to improve her game. But in Europe, women's cyclocross gets an almost frosty reception. Indifferent. Subdued. And the start money is minuscule compared to the men's.

In the U.S., the energy, spirit, and numbers of women racing are eye-popping. At a big U.S. cyclocross race, the women's start is as rousing as the men's.

After the race, I hand Katie her 350 euros travel money and congratulate her on the good job. Mission accomplished. In the absence of spectator fervor and big payouts, at least there are the UCI points: 260 of them, to be exact.

During the downtime between races, I watch Bart Wellens, the underdog, take some warm-up laps. Back in 2005, at the World Cup in Nommay, France, he hit his nadir—totally empty, listless, depressed. After two years in the rainbow jersey, he had fallen off the mountain. Since then, he has fought his way back. Nine wins in 2005-2006, seven last season, including his hoofing epic—they actually put plywood down on top of the mud in hopes of increasing the rideability—to take the Belgian title in sodden Hamme-Zogge.

But there was a time when Bart didn't need to fight. He was too good.

Never, not ever, have I seen excellence like I witnessed in Bart Wellens circa 2003-2004. Only 21 wins, yes. But it was the way he won. Standing up. Just hammering the bejesus out of his pedals. Out of every corner. People still talk about Bart riding one of the toughest climbs in international cyclocross, the climb on the Asper-Gavere circuit in 2003.

In the big chain ring.

Ne plus ultra.

Some of the best footage from the three-year Belgian docu-soap *Wellens en Wee* (notwithstanding some of the locker-room humor segments) is the episode from the Pontchateau, France for the World Championships of 2004. At one point, during a pre-ride training day, the cameras capture Wellens's supporters—replete with Viking helmets and Belgian flags—singing in the rain. The melody is "Sur le Pont D'Avignon." But the words are "Sur le pont, Pontchateau, Bartje

Wellens, Bartje Wellens, Sur le pont, Pontchateau, il veut son nouveau tricot."

And voilà. He does get his new jersey, just like the song says.

Bart outsprints Mario De Clercq by the width of a valve extender.

The best part—cameras rolling—comes with the separate reactions of Bart's parents as they scramble toward the finish and learn the outcome. Bart's second consecutive rainbow. Mother Wiske collapses in father Lucien's arms.

"*We hebben 'm,*" goes the audio. We have him.

Strike the music. Bring on the pandemonium.

Veldriligion.

So far this 2007 season, though, Bart's struggling. He's not too happy about teammate Zdenek Stybar outsprinting him in Ruddervoorde, and as the race starts here in Kalmthout, he's already forced to play the Fidea loyalty card by blocking for an off-the-front Stybar.

From the pit, it's clear that the crowd both loves their Bartje and disapproves of this subservient role. Wellens's supporters would clearly like to see Bart ride more selfishly and chase down his teammate Stybar.

On the penultimate lap—with Stybar long gone—Bart punctures. As he rides into the pit, the collective sigh of deflation from fans is audible. Palpable even. Bart's not back. Not yet.

Farther back in the race, Jonathan Page and Ryan Trebon dogfight it early on in the teens, scrapping between 13th and 19th place. But Ryan has all kinds of problems, coming into the pit several times—too much tire pressure, too little tire pressure, an ankle twist, a gratuitous bike change—while Jonathan fights to keep ahead of no man's land, just off the back of the first group.

In the middle of the race, Erwin gains ground from his poor start position and then snaps his derailleur for the second time in a month. He doesn't realize his mechanical until he's at the midpoint of the pit, in the parallel race lane. I can tell he wants to jump over the course tape à la Groenendaal in Loenhout 2005. But that incident precipitated the UCI rule prohibiting such behavior, and Erwin knows it. So he has to beat it, backtracking in the race lane, to get to the pit entrance per the rules.

Meanwhile, I'm in Box 12 focusing on my guys. Suddenly, from behind me in Belgian Box 13, Erwin's dad, running toward the pit entrance with Erwin's spare bike, gets hung up with me and with Ryan's bike cables, nearly knocking me over. I've known Erwin's dad for years. His colorful language is a known quantity.

Verdomme. The all-purpose Flemish expletive for any stressful situation.

As quickly as it comes, it diffuses. We untangle. Aboard his new bike, Erwin gets underway again. But his fire is gone. He takes 22nd place.

When I talk to him later, I'm simultaneously complimentary and realistic. Erwin clearly still has the stellar spurts in him, but I'm not convinced he's got it in him for the whole hour. At least not right now. His troubled results to date bear it out. Normally he's in the top three on the overall UCI ranking. After Kalmthout, he's only eleventh.

Wearing the world champion's tunic must be an incredible burden when you're not going well, I realize. It must be a tremendous responsibility even when you're winning.

Part of me thinks he hasn't trained like he used to—how easy, how subtly the mind succumbs to making a four-hour training ride a 3.5. In the press, he's already wondering out loud if it's his *rotseason*—literally, rotten season—like Bart's of 2005.

The drive back to Izegem is over roads I've come to love for their proximity to where you want to go, unlike the tyrannical distances of Montana. One of the mechanics and I talk cycling and technique. Infinite yellow overhead highway lights flash by—a flicker comes on in my head. In the race that day, I realize, just after Pit 1, the riders zipped by us in the race lane, shifting down two to the best gear for acceleration after the redirecting turn. But with Ryan? No click-click. Instead, after the turn, he's engaged in a full-on muscling to get his bike back up to speed.

Regardless of what other problems he has in a race, there's no way he can snap it that many times to be up there at the end. I make a mental note. Something to coach.

But what about Jonathan's feistiness? During the race he kills himself to stay close, yo-yo-ing to ultimately place 11th. What is that and where does it come from? I make a mental note. Something you can't coach.

Back in Izegem, I help the mechanics unpack. Back and forth to the van. The wind comes up.

After his massage and dinner, Ryan and I talk until after midnight. I mention the click-click, that it's something he should work on. He agrees. We discuss the challenges of living in Belgium for an extended period of time, most of it alone in the U.S.A. House—the home available to national team riders racing in Belgium. He's the sole person there this October, with the road racing guys having finished their seasons.

"People always say, 'Oh, you're racing in Belgium. That's awesome.' But racing is only a small percentage of my time here. Granted I have good friends here, good support. These guys—they're good, honest people, they work hard—but it's pretty tough to come home to an empty house."

"But you would have the same situation in Bend. An empty house, no?"

"Yeah, but at home, it's not like every person I know is involved in cycling. Here, it's all about cycling. And when things go badly, it's easy to dwell on it here."

"What pushes you then?"

Uneasy laughter.

"That's something I ask myself all the time. It's easy to know why you do it when it's going good, and it's hard to figure out why you do it when it's going bad.

"It's easy to be a big fish in a small pond, but it's really hard to be any kind of fish in this pond. Either you suck or you don't, man. That's what people don't get. Like Sven—the dude is good in every race. And because he's at such a high level, when he's bad, he finishes like fifth. Which is like a national catastrophe."

Another laugh.

It's great racing in Belgium, where people understand the sport and know how hard it is, he says. "But my problem is I can't live here.

Getting a massage the other day, I was talking to Fox (Chris De Vos) asking him, 'How do you guys live here?' I mean, I guess I didn't grow up here, so it's different, but it's not pretty here. There's not a ton of shit to do."

He pauses. "For me, living some place nice, desirable, where you're happy rather than just living around your family—that's more my style. And I'd rather have a crappier job and live someplace nice than have a good job and live someplace I don't like.

"I admire the Belgians for being content with what they have. I think in the U.S., a lot of our problem is that people think they can achieve everything, which isn't true," he says. "The people here, they're like, 'This is good enough.' They don't have to be a millionaire, which I like. I get tired of people always striving to out-do each other."

It's late. Wind rattles worn window coverings. Sporadic cars cruise empty Kortrijksestraat. I let Ryan's contradictions be. It's all part of it, the soul search.

To have a good job, but in a place he doesn't like. To admire people's humility and contentment, yet long for a higher place in the biggest show in town. To turn down a season-long series contract for fear of cracking, yet fly to Europe for a brief period and achieve only the occasional good result. To be here, but not want to be here.

It comes to me as I drift off. Hamlet again.

Toward the end of the play, with Hamlet's waverings at full amplitude, Fortinbras's Norwegian army marches through Denmark en route to do battle in Poland. Hamlet comes upon one of Fortinbras' captains and asks him the reasons for the attack. Surely Shakespeare had only cyclocross in mind when he penned the captain's response—

"Truly to speak, and with no addition
We go to gain a little patch of ground
That hath in it no profit but the name."

Ryan Trebon, one of the best cyclocross riders in the U.S., can't quite accept the actions he must take to succeed. He'll compete for a patch of ground, but it will be on his own terms.

Another of the nation's best—Jonathan Page—battles and claws for every clump of ground, and it will be on the sport's terms. He's an American living in Europe because there's a job to do, and that's part of the bargain.

Mario De Clercq   PHOTOPRESS.BE

Ryan Trebon, (Kalmthout 2007)

Jonathan Page, (Lievin 2008)

PHOTOPRESS.BE

15: UP AND OVER

Given that cyclocross got its start in France in the early 1900s as a way to keep the French army fit, the element of stealth in the sport has always been in some way linked to its pedigree. These days, though, the opportunity to pull one over on a cyclocross rival is fairly limited. With the standardization of courses fostered by UCI regulations, it's increasingly unlikely to see bombshell moves like Sven's Zolder tree move at the 2002 Worlds or Sven's trademark bunny-hopping acrobatics.

Which is precisely why UCI point leader Zdenek Stybar's throwing down in the Tabor World Cup on October 27, 2007 is pure cheek. On the second of nine laps, just as the race has settled into that redline fug of oxygen depletion—guys top tube to top tube—Stybar, the strong Czech rider, throws down the gauntlet by bunny-hopping the two hurdles while still on his bike. He gains precious seconds on the uphill section and Sven—some six guys back, just rounding a corner, his view obstructed—doesn't see the hops. But, Sven being Sven, he senses it. How else could Stybar have gotten the gap?

To get back, he must answer. He must replicate Stybar's move. Up and over. Up and over. Through traffic. He gets himself right back in it.

Few aspects in cyclocross are as rich as the maneuver of clearing a hurdle while remaining on the bike. Patrick Bassez of the Flanders Training School, one of Belgium's many provincial training centers, even has a few chapters on the topic in his 1999 dissertation entitled *Biomechanica Van Het Fietsen* (The Biomechanics of Cycling).

Bassez describes the three different methods of clearing hurdles in the minutest detail. The first requires a full-sail, full-speed clearing of the barrier or hurdle. Bassez labels this *de zweefsprong*, or "the glider jump." The second is a technique Bassez calls "the double jump." Popularized by Danny De Bie in 1989, it calls for the rider to seesaw up and over a log or hurdle with front and rear tires making contact. Bassez likens the third technique—the "Sven Nys jump"—to the Fosbury Flop in high jumping, where the rider combines elements of the first two methods (the clean clearing and the seesawing) to achieve virtually no contact with the barrier during the up and over.

For better or worse, in January 2000, the UCI unequivocally acts to foil the kangaroo-like prowess of a certain Sven Nys. Implementing regulation 5.1.024, the governing body mandates that an obstacle section have two planked hurdles 40 cm high, with 4 meters between each plank. The regulation renders the first method of full-clearance launching impossible due to the close succession of the two planks. It also seriously constrains the slower "bunny-hopping" moves due to space limitations between hurdles. In essence, it becomes faster for a rider to run the obstacles than to attempt such athletics. Long gone now is the original regulation language: "No acrobatics on the part of the riders shall be required to overcome the obstacles." Some still refer to it as the "anti-Sven rule." (Note: In 2010-2011, the UCI Cyclocross Commission relaxes the distance between planks, allowing for a distance of 4-to-6 meters and "up to 40 cm high," thereby increasing the probability that riders might again jump the planks while on the bike).

Most hard-core 'cross students know the legend of Belgian Eric de Vlaeminck. Maybe they've seen a photo of his *zweefsprongen* prowess back in the day. He was the only pro cyclist actively hopping obstacles on his way to winning six consecutive pro 'cross titles from 1968 to 1973. Belgian old-timers still recall seeing Eric ride several hundred meters on a very narrow edge of a sidewalk and jumping over logs and hurdles. His brother Roger—Mr. Paris-Roubaix for his victories there—could certainly pilot a 'cross bike, too, but he never resorted to jumping the barriers like Eric, for fear of an injury.

Eric, on the other hand—the dude could hop.

Very few know—except perhaps for Bassez and a few Americans—that probably the first guy to successfully achieve the hop in World Championship amateur competition is none other than American

Laurence Malone during the 1977 Worlds in Hanover, Germany. And even fewer people are probably aware that Laurence didn't think he could jump the 40 cm beam until he actually did it—in the race.

"Yeah, it was pretty high, but nothing any American BMX kid couldn't handle," he tells me. "You know, you train in Santa Cruz, there's plenty of logs to hop over. In Hanover, I was a bit nervous—the sport is bound by such tradition. But once the race begins, you find you can do amazing things."

The photo and caption in *VeloNews* are priceless. Dubbed "The Flying American" by German newspapers, Malone "amazed the crowd by staying in the saddle and sailing through the air at high speed, gaining about 20 meters on his opponents each lap. His acrobatics were the greatest attraction in the race and when he entered the stadium for the last time, he received more applause than the eventual winner," the story reads.

The funniest part, Laurence says, is that "there was a huge photo of me in full flight, clearing the barrier in the big French cycling magazine *Miroir du Cyclisme*. Accompanied by a typically snide French caption. Something to the effect of, 'For 32nd place, he didn't have much to lose.'"

Fast forward to Danny De Bie hopping his way to the 1989 world pro title in Pontchateau, France, breaking the legs of perennial bridesmaid Adri van der Poel in the process. Ponytail flopping with each hop over the toughly placed single planks, Danny literally steals the title from the clearly stronger Adri and wins the hearts of cyclocross fans the world over. It is Adri's third of five silver medals until—finally—he clinches a victory, his only, in Paris 1996.

For Danny, doing *de doublesprong* to the rainbow jersey is his career's greatest moment.

"Everyone knew I could jump the barriers. I already had nine or ten victories that season. And I would jump when I could. But the way I did it—the spectacle in Pontchateau—that's what the spectators loved," he says with pride. "It's not right that they make it so difficult to do now. It's good for the sport."

The next time a world title is won by virtue of vaulting a barrier comes in the 1997 Under 23 title race in Munich's Olympia Park stadium track.

By a kid named Sven Nys.

I've watched the video a hundred times. It's something to behold.

On the same athletic oval used for the snowy 1985 World Cyclocross Championships and built for the 1972 summer Olympics, Sven kills it over the two separate single hurdles spaced maybe 10 meters apart. Compatriot Bart Wellens keeps it close for a while, but Sven's hurdling ability is superior. He's easily going 35 km an hour as he launches.

In *Ik, Sven Nys*, Sven shares his thoughts about that race, that move. "It was the first time in my life that I was in a position to win a world championship," he writes. Jumping the beams, a "secret weapon" that his coach told him not to reveal to anyone, "gave me tremendous strength. After the first lap, we came in and the other riders were hitting their brakes. I made the jumps perfectly. Adrenaline surged through my body and the Belgian supporters who were in the stadium shouted with joy."

It's a scenario that has played out again and again in races big and small since Sven first came on to the scene. Sven's ditch jumping in Loenhout, Belgium, a few years ago prompted organizers to replace the ditch with pallets, deeming that Sven's chasm-jumping gave him too much of an advantage. Sven's victory in the 2006 Belgian Championships in Tervuren, where the barriers were placed very close to the end of the lap, is another memorable example of the up-and-over. When Sven shows me the footage of that race on his big screen, it reminds me of watching Todd Wells win the 2001 National Championship in Baltimore, where his hops helped him defeat Tim Johnson and Marc Gullickson. In both these races, the move significantly enhances the chance for victory.

In essence, feats of acrobatics have always endeared athletes to the crowd. One of America's best cyclocross pros, Jeremy Powers, always receives huge cheers when he takes the barriers from the saddle. While the 2000 ruling means the full-sail days are gone for good, it at least grants room for the possibility of hopping in certain situations.

And that's exactly what transpires in this Tabor World Cup of 2007.

Game film:

By the third lap, with a selection needing to be made, Sven and Stybar fan out the width of the double-wide *balken* and take flight.

Gutsy Stybar already has one World Cup victory this season, in Kalmthout. He wants more.

Sven has never been one to heap praise on the Tabor course. Not enough challenge. Low ambiance. But, as future hosts for the Worlds in 2010, the Tabor organizers have added some spice—a sand stretch—to give the course more dimension.

Sven adapts. In what has become his trademark, he determines the toughest section of any course—in this case the leg-sapping sand—and brings out his hammer. Serene to the challenge.

Lap six, Sven hits the sand first, followed by the selection—Stybar, Klaas Vantornout, Lars Boom, a dangling Bart Wellens.

Just after the sand, Sven pounds forward, pouring out the wattage. The kind of attack at the heart of all bike racing for its capacity to electrify.

Sven's legs do the talking. As if to say—"Not only will I jump with you, I will attack you when you're on the red wire."

42:04 into the race. Another lap.

Now, 48:45 and it's only a matter of time. They're at the sand again.

Vantornout and Stybar are still there. But their tongues are wagging like heatstroked dogs.

Sven bangs them again. Same place. He seems to be working in his own forge. A couple of tight turns.

Out of the corner of his eye, a slight gap.

Time for the kill.

A little extra pressure.

Space between wheels.

Time to ram things home.

To the toolbox once more.

49:48.

In the heat of the moment, where the race needs to be won, Sven reaches for the move.

Most—if not all—'crossers, when approaching a run-up, swing the hindmost leg around and "step off the back" of the bike onto the back leg. They then square things up with another step before propelling themselves upward, with bike in hand or on shoulder.

For the majority of riders who dismount off the left side of the bike, it's a fluid one-two and up: Step off the back with the right, then onto the left, and then take the first stair step with the right.

One-two and up. So say all the textbooks and videos.

Stybar, Vantornout, Lars, and Bart do the one-two.

Watch there, though. Just there.

In one balletic swing, Sven "steps off the back."

One. But no two. No square up with the left.

Instead, it's—bang. Straight to the stair on one. With his left—as in, his second—foot.

Sven is literally one step ahead of the competition.

The fact that he's been doing it the whole race is immaterial. When it counts—when the race is on the line—he will pound you. Nails to your coffin.

The last two laps, with a commanding lead, he hops the barriers unnecessarily. The potential reward worth more—apparently—than the risk. Confidence. Unadulterated.

They don't call him the Cannibaal for nothing.

Sven Nys, (Tabor 2007)   PHOTOPRESS.BE

Zdenek Stybar, (Tabor 2007)

16: LOU-A-VILLE

OCTOBER 27-28, 2007

With the exception of Page and Jonathan Baker making the trek to the Czech Republic World Cup in late October, the best American racers meet on the same weekend for the U.S. Grand Prix of Cyclocross (USGP) races in Louisville, Kentucky. The USGP series, started in 2004 by director Bruce Fina to bring the best American racers together, has become the preeminent U.S. national cyclocross race series, with 2007 events in Louisville, Kentucky; Mercer, New Jersey; and Portland, Oregon. I've been a part of the series since its inception as its technical director, in charge of course construction and adherence to UCI regulations. In this instance, I'm also in Louisville as national team coach, keeping an eye on the younger riders especially.

The racing is hot and bothered.

Tim Johnson and Jeremy Powers—affiliated by their New England roots and their shared sponsor, Cyclocrossworld.com—get the better of Kona duo Ryan Trebon and Barry Wicks, but all four are clearly on a higher level than the others at this point in the season.

Despite some entertaining smack barbin' in and out of the press, this two-on-two is good for the sport. And it's definitely an "on any given weekend" scenario for domestic American 'cross. The guys are pretty evenly matched. They all bring some super skill-sets to the table; winning is often decided by who has the best legs.

But for me, the real barometer in Louisville is who shows the most desire. Which guy can go out and lay down the pain for an hour? What I look at as a coach are the strengths and weaknesses. I try to stay in the background, sculpt their planning if they ask, and try to boost their motivation so that we can eventually have strong World Championship performances. That's the objective, anyway.

Because a funny thing happens when you go to Europe and race against the world: The trash talking and tensions subside and previous rivals on the domestic circuit draw collective strength from each other to try and blow down Euro doors.

I'm encouraged by another Louisville impression: A quarter of the elite men's field is composed of espoirs, and over half of these Under 23's have raced 'cross in Europe. What's more, two of the top five elite men and all five of the top espoirs on both days are EuroCrossCamp alumni. I feel a sense of accomplishment that my camp in Belgium is achieving its goal to help develop top American riders.

My final thought from the Louisville weekend comes in a conversation with an old friend, the ever-casual Giant pro Adam Craig. Adam has always done a few 'cross races since becoming one of the world's best mountain bikers, and the topic of U.S. Olympic mountain bike selection is very much on his mind. Over some quick hors d'oeuvres at the USGP number presentation in the posh Kentucky Derby museum, where the top riders are presented their racing numbers by local cycling club kids, we talk about some of the disgruntlement he'd recently voiced in a Cyclingnews.com article that criticized the selection process and the Olympic mountain bike circuit in Beijing.

"Pretty pointed comments," I posit.

"Do I come off sounding bad?"

"Well, the text describes you as 'irate' but 'diplomatic.'"

"Yeah, well, it is a bummer."

He's referring to the end-of-season national rankings, which decide whether the U.S. will get two spots in the Olympics, or three. The cumulative point total for a nation's top three riders depends to a certain extent on the commitment among a country's top riders to accumulate as many points as possible. Adam is frustrated by the fact that some of the other top U.S. guys aren't chasing UCI points the way Sven has done it for Belgium. He wonders if the Americans will even bother going to Chile to chase the points they need.

"Maybe it's a longshot for you guys to win enough points down there anyway," I offer.

"Yeah, true. But I can't do it all alone," Adam replies.

Our conversation becomes drowned out by vibrant race announcer Richard Fries as he opens up the ceremony. A classy number presentation gets underway and a crowd of 150 hungry racers and cyclocross paparazzi scarf down artichoke appetizers.

American cyclocross has come a long way, I think to myself.

Through the din, I shift subjects. A month before, Adam traveled to China and struggled to a DNF (did not finish) in the Olympic mountain bike test event. I've heard all about the air pollution problem, but I want to know about the circuit.

"How did the course ride there?"

"Ah, not too technical. A few steep climbs. Pretty basic."

"Could you do it on a 'cross bike?" I ask, remembering Sven's penchant for racing mountain bike races on his 'cross bike.

"Maybe. Maybe," he says, eyeing me quizzically.

Photo: Tom Robertson

17: FIELDS AND FARMERS

OCTOBER 31, 2007

Flanders fields lie fallow now. Cold west wind pours down your neck and you pedal faster to keep warm. North toward Koolskamp, Lichtervelde, the roundabout toward Diksmuide, past the many military cemeteries in and around Hooglede, and back to the chateau in the Ardooie, home to Izegem.

Piles of cauliflower and carrots harvested the same morning lie in heaps next to the road. The scent of onion jets into your nostrils, driven by dirt and wind.

Like the 'crossman.

Farmers. Farming. Cyclers. Cycling. You can't escape the affinity.

Working the fields; working the earth.

I love the connection.

The development of the sport in the U.S. isn't tied to these agrarian roots; the typical American cyclocross course derives from city parks and municipal open spaces.

Even in Europe, the sport's pastoral ties are being transformed (some would say transmogrified) by more open, faster, standardized circuits, morphing toward modernity and pristine precision, leaving old connections behind.

But, the connection is still there. To feel—with tires and feet—the texture of the mud, the glide of the sand, the slickness of the grass. To hear the wind blow through leafless trees. To smell the compost, the wood smoke, the air just before it begins to snow.

"When I'm training in the woods on my circuit, alone, I feel the most alive. More even than when I'm racing," as Sven puts it. "When I'm alone, it's me against nature and me against myself."

Says Lars Boom: "The old-fashioned races—Koppenberg, Niel, Baal—the heavy ones, where it's me against the course—the mud, where the course is so wide that I can ride or run pretty much anywhere, trying to find the right line—these are my favorite moments in cyclocross."

Adds Jonathan Page: "Once in a while, when I have a magical day, I feel totally connected to what I'm riding on. But those days are vastly outnumbered by days when I feel not like a farmer but an overworked pack mule. No matter how hard I work, I'm just going to end up back at the barn with another load to carry."

Wouter Van Driesen has a better view than most when it comes to the concurrence between earth and cyclist. His grandfather's house is one of the last structures on the rider's right before the ascent of the famed Koppenberg race, outside Oudenaarde. It's still a few days before the kings of 'cross will battle up its slopes in the Koppenberg Cross GVA series race and it will be six months before the likes of Tom Boonen and Stijn Devolder thunder up the cobbled incline again in the Tour of Flanders, the famed spring road classic known simply in these parts as De Ronde.

Brown and white cows look cold in the flecking rain. Fences and posts stand upright. The fields will be littered with plastic beer cups in a few days time. Meadow grass seems to moan with each passing minute.

I ask Wouter about this mythical hill and the metaphysics of it all. Are the farmers who own this land happy to host such big races?

"Of course. There are big memories here. The big stars climbing the cobbles. Jesper Skibby getting run over by the official's car in 1987."

The incident he refers to kept the Koppenberg out of the Tour of Flanders from 1988 to 2003, due to the unconscionably steep cobbles. If De Ronde Van Vlaanderen comes with rain, as it often does, the cobbles become impossibly slick and road riders have to dismount like 'crossmen and slip-slide their way up.

"Besides, it's good money for the landowners."

"They're paid?" I ask, somewhat incredulously.

"Sure. That's a lot of beer cups to clean up."

I ask him about my musings about farming and cycling.

It's a connection some people wouldn't like, he says. "Modern Belgians wouldn't necessarily want to be associated with farming. The connotation is old-fashioned."

On the other hand, there's truth to it. "It's sort of like road racing and the 'crosses here in Flanders," he says. "Road racing—it's seen as heroic, larger than life, but cyclocross is seen as maybe more authentic. Like farming. And, you know, there aren't so many things that are really authentic anymore."

Cows chew cud across vacant tracts.

Clouds deepen gray.

Cobbles glisten.

As I walk back to my car, I wonder if only an American can feel this—this romanticized notion about a sport's link to farming fields. After all, according to cyclingrevealed.com, the sport was born as a military exercise in the late 19th century, allegedly after a French soldier rode his bike through the fields. Officers watched him and began to realize the potential usefulness of the endeavor. Eventually, the French Army started doing drills on bikes. France held its first National Championships in 1902; Belgium followed suit in 1910. The sport's first big event, the "Criterium International," took place in France in 1924, complete with a descent known as the "Trou du diable" (the hole of the devil). In 1950, the legendary Frenchman Jean Robic won the first World Cyclocross Championships, the only rider to ever win both that prize and the Tour de France.

The Koppenbergcross, with its climb up the cobbles and serpentine descent, is no cakewalk either. I once asked Jeremy Powers, a two-time Koppenberg survivor, to describe what it's like to race cyclocross here.

"It's the hardest of all the Belgian races I've done. It's the worst for me personally. A really, really hard, fast start. A straight-up sprint to the first hard left. Then drag race to the cobbles. Then the 18 percent climb is crazy demanding and slimy. ... Off-camber, lumpy cow field grass. On the big climb, once you're done pedaling squares up to a certain point, you usually have to get off and run. About two seconds after you get back on your bike at the top, you start pedaling again and come to the trickiest technical descent in 'cross. Left. Right. Left again, and onto the road that brings you to the field, then the pavement and then up the cobbled climb again. No rest. ... A complete sufferfest. Twenty thousand spectators. Nothing like it."

Flanders field   Photo: Tom Robertson

Photo: Tom Robertson

18: PRESSURE POINT

NOVEMBER 1, 2007

A holiday crowd in the tens of thousands drapes the Koppenberg fields. The big guns batter each other in the mud—changing bikes every half-lap—until in the last lap, Sven and Bart are the only ones left standing. Bart has come back from a sensational crash to draw even with Sven as they head up the cobbles one last time. Just before turning off into the field—halfway up—Bart comes through on the inside, stuffing Sven to such an extent that he has to wheelie around the precipitous right-hander.

It will be Bart's best and last moment.

In the hardest section—uphill grinding through tufted clay—Sven pistons forward, then transitions off to a churning run toward the top point of the course.

Game over.

"Your fifth Koppenberg victory, Sven. Chapeau," I congratulate Sven that evening by phone.

He graciously responds by giving credit to his foe. "Bart was just killing me on the slippery descent, taking all kinds of risks," he says.

Still. Sven's batting .500 this week with two huge wins, Tabor and Koppenberg, out of four races; he'll score another big victory the following day at the Superprestige in Hamme-Zogge. Five wins in nine days. Steady as she goes for the man in the new-and-blue UCI leader's skinsuit awarded to the world's number-one ranked rider.

Before I end the call, I have to follow up with the key question: "What tires were you running?" I ask.

"Rhino 34's. But it's always a hard choice. Bart was running lower pressure and was way better than me on the downhill. I wanted more pressure for the road and the climb. Sometimes you have to choose, eh?"

It would be an understatement in European cyclocross to categorize tires and tire pressure as simply a consideration. A science would be more apropos.

Take the scene at the 2002 Wetzikon, Switzerland World Cup. I'm there coaching the Americans. Adam Craig, a bright-eyed young rider who would go on to finish a brilliant eighth at the U23 Worlds in Zolder a week later, comes through the pit during his first warm-up lap with his Michelin clinchers brick-hard. My practice is to be in the pit during the warm-up, with extra wheels and a pump for the dialing in.

"Adam, you've got to run less pressure."

"No, I'm good."

"Adam, less pressure."

"We'll check 'er out."

A lap later. Muddied from a few tumbles—

"Geoff, we've got to run less pressure."

The science and pseudo-science of it is incredible. The top guys? Stowed away in their campers—some 20-30 sets of wheels. Philippe Maertens devotes a whole chapter to the topic in his Fidea book.

Different treads: Slick. Semi-slick. File. Knob. Diamond. Chevron. Combo.

Different widths: 28. 30. 32. 34.

Different rims: Carbon. Aluminum. Dished. Traditional.

Remarkably, very few of the top pros use a pressure-gauged pump. Erwin uses his thumb and forefinger. Sven and Bart simply bop around the parking lot prior to going out on the circuit. As they ride, they push down on their handlebars, divining whether their tires are too hard, too soft or just right. If there's too much pressure, they stop and let some out. It's funny to watch the faces of mechanics who have precisely pumped their rider's tires to a certain pressure on the dial, only to have the riders then deflate them according to some internal prognostication.

Fork travel, volk-style.

Directly related—but far less discernible to the passionati—is the utilization of the pit zone during the race by the most experienced pros. Assuming the rider doesn't lose too much time, it's not unusual for the top guys to spend the first half of the race coming into the pit each lap to figure out the best tires and tire pressures for the day's work. On courses like the famed Hofstade circuit, which combines moist beach sand with woodsy slick mud, it's standard to hear riders barking orders to their pit crews. The more vacillating a course's surface, the more fluctuating the temperatures, the more varying the precipitation, the more range for tire and pressure options.

I've always been impressed, especially in Switzerland, by the way European clay-based soil freezes and unfreezes. Often, when temperatures rise throughout the day, an afternoon's race conditions will be completely different than in an early morning junior race. If you hit it just so—when the top layer thaws above the frozen under-turf— you've got a recipe for a real yard sale. It's usually one of the foremost experiences for American understudies when they hit the continent.

In the pit, box-to-box with the Belgians, the Dutch, the Czechs during a race, it's riveting to hear the riders—totally gilled—mustering monosyllabic instructions to their mechanics.

"Too high," they stutter.

"34's," they stammer.

"Slicks," they splutter.

The best tire tale of all-time? The moment-by-moment action from Koppenberg 2006.

Deceitfully tricky. Deviously hard.

The K-bomb. The Koppenberg 'cross.

Sven tells the story.

"When we do our warm-up laps, the track is dry. But it rains right before the race and again on the first lap. We all start with our tires for dry"—Dugast Typhoon with the standard chevron and side knob tread—"and everyone crashes in the first laps. So, I ride the first laps with the same tires and I say, 'Shit—this is a problem.' Because the tires I need, they're back at the camper. So I yell to my mechanics to go get the tires. But with all the spectators, it takes them a lap to get to the camper. So, what do I do? I decide to stop right there after the cobbles and let out some air."

But stopping—seemingly interminably—in the race course, on the big climb, to deflate his rear tire? In the middle of the race?

That's Sven.

Hoping to capitalize, the Frenchman John Gadret drills it at the front. He smells blood. He's ahead by 25, 26, 27 seconds—the gap!

Sven is now 30 seconds down with 6.5 laps to go.

"By the time I get my new bike, I'm way behind. And then I win the race. I still can't believe it."

Lead group, (Koppenberg 2007)   PHOTOPRESS.BE

Lars Boom, (Koppenberg 2007)

PHOTOPRESS.BE

(Koppenberg 2007)

PHOTOPRESS.BE

Erwin Vervecken, (Koppenberg 2007)

Lars Boom, (Treviso Worlds 2008)

Sven Nys, (Hofstade BK 2008)

Bart Wellens, (Niel 2007)   PHOTOPRESS.BE

Erwin Vervecken, (Pijnakker 2007)

Izegem   Photo: Tom Robertson

Izegem   Photo: Tom Robertson

Jonathan Page, (Hofstade 2007)

Ryan Trebon, (Ruddervoorde 2007)

Going deep   Photo: Tom Robertson

19: TEAM-VERK

Everything is about the race, and the next race is always coming.

For Sven, there's a Tabor win; a bad start in Zonhoven; a tired recovery day plus massage; training, training, and massage; a Koppenberg victory and massage; more training and massage; a 7th place finish in Eernegem and a massage; then a 40th victory in a Superprestige in Hamme Zogge.

Competing teams all have their individual dramas. Sven's previous teammate Richard Groenendaal departs from Rabobank and now rides for a new Dutch team AA Drink. Meanwhile, Lars Boom moves up to the elite ranks and now rides alongside Sven to form a dynamic Rabobank duo.

"It's really good to have another guy," Sven says about Lars during our regular midweek phone call. "I made a mistake to assume Lars would be good enough to help me chase down Stybar in Kalmthout, but he wasn't good there. But in Tabor, Lars was at the front every lap. He's good on the fast courses—hey, he's world time trial champion—but not so good with technique yet."

Though he's the veteran—eight years older than Lars—he's not a mentor to Lars the way Adri van der Poel once was to him, he says.

"Lars is on a completely different summer program than I am. And, Lars, he's less timid than I was when I was younger. Lars, he's not the kind of guy who looks up to another guy. He's very good in his own right."

"So it's you two against the Fideas?"

"You know, Fidea is not the team that everybody makes out," Sven says. "With so many champions—Wellens, Vervecken, Stybar—they're riding for themselves. All individual egos. They should be riding for Bart right now"—because he's the strongest—"but they don't." Rumor has it that Stybar and Klaas Vantornout are thinking of signing contracts with rival team Sunweb-Pro Job the following year, he adds.

I pause and think about Richard Groenendaal's departure from Rabobank and the famous January 2007 photo from Hoogstraten before he left. Despite their being teammates, Richard flips off Sven for out-sprinting him in a race Sven essentially cannibalized (the two rode together way out in front and obviously didn't agree beforehand who should take the win).

"How is it different with Lars rather than Richard?"

"Oh, it's totally different." He pauses to choose his words carefully. "Richard is not a guy who rides for another guy. He only rides for himself. He's a special guy that way."

The talk about teamwork makes me wonder: Is there no place for sacrifice in modern cyclocross, as there is in road racing? No mechanism for dutifully laying it down for one's team leader? No invoking of Shakespeare's Henry V "band of brothers" speech—or, better, the soliloquy from the resolute Wiglaf, last warrior standing in defense of leader Beowulf against the final dragon?

"I would rather my body were robed in the same
Burning blaze as my gold-giver's body
Than go back home bearing arms.
We must bond together
Shield, helmet, mailshirt and sword."

In terms of the race and team structure, of course, road racing is very different than cyclocross. In road racing, the demands require a significant collective ethos. Worker bees pack and haul, shelter and pull for the designated leader. A domestique is paid to do his work within the greater context of the race and the team hierarchy. And, over the course of an event, the kings of the finale are the ones who have been piloted by their teammates to stand above. The entire team regularly shares the winner's prize money.

As a result, when road race team directors mull the lineup for a stage race, they look at their best climbers who can time trial, their best time-trialers who can climb, and their best sprinter for team-building. Then they look for their best rouleurs to complement whatever objectives the team holds for the race.

Road cycling is all about filling roles for the greater good. As riders come up through the pipeline, their strengths and fissures are duly noted. They are commodities, prized and paid for their talents—a skill, an ingredient, a role. By the time they go pro, they've been shaped by the caste system. The reward, at the top, is a bit of comfort. Lord knows they still have to hurt. And they still have to prove themselves to earn the next contract. But their roles are established—as leaders or, more than likely, supporting riders.

Cyclocross requires no such martyrdom. But the sport does value teamwork. A while back, I asked U.S.A.C Vice President of Athletics Jim Miller what Rabobank saw in talented Tejay Van Garderen, an up-and-coming American road racer, whom I'd seen develop on the Montana roads of his childhood.

Jim, also Tejay's coach, gave me his answer: "Rabobank knew Tejay could time trial and climb. What impressed them the most, though, is that they saw he could still do these things after working for someone else the whole race. That's what got him his first Rabobank contract."

In modern cyclocross, there's no room for commodification. It's all. Or it's nothing.

The discipline hasn't got the same evolution or compartmentalized demands of road racing. The nature of the racing isn't fashioned from a collective cloth.

Cyclocross riders are not paid to merely sprint well, climb well, ride solo well. These are the prerequisites for going pro. Quite simply, a cyclocross rider is paid to do one thing.

Win.

The only required aggregate effort is helping teammates at crunch time—when there's no chance for personal glory, and it's time to help a colleague reach the podium. In other words, the only requirement is that teammates pitch in, when necessary, to block a rival team, if it will put one of their own on the podium.

What that means for 'cross riders is more room for personal triumph. What it also means: Their own performance is to blame when they blow it.

There's no place to hide.

Photo: Tom Robertson

20: WAVE THEORY

Fifteen clicks from Lichtaart, home of Sven's trainer Paul Van Den Bosch, I pull the Saab over at a truck stop. I've come to Belgium for a six-day trip, one I've been looking forward to for weeks. The early November air bites shrewdly. Overcast. Trees like sticks to the sky. Birds flock to fields plowed under. The traffic on the Antwerp-Eindhoven 313 drones in the background. Bedraggled trash litters the wet grass. I take a leak and wonder where Festina soigneur Willy Voet was snagged during the infamous traffic-stop-turned-drug-bust that face-planted the 1999 Tour de France. It was probably at some nondescript Belgian outpost like this one.

Making my way back to the car, my thoughts leap, unaccountably, to a book that informs my classroom teaching, *Rhetoric: Discovery and Change*, written by three University of Michigan professors. One chapter examines how physics principles can be used by writers to uncover alternative perspectives. In this view, "A unit of experience can be viewed as a particle, or as a wave, or as a field. That is, the writer can choose to view any element of his experience as if it were static, or as if it were dynamic, or as if it were a network of relationships or a part of a larger network."

As I slide into the steady stream of traffic, I realize what I'm after on this November trip. Where before I've sought and experienced infinite amounts of static perspective (particles) with the world's best 'crossers—pre-season interviews, individual race interactions, Christmas camp immersions as national coach, week-long World Championship build-ups—this time I'm compelled by what the Michigan professors call "the fusion and absence of distinct boundaries." In this case, between training and racing, living and competing.

I don't want seams. I want smear.

In essence, I want ... the wave.

Backstage.

Embedded.

A week in the life.

***

On the side of a sandy incline on a forested loop, Paul Van Den Bosch and I talk as we wait for Sven to come 'round the circuit again.

Having worked together for several years now, Paul and Sven enjoy a certain significant symbiosis. Paul is Sven's trainer—designing programs throughout the year and monitoring daily Sven's fitness. But both men confirm that he's more than that. Paul is Sven's chief confidante and motivator, as well.

It's a Wednesday morning. Sven is *bos* (woods) training in the forest. Paul and I take a short walk to the top of a precipitously steep, sandy ravine. Sven makes the first of many approaches. I peer over and ascertain that it's a climb I don't think I could ride up.

Paul—eager—shouts encouragement.

"Up ... Up ... Up ... Komaan ... Up ... Up."

Orange and blue Rabobank tights wrap churning knees as Sven powers upward and over the lip.

"The first time we came here years ago, Sven couldn't make it up," Paul says. "Now, he's doing these explosions every week. Some weeks, harder, longer sessions. For example, four sets of three explosions up this little hill. But this week, just one hour with two sets of three times up. Short efforts. To keep the feeling, to have contact with me, to have the good feeling in his head. That's why he comes here.

"Most don't start training on the cyclocross bike until August. But with Sven, we start all the way back in April. To never let the feeling go away. Even when he's in the middle of his road racing, we come here."

Sand shifts under my feet. I reposition and watch Sven come up again.

Paul tells me Sven also trains on a larger circuit. "When we're training hard, I have him do five laps"—around the big circuit—"at around 3:50 per lap, then four laps at 3:40, then three laps at 3:35, then two laps at 3:30 and then one lap flat out. His best lap time ever is 3:18, but it also depends on the conditions, of course. So, you see, this method of descending intervals is very much similar to track and field. I borrow a lot of my training principles from athletics."

Another pass from Sven—his breathing labored but still well within himself.

"167," Sven grunts to Paul.

"Not so high heart rate you see," Paul says to me. "Still, I hope he won't break his chain. Look at that power."

"Super, Sven," Paul shouts.

"You see, this is not work for Sven," Paul turns back to me. "When you love what you do, when you have such a good condition from the big base of the summer, it's not work. I coach Mario Aerts [the Lotto road pro] also. For Mario, it's work. For Sven, I always make his training instructions on the light side, because I know that he will always do more. Okay, it's not always fun. Training in the atmospheric chamber in Leuven, that's work. But to come here, in the bos, it's fun for Sven.

"Komaan, eh Sven…Up…Up…Up," Paul yells.

"Why the Leuven chamber training?" I ask.

"We've found that Sven can do harder workouts in Leuven without as much stress on the muscles," Paul says. "You only have to do 260 watts to achieve the same result as 300 watts outside of the chamber. And we can adjust the climatic conditions to whatever we want. When he's sleeping at home in his altitude bedroom, it's to make his hematocrit higher. When he's at 41, you can get it to go up … but his hematocrit never gets above 43.8 or 44. Never higher."

Sven is at the other end of the ravine. Vapor and mist steam off his shoulders.

"Sven, one more," Paul encourages.

Sven nods and does one more.

And then adds one more.

"You know," Paul says, "people ask me why I put Sven's training schedules up on my blog, which gets 2,000 visitors a day. I say it's no problem. I know that nobody is able to train like Sven. They can't do it. They are broken if they try.

"When you combine love of something with success, then it's easy to train," he repeats. "Especially here. It's quiet. It's peaceful. It's special."

Sven heads off to cool down, the session over.

Leaves crunch underfoot as Paul and I walk back to the car. What happens next couldn't be better scripted.

In the distance, a rider in the Belgian tricolor whizzes past on a dirt path.

We both know immediately that it's Bart. He lives in nearby Vorselaar.

Paul smiles.

"He knows we're training here," Paul says quietly.

In my mind, whether Bart does or doesn't know is beside the point. What's important to Paul is that in his head, in Sven's head, Bart is in some way following their lead by coming here.

To the bos. To be the boss. Of 'cross.

A few moments later, we climb into the car.

"It's a battle," Paul says, moving onto a touchy subject: the media. "Everyone is always trying to crack Sven in the press. Always trying to get the edge. The other day, a story in the papers about how Vervecken thinks Sven doesn't need me as his trainer. Or Hans Van Kasteren saying how Sven isn't going to win 30 races this season. ... I think it's just frustration."

"Well," I suggest, "nobody likes a kingpin. Someone always trying to knock you off."

"Yes, but it's crazy." Paul says. "For me, with Sven winning, it's good for Sven, his supporters, for me ... but I admit it's not good for the sport." Paul seems to be implying that a certain fan base is lost when only one guy wins all the time. "And you know, it's hard now for his parents, for the supporters, because they don't understand anymore that

Sven can lose and he will one day lose. That sport is about winning and losing. They have forgotten that."

We arrive back at Paul's stately home, tucked away on a quiet side street. It's noon. Sven, having arrived by bike, takes his first shower of the day upstairs. He'll take another one later, after his second session of the day—a two-hour steady road ride behind the moto. For the souplesse. There had also been two sessions the day before—a 40-minute run and a steady ride on the road. It was one of the first, actually, that Sven did with an SRM—short for Schoberer Rad Messtechnik, a road measuring system invented by Ulrich Schoberer that measures watts of power output in each pedal stroke. I ask about his numbers.

"3.5 hours. 35 kph. 144 bpm. 277 watts. Averages."

Two big races loom this weekend, the Niel GVA and the World Cup in Pijnakker, Netherlands. No need to overdo it.

Sven sips a recovery drink, Paul and I, a Coke. Paul gives me copies of several of his training books. Across a coffee table, we talk more about training, the upcoming races, how it's harder for Sven to win the faster, tactical races where it's more of a crapshoot, and how the season bodes well, with the calendar full of tough, heavy races. Just the way Sven likes them.

Serendipitously, we end up on the topic of the Olympics. The Americans went to Chile to chase points for it, Sven mentions.

"I saw this past weekend an American guy in Chile. But he's standing fourth in the UCI ranking of Americans, so it's not a problem for us."

"But it's still 15 points he won," Paul interjects.

"No, it doesn't matter. It's the same as if our fourth-best guy from Belgium takes points. It's only the top three guys from each country that count," Sven says.

"Yeah, I think our U.S. chances are over for trying to qualify three guys," I agree.

"No? For sure?" Sven fires back, eagerly.

"I'm pretty sure our guys aren't pursuing it."

"Yes, they would have to—all three—go for two weeks to Chile and finish one, two, three," Sven says.

A beat.

Then, Sven's eyes seem to ignite. It's a eureka moment. And I'm there to witness it.

The realization. The actualization—

Sven's going to the Olympics.

It's classic Sven. He's obviously done the calculations in his head—probably over and over—yet he's never allowed himself the luxury of letting their meaning sink in.

Until now.

I see in his restrained excitement an incredibly important athletic trait—the ability to train one's mind to focus only on the task at hand, only on what one can control. The discipline to acknowledge the possibilities, weigh them daily, while publicly appearing off-hand and even somewhat helpless, as if snagging a berth at the highest level of competition is beyond one's ken. To manage all that represents exceptional self-control.

Surely, all Olympians remember—indelibly—the moment they realized they made it. That they were going to the big show.

I'm fortunate to be there for Sven's.

"The most important thing I did for my Olympic chances," Sven gushes, "is the Gieten mountain bike race. It was a stupid race. I did it on my cyclocross bike. But it was so important. The sixty points. Since then, every weekend, I've been studying the American results. I look to the Chile races and I say, 'Oh shit, an American guy, who is this guy?' But now, it looks clear that Belgium will finish ahead of the Americans on the ranking, so we can send three guys."

"So, are we now sure we can go?" Paul asks, not quite ready to believe it.

"Yes, I think so. I'm our third guy," Sven beams, on the edge of his seat. "With these developments, I'm beginning to have the feeling that we can go to the Olympics."

Sven Nys, training (November 2007)

Sven Nys and Coach Paul Van Den Bosch, hill repeats, (November 2007)

21: THE DUTCH WAY

As I pull out of Paul's driveway, direction the Netherlands, nothing's working. My cell phone dies and the GPS is on the blink. And I need to be in the little border town of Alphen-Chaam by 14:00. That's where part-time Rabobank Coach Nico van Heste meets all the top Dutch riders for his legendary weekly training sessions.

Every Wednesday.

From September to February. Each and every year, for at least the last decade.

And all the riders know: With Nico, you can't be late.

Sven used to religiously attend these trainings, but now the drive takes too much time and he prefers the solo work with Paul closer to home.

I phone Rabobank pro Gerben de Knegt for directions. Left at the church, right at the roundabout, right at the school.

No address.

No problem. I step on it.

Ever since I first learned about these ardent sessions some 15 years ago, I've always wanted to go to the *Chaamse bossen*, or "forest of Chaam." To this mythical athletic place of quiescent paths, dense trees, and grassy meadows. A palimpsest of Dutch cyclocross greatness.

I arrive at where I think I'm supposed to be, but still can't find the exact place. Fortunately, I'm clued to the whereabouts by young Rabobank continental pro Ricardo van de Velde, son of Tour de France great Johan, and Lars Boom's dad, Walter, with the big orange-and-blue Rabobank truck, who are unpacking in the pavé parking lot. An anonymous one-story brick locker and shower facility—omnipresent in sport parks across the Low Countries—stands in the distance. Walter Boom is one hell of a mechanic, working on bikes for Lars for the entire cyclocross season and recently hired to wrench for the Pro Tour Rabobank team next season on the road.

Given the price of flying a bike to Europe these days—anywhere from $75 to $300 depending on the airline—I've left my 'cross bike at home. What I do have is a road bike I've brought from Izegem, and it will have to do. No worry. I'm here to observe, even if it would be fun to rail around the bossen with these guys.

Soon others trickle in and we ride the two kilometers to the inner part of the forested park, to the secret garden. My road tires don't hold a line very well on the moist, mudded paths, so I sag ride, starting with Lars and gradually sliding backward. It's okay. I won't be dropped. I'm surrounded by a pack of at least thirty of the best cyclocross riders in the Netherlands.

We arrive en masse to a big grass clearing at the head of a small lake used in summer for swimming. A small three-sided brick shelter flanks the field with graffitti splashed on the fading mortared walls. A bunch of sturdy three-speed fendered Euro commuter bikes lean against one wall. Orange-and-black 4,000-euro Colnagos commingle. On the lee side, some twenty-five old-timers flick and chomp a smoke. Retired, out of work, or enjoying a day off, they huddle beneath a penumbrous sky.

I cross paths with one of the pocked and grizzled codgers.

He asks, "You here special? Journalist?"

"No, I'm a coach. National team. From America."

"Ah, U.S.A. Espionage, eh?" He winks.

He's not far from the truth, I guess.

Nico, the czar of this weekly ritual, is a schoolteacher. His presence like a hunk of granite. Hard and intractable. It's a surpassingly high compliment to him that all the Dutch best are here. Lars Boom, Richard Groenendaal, Gerben de Knegt, Bart Arnouts (Belgian, but on the Dutch Rabobank team), Wilant van Gils, Thys Al, Ramon Sinkeldam, Boy van Poppel, Ricardo van de Velde, Thijs Van Amerongen, and retired Erik Dekker on a mountain bike. Netherland's top women are also here, including Daphny van den Brand, Mirjam Melchers, and some thirty other amateurs and juniors.

Knowing that training can often be toil and drudge, Nico subscribes to the theory that group training can mollify mental maundering.

Hence ... the Wednesday constitutional.

But as the now forty-strong group begins its first block of warming up around a coned, grassy rectangle maybe half a soccer field in size, Nico is not happy.

In the distance, by the lake, Lars has been roped into an interview with a Dutch television crew, replete with a big fuzzy phallus of a microphone. The fact that Lars has brought apple turnovers today for some excellent post-workout snacking doesn't seem to assuage.

"Komaan, it's time for training," Nico snarls to no one in particular. He turns to me.

"You see, even here, they find Lars here. Nothing is sacred anymore."

When it comes to training, there's only one word for Nico: trenchant. For their esprit de corps, group cyclocross workouts are somewhat common throughout the sport. Seeing your mates out there grunting and groaning is empowering. But it's pretty unusual to see this many of the world's best in the same place at the same time.

Eighty pedals unclip and clip in unison.

Thoroughbred lungs swill heavy air.

Brakes squeak on carbon rims.

The pain session gets underway.

Maybe twenty laps around four corner cones on flat grass; Nico whistles with his lips; Tweeeet—dismount—jog—tweeeet—mount; tweeeet—accel on the bike—tweeeet—easy on the bike; tweeeet—ride to the corner cone and sprint one side; tweeeet—wind it up for a big sprint to one final cone.

Then—easy laps; talking. Ten minutes. Lars joins up about halfway through. Nico shoots him the evil eye.

Next: a short, three-minute lap; combination of open flat grass and bushy single track. Ten minutes. Semi-hard. Nico leads for a lap, demonstrating what to do, then turns them loose. (Each Wednesday, he chooses terrain the riders will see in the upcoming weekend race.

In today's case, the workout is tailored for the upcoming Dutch World Cup in Pijnakker.)

Nico and I stand together watching. Nico narrates. "I want them at 130 to 150 heart rate. No more than that right now. That's still ten to fifteen beats higher than training on the road. So, you see, this is better training."

Then, turning to the riders, Nico yells, "Komaan! Concentraat! Pijnakker! Pijnakker!"

Next up, the pack attacks a medium lap—maybe five minutes in duration; mostly in the woods; down and up by the lake. Nico again leads for a lap. Camaraderie. Fifteen minutes. Hard.

"Watch Groenendaal," Nico says to me. "Always pushing."

Regrouping on the flat grass field. Stretching, hopping, laughing. Stragglers rejoin. Ten minutes.

Clouds hum by. A jet scours the sky. Rain sputters.

Nico briefly huddles the riders up and delivers Pijnakker nuances—sectors in the race where they'll have to be on it. Then quickly they disperse.

Always moving.

Next, a long lap—a greater circumference of the wooded trails and open fields. Some coned S-turns, slalom-style, and a sandy running section down on the beach. I watch from the sidelines. Television cameras scurry down for a better angle. Twenty-five minutes. Hard.

Richard and Lars just killing each other now.

Across the grassy flat sections, Richard driving it.

Huge digs.

Unremitting.

A lake loop—three laps along the periphery of the water, bobbing up and back down to the shore. Twenty minutes. Hard.

Walter Boom joins me.

"You not training?"

"Wrong bike. Need a 'cross bike."

"Ja, it's nice training here, eh?"

"Is Richard always like this?

"Always. Always trying to drop the others."

"But it's good for Lars?"

"For sure."

Cool-down laps on the field. Chatting. Work done. Fifteen minutes. Total work time: two hours. Tickling the red zone.

The group begins to head back to the changing rooms. The cluster of old men disperses as well.

I catch up with Richard and we ride back together.

"Good effort?"

"I don't know. We see this weekend," he says.

The guys shower and pack up, and I wait to talk to Lars.

When he appears, he's—as usual—all brio. The guy just resonates with energy, vivacity.

"How's the season so far?" I ask.

"Ups and downs. Kalmthout was very bad. That circuit—not my thing. Koppenberg, I was not good in my head. I broke up with my girlfriend. But Tabor was good."

"Will you switch to road racing soon?" The rumor is that Lars will go to full-time road racing in the next few years.

"Next couple seasons I give 100 percent for 'cross," he says. "I want to be world cyclocross champion in the elites. That's my goal. I love cyclocross—the shorter races, the less stressed ambiance, less tactics. You can count on one hand the number of 'crosses decided by tactics. Okay, compared to the road, cyclocross is still, we say in Dutch, a *tweederangsport*, or second-rung sport. But what makes it great—man against man. Also, training in the woods, away from the cars, like today. I love it."

"And in five years, the Tour de France?"

"Of course. But I'm not thinking about that now."

Lars says he likes riding with Rabobank. And the relationship with Sven is a good one, he tells me. But when I ask if Sven is his mentor, or someone he looks up to, he brushes it off.

"I want to be looked up to by the other riders, but I don't have idols. Of course I have respect for guys like Wellens, but sometimes you have to push that away."

"What do you mean?"

"Like in Tabor, Bart was yelling at me to chase—'Go, go, go!'— but Sven and Stybar were off the front. So I said something like 'Fuck off,' and he started talking bad about me in the press, how I don't have respect. Of course I have respect, but sometimes in the races, you need to say, as a young rider, 'Fuck this guy, fuck that guy, I'm working for myself,' and that's important. You need to respect the top guys, but not that much."

What about Niels Albert? He's another big rival: Lars beat him last year for the espoir world championship, I point out.

"For sure. We fight hard in the races, but we can always talk after. It's good financially when we play hard out there."

Louis Delahaije, the Rabobank trainer, has Lars training twenty hours on the bike these weeks, with two-plus hours behind the moto with his father. "Sometimes after two hours we have already 100 K's," Lars says. That's in between lifting weights two or three times a week.

"Some day, I hope you can come race 'cross in the U.S.," I tell him. I can't resist making the pitch. If Lars and Sven and Bart came to the States, it would be a huge boost to the sport.

"There's a lot of Americans racing. We'll have 2,000 racers at our Nationals," I say.

"No."

"Yeah, 100 masters in every five-year age category."

"No, really?"

"Yeah. Really."

(Pijnacker 2007)   PHOTOPRESS.BE

Lars Boom, (Pijnacker 2007)   PHOTOPRESS.BE

22: ERWIN AT EASE

NOVEMBER 7, 2007

After the quick trip from the Netherlands back to Belgium, I sit down to a nice meal at a Lille café operated by Erwin Vervecken's training partner, Sten Raeymaekers, and his family. Fifty years ago, this area was one of the poorest parts of Flanders, but now the neat brick homes, busy streets, and green fields reflect the burgeoning middle-class feel to Flemish-speaking Belgium. Throughout our meal, Erwin's phone rings with interview and sound-byte requests. Ever the polite one, Erwin obliges. Later, Erwin's wife, Liesbeth, joins us.

In this casual setting, it's easy to see the wisdom, the confidence that Erwin has gained. When you've been in the game as long as he has, you come to terms with who you are.

On the monk-to-immoderate continuum, Erwin positions himself somewhere in the middle. With Sven Nys and Sven Vanthourenhout on one uber-disciplined extreme, the fleeting, struggling Tom Vanoppen on the other (Vanoppen is released by Sunweb in December 2007 for missing a training ride and returns a positive test for cocaine in January 2008). Erwin ascribes to a centrist attitude, hardworking sans obsession.

"Everyone is always saying that Sven, Bart, they're living 105 percent for their sport. So, no glass of red wine on a Monday evening to relax after a hard weekend, or frites post-race for some occasional fat," he says. "The stress of having eaten those things on a Monday would haunt them the whole week. Sven Vanthourenhout will do like a five-hour ride and then come back and just eat a yogurt. It's crazy. If you live 105 percent for your sport but lose 10 percent of that due to stressing about being perfect, then you're back where you started from."

I wonder about this. "Maybe if Sven lived and trained at 95 percent and achieved top results, he wouldn't be satisfied because he'd think he could have done even better if he'd lived and trained at 100 percent," I say.

"Two ways to look at it, I guess."

"What about Bart?"

"Ja," Erwin continues. "Bart thinks he lives for the sport. But he's always promoting himself, and for a few weeks he's living super fanatical, but then sometimes he lets himself go, drinking wine and beer."

"And that," interjects Liesbeth, "is Bart. But the real thing is the fans. These guys are living under a microscope. The fans want to see that 100 percent fanaticism all the time, and they don't like it when they see someone like Erwin take everything with ease."

"I got a lot of reaction from the article in last Saturday's paper where I said that Sven Nys doesn't really need his coach," Erwin says. "Hey, Sven knows what to do. He's been on the top for five years. If his coach dies tomorrow, he'll still be Sven Nys."

Maybe 80 percent of the riders need a coach for support, Erwin says. "But it doesn't work for me. I know how to be good in my head. I don't need someone like a mental coach. I'd say, 'I don't need your pep talk.' I'm at my best when I'm relaxed.

"But maybe that's bad," he adds. It's an uneasy attempt at humor about what might be called his rotseason. A few weeks earlier, just before my visit, Erwin and I had talked by phone, and I'd never heard him sound so down. Hamme-Zogge and other recent races had not gone well. The Fidea team was struggling. And Erwin seemed dejected about his own sub-par performances. He'd been making mistakes in the first two laps of the races, he told me. He'd been racing too much, and that didn't leave enough time for training.

Now we chuckle, but I can see in Liesbeth's eyes that the rotseason is weighing heavily.

Late, at around 11 p.m., I climb the rickety stairs to my lodging for the night, an apartment above the restaurant where we've just finished dinner. Carving out a spot on a rather seedy couch from some bygone era, I wrap up in a mangy blanket, plug in the tape from the Hamme-Zogge Superprestige, and try to sleep. Most times, quite ironically for someone so entranced by cyclocross, a race DVD will cure me of any hint of insomnia. This time, far from home, missing my family in pursuit of trying to write a book about this crazy sport, the race tape doesn't do the trick.

My mind races.

Every top rider has to manage the stimuli around him—from supporters, from the press, from his team, from himself—as best he can, I think to myself. But sometimes the character of the sport itself gets overwhelming.

Cold. Arduous. Hard.

Unable to sleep, I flip open Paul Fournel's nifty chapbook, *Need for the Bike*. Fournel describes one of the most famous road cycling ascents in history—the Ventoux. He might just as well be writing about the power of cyclocross to force self-reflection. Riding the Ventoux, he writes, is "the greatest revelation of yourself. It simply feeds back your fatigue and fear. It has total knowledge of the shape you're in, your capacity for cycling happiness, and for happiness in general. It's yourself you're climbing. If you don't want to know, stay at the bottom."

Erwin and Liesbeth Vervecken   PHOTOPRESS.BE

Erwin Vervecken, (Gieten 2007)

23: FOLLOWING FIDEA

NOVEMBER 7, 2007

Thursday dawns gray. I'm as tweaked as a stiff dog from the restless night. But a chance to ride shotgun with Fidea coach Danny De Bie on the team's morning training ride has me up and hungry early.

In separate cars, Erwin and I drive the twenty minutes to meet up at the De Residentie, a stately private hotel and spa nestled amid tall pines near Lichtaart, Province Antwerp.

It is these once-a-week sessions that define Fidea's ethos, giving the team a dimension no other pro cyclocross team approximates. The half-hour pre-ride coffee session on roomy restaurant lounge couches—full of colorful repartee in several different languages—and then the training ride itself and an ensuing noontime meal and massage form the foundation of Fidea's emphasis on team building. The Dutch may have their weekly training sessions, but with upwards of forty riders of varying levels, there isn't the same small unit pulse as in these Fidea trainings. The Residentie sessions are for Fidea team riders and their director only. No tag alongs, no distractions. I wonder how many outsiders like me they've allowed into their Residentie world.

"Everybody knows cyclocross is an individual sport," Danny tells me as we climb into the blue stickered team car, Danny at the wheel, me riding shotgun, "but these training sessions are my idea to help make all the team a group of friends. Every week"—usually on Tuesdays—"we do this to make a good group, a good team. We talk about the previous race, laugh, joke, with no pressure—it's all good for the riders."

Soon, we're out on the road, Bart having just announced the route he's chosen—100 kilometers through quiet roads, bike paths, and village streets—just prior to leaving the Residentie. Locked and loaded, the blue train of Fidea slides into formation.

Ten guys, two abreast in an echeloned pace line, the point man easing off in what for group cycling is a familiar and timeless rhythm.

Not a helmet to be seen. Some habits die hard. Black knit Fidea hats all around. Sunglasses' arms wrap around the outside of the hats. Each rider wearing thermal jackets, leg warmers and booties.

All the Fidea team riders are here: Scrappy Zdenek "Styby" Stybar; elongated rebel Klaas Vantornout; rainbow-banded—all legs and arms—Vervecken; green and relatively untested Quentin Bertholet; convivial rookie Tom Meeusen; black-on-gold-on-red jacketed Bart Wellens; peaceful, reticent Kevin Pauwels; yuckster elder statesman Peter Van Santvliet; suave-looking Luxembourger Jempy Drucker; cajoling youngster Vincent Baestaens.

Spirited, they stroke the bleak landscape.

Five in the top ten this past Sunday in Hamme-Zogge.

Bertholet 6th and Drucker 7th in Hittnau, Switzerland at the European Espoir champs.

Danny drives. Danny smokes. Danny talks.

To be a rider, sure, you have to love it. But at least you get the satisfaction of pumping blood.

To be a director? Even a cyclocross director like Danny? There's still four months behind the wheel in the summer road races.

That's some serious seat time.

Short and trim, Danny still looks like he could hop a barrier or two, albeit with a smoker's hack. But his eyes—vigilant, tough, inured— are the eyes of a manager. It's hard to know what's behind his gaze. While I find it easy to talk to him about his proudest moment—his 1989 Pontchateau world's win—I can't muster the courage to ask about any of that era's dark side.

Instead we keep it light. We laugh about Erwin's bachelor party a few years ago, when Erwin was forced to ride down his hometown street—in drag on a tiny bike dragging clanking tin cans.

"She [Erwin] was cute," Danny yucks. And after a pause, "People really don't know the crazy side of Erwin."

At one point, a foreboding cell ring tone—like a thousand angry wasps—interrupts our conversation. It's the Boss, Hans "HVK" Van Kasteren, to follow up on a discussion they had earlier in the day. A discussion about how they'll do whatever it takes to keep Stybar under contract and set Klaas Vantornout free to test the waters. I feel awkward that at this moment I might know more about Vantornout's fate than he does.

"The Boss is the boss," Danny shrugs.

We talk about training, about the team's make-up, about how Petr Dlask prefers to train at home in the Czech Republic and make the nine-hour drive each way each week rather than live in Belgium, about Danny's preferred coaching style, and how he never pressures riders to perform.

"A rider has to do it on his own."

Two hours in 32 kph. Easy tempo.

I roll down the window.

Erwin says the legs feel really good. Then he's back in the pace line.

Watching professionals ride in a pace line, a formation where half the riders move forward in each other's slipstream while the other half move slowly backwards, is a pleasure to behold. The key place to watch is the point at the front end where each rider, in succession, takes that brief pull, thereby breaking the wind, before smoothly sliding to the side and drifting back as the next guy takes the front. If you watch just there, at the front, you get a sense of who's feeling good and who's not. The guys who are strong will either intentionally or unintentionally amp it up ever so subtly.

Today, it's Erwin and Stybar pushing the envelope. Since they're not riding hard, no one is going to be dropped. But it's these very slight accelerations that stamp a rider's authority on the others and become part of the mind games riders can play on each other.

Toward the end of the ride, going on three hours, it's time for a pit stop. Erwin tells me he'll ride some more later on. Danny and I take a quick zoom ahead to a bakery to pick up a cake for dessert. It's Danny's way of saying, "Way to go, boys."

Got to keep everyone happy.

At lunch back at De Residentie, white tablecloths, pasta followed by chicken, and ample portions of sophomoric humor. Peter Van Santvliet provides anything off-color. Tom and Vincent pepper me with questions about racing 'cross in the U.S. I parlez my best French to include Quentin, who speaks no English. Clearly it's tough for him as the lone Walloon on a Flemish-English speaking team.

I enjoy talking to Styby about his struggles to set up shop in Belgium, to learn the language, to choose one discipline (cyclocross) over another (road racing), even though he's top-shelf in both. He says he owes a lot of his maturation to his Flemish girlfriend and the support he and the other Czechs receive from their Belgian support system. I tell him about the little known fact that he has quite a following back in America because he chooses to do his post-race interviews in English.

"I do that because my Flemish is not so good. But it doesn't make the Flemish commentators too happy," he says with a grin.

Bart is absent for most of the meal, preferring a longer-than-usual massage to work out the kinks—his problematic back, his upper legs— along with some special stretching. When he arrives, he bolts down his food, long after we've all finished. But he looks relaxed, so once he's done with his meal, I figure it's a good time to ask him to a cup of coffee. It's time to get to know this rock star better—to see if I can get this cyclocross icon to speak.

Not that he's press-shy. The process and product of a public upbringing is perhaps more visible in Bart Wellens than in any other top 'cross rider. Like Sven, since the age of nine, "Bartje" has shown the world—his world—his proficiency and wizardry on the 'cross *fiets*. His four world titles—two as an espoir and two as a pro—represent confirmation more than surprise. Even when Bart and Tom Vanoppen came to the U.S. to race in the New England road scene during the summer of 1999, Bart just tore the legs off the competition, routinely lapping the field, according to house-host and friend to both, Tim Johnson. And Bart and Tom were on holiday, to boot.

But, unlike Sven—his big rival, the man he's pitted against in the public eye—Bart says he's always felt comfortable sharing his personality, his extroversion, with his public. In the three years of the *Wellens en Wee* reality television show, Bart was always in the limelight. And he wouldn't want it any other way. Nor would his many, many fans.

As a sportsman, Bart's thirst for fame and fortune is palpable. You see it especially on days like these Residentie sessions.

Bart loves—no, thrives on—the elixir of attention.

From his teammates. From Danny. From the hotel help. From the media.

In fact, when I do manage to talk with him after lunch, I see two other journalists eyeing us, waiting for us to finish our coffee.

Waiting on the man.

"Yeah, it's part of my job, to speak in public for the sponsors, to sign autographs, to be there for interviews, for the TV show," he says. He looks relaxed in his aquamarine team polo and jeans with Fidea inscribed on each rear pocket. "But if I don't have all those requests, then I'm not important enough and that's not good for me. When I'm in demand, that's the most positive for my head.

"And, it's about me, yes, but it's mostly about our sport of cyclocross," he says. "The top football [soccer] guys, after the game, they get on the bus and that's it"—they disappear somewhere until the next game. "At the Koppenbergcross a week ago, 18,000 people could touch me or come by before or after the race. And the television show, the good thing about that was it showed the people of Belgium who maybe don't know cyclocross, it showed them what it means, what it's all about."

I ask him about the claim that Fidea has too many leaders. He acknowledges that it is a problem in the faster races where there's usually a bigger group present at the end of the race because the conditions don't make more of a selection. But he says in the heavier races, the muddier, slower races, things sort themselves out.

"Already, there's been a lot of talk about the problems with Styby and Klaas riding so fast and how we have too many leaders in our team.

But really, in the end, the strongest wins. ... As we get into the heavy races, it all becomes honest."

I force myself to ask about his performance this year, which, there's no overlooking it, has been lackluster compared to the past. "Do you struggle with how good you were a few years ago?"

Bart answers without hesitation. "Well, obviously it would be nice to be as strong as I was in my super years, but you have to take the good with the bad. I don't have a trainer, but I do have a psychologist who helps me through these tough periods."

"It's interesting that you don't have a trainer," I tell him. "Erwin says he doesn't have one, either."

"Well, for sure, Erwin is a special guy." But Erwin would do better if he focused more on riding, Bart says. "When he lives 100 percent for his sport, then he's one of the most talented. But he has so many interests, and he does good things like go to race in the U.S. While it's good for cyclocross, it's maybe too much and he might be better off to stay home and train. When you see, like, Sven and me, it's cyclocross and nothing else."

With Sven and Bart, it's not only cyclocross and nothing else—sometimes it's cyclocross with too much else. In December 2005, television cameras catch Bart giving a karate kick to a harassing spectator in a big race in Overijse, Belgium. Bart wins the race but is later disqualified and suspended from racing for a month. Yet, some ten months later, in September 2006 at a race in Aalter, Belgium, Sven claims a fan moves some fencing into his path, causing him to crash. In retaliation, Sven punches the fan. After the race, according to cyclingnews.com, Sven files a report with the police, and when the instigator is later determined to have given a false address, no action is taken against Sven.

"Ja," says Bart, "the problem was, I did that kick in a big race and it was on television. But Sven, he actually hit a guy in the face with his fist. But it was a small race, so nobody saw it. That's not right that I am so punished and nothing happens for Sven."

"But aside from that, the sport feeds on the rivalry between you two, no?"

"For sure. Like in Hamme-Zogge last Sunday. I had a terrible start. I was maybe 22nd or 23rd place after the start. And everybody is saying, "There's Sven at the front, but where is Bart?' It's always like that. I wouldn't say Sven is my best friend, but he's a good colleague. ... We've grown up together in this sport. He needs me and I need him."

Coffee cups stand empty. Idle journalists shoot me the eagle eye. It's time to stop. I wouldn't say—by any stretch—that I've gotten show-stopping disclosures from Bart Wellens. But I do feel a better sense of affinity with the spark plug from Vorselaar.

It also gives me an inkling of what draws fans to this sport, to this or that race, in the rain, or snow, in bleak winter.

Invariably, their first response is—"Wellens" or "Nys."

"But why do you go to such lengths? Why the jackets, the buses, the partying, the cheering?" I asked an ardent Wellens fan at one point at a race in Baal a few years ago. She stood in a downpour, her umbrella kaput, face splattered with mud, shouting Bart's name. Perhaps the mud came from Bart's own wheel spray. I doubted she'd ever wash the mud off.

Her responses still resonate.

"In Belgium, we don't have so many things to do on a rainy weekend," she said.

"How do you pick your favorite?"

"We choose the one who fits our personality."

Hero worship. Identification. I'm suddenly in a college Psych 101 class from twenty years before. People admire those they want to be like; they condemn others for weaknesses they recognize in themselves. There are enough different personalities in top-level European cyclocross to suit the loving, condemning fans by the thousands.

During winter's darkest days, not only does the sport bring color to people's lives, but supporters offer oblation as well. The whole symbiosis between rider and supporter borders on the numinous.

Oh, and one more detail: It makes for one hell of a business model.

Recipe for success:

1. Take thousands of supporters who travel by bus to the races to drink beer and cheer on their favorite rider;

2. Add thousands of VIP's who attend the races to network, eat, and drink in huge, fancy temporary tents outfitted with televisions for watching the race;

3. Sprinkle in the merchandising of everything from posters and clothing to fritjes (french fries) and beer;

4. Add in the television rights and gate fees, and you have all the necessary ingredients for a booming sports business.

Bart Wellens And Danny De Bie, (Igorre 2007)   PHOTOPRESS.BE

Top and above: Training with the Fidea team

24: OVER THE LIMIT

Behind schedule, I zip west toward Izegem, lost in my impressions of the day. The Ghent viaduct speed camera, a little box mounted on a tall light post, catches me unaware. Even had I known about it at the time, I would have considered the 75-euro speeding ticket worth the price of a day with Fidea. Seeing Bart—the animated Bart—spinning effortless circles around east Flanders, his teammates, the press, I sense he's on the verge of something new. A spell of good fitness, perhaps. Yesterday, when Sven, Paul, and I saw Bart in the woods, he was midway through 5.5 hours of training, half of it in the woods, half of it on the road. Perhaps the upcoming weekend racing will bring Bartje and the Bartje-faithful the season's first big smile.

In the meantime, all is not well in Camp Page. On Thursday evening I ring up Jonathan to set up a visit with him on my way to Niel. The shit has hit the fan, it seems, and his wife Cori is justifiably upset.

Cori tells me that Sunweb manager Jurgen Mettepenningen has been publicly raking Jonathan and the family over the coals, and the newspapers have played up the tension. She says the local newspapers have made the claim that she is not a good wife and that, because Jonathan is occasionally seen with baby Milo in a sling around his neck, her husband is burdened with having to raise the children. Mettepenningen has been quoted as saying that Jonathan is a disappointment and that he hasn't been working hard enough. A week and a half later, the team will publish a press release stating that Page can't handle the discipline of a professional team.

"Not only are his results disappointing—Page never finished top 10 in a big race—also his approach has raised some questions," as CyclingNews.com quoted the release.

The family has responded by holing up in their Oudenaarde home and seeking support from their friends—Toby Stanton from the New England team Hot Tubes, road pro Christian Vande Velde, and mechanic Franky Van Haesebroucke and his wife.

"The folks that matter," says Cori.

They've stopped reading the trash in the newspapers. It's gotten so bad that Cori plans a weekend getaway with the kids to Ireland to visit friends and escape the negativity.

"They're really hurtful personal attacks," Cori says.

And, finally, they have it out with the guy caught in the middle—the coach, but also the Sunweb Director Mario De Clercq.

Cori continues the story:

"We had Mario come to the house. I said, 'Mario, if you're going to be a jerk about this, there's the door. You signed Jonathan because you believe in him, but this kind of pressure—it's not working. It's good to have a sponsor who wants results, but this trash, this personal affront, is not positive.'"

Mario did not walk out. Instead, they had it out, with Mario telling Jonathan he needed to be more serious, and Jonathan saying he was coming under too much pressure.

Cori tells me the air is a bit clearer now, but she's wary.

Two days later, with Cori and the kids on their way to Ireland, I stop by to say hello to Jonathan. His resolve to work hard and win, his way, is as palpable as ever.

"I don't think very many people know how hard this is," he says. He sits on his couch, drinking a cup of coffee. "This contract with this team—it's a milestone—but the way they work, the pressure, the lack of communication, it doesn't work for me." Finally, he says, he reached a limit. "I just shut down. Yes, the money is great, but really, they can take it and shove it up their ass. Mettepenningen, he doesn't talk to me. But he talks to the press about me. I've tried to set up a meeting, but Mettepenningen hasn't responded. It's crazy."

(Mettepenningen would later offer CyclingNews.com his version of events. "Presenting all of this as a pester campaign," against Jonathan "is incorrect," he is quoted. "It's too bad Jonathan can't handle the pressure that is related to a top team.")

I tell Jonathan how different this all sounds compared to Danny De Bie's hands-off style with Fidea.

"That's the thing," Jonathan continues. "I need to do it my way. I don't respond well to Sunweb's methods." The team constantly demands his attention, he says. "The team website guy even got pissed because I didn't answer an email when I was in the Czech Republic at the World Cup. That's ridiculous."

Then he turns more reflective. "My results aren't super bad so far. I just haven't had a good run yet. I need to get everything to mesh. I'm just off the first group, which is a really tough place to be."

"And you've got everyone in Flanders armchair quarterbacking your every move."

"For sure. Always got to do it the Belgian way. It can be infuriating. That's part of the problem with Mario. He hears from someone else that I walked my son Milo in the stroller to the bank. And then it becomes this 'he said-she said' shit. When that happens, I just put up a shield."

I try to think of something positive to offer. "But maybe all this shit, this adversity—it's what you thrive on?"

"I do think about that. Continue to think about it. How I need to get my ass kicked sometimes."

We're silent for a moment. It's hard to know what to say to someone on the edge of ... what? Leaving his team? Even if that happened, I know Jonathan won't stop trying to win.

"You ready for tomorrow's World Cup?" I change the subject, asking him about the upcoming race in Pijnakker.

"I'll be ready. But I'm also going to go to a media gathering tonight in Brugge. These types of media appearances are important, too. I'm sure I'll get shit for it from my team. For staying out, not being in bed."

"You're going tonight? Really?"

Yes, really, he tells me. "I guess I just learn things the hard way sometimes."

Photo: Tom Robertson

Photo: Tom Robertson

25: THE ENGINE ROOM

NOVEMBER 10, 2007

To cut below the crust and mantle and go straight to the iron core of cyclocross—Belgian field riding—is to go to a race like the Jaarmarkt 'cross in Niel, just south of Antwerp. The race is a showcase for the GVA series, named for sponsor *Gazet Van Antwerpen*, the Antwerp newspaper, whose offices are perhaps 20 kilometers away. For the *Gazet* and everyone else in Belgium, the race says only one thing—

Bring it.

Combine a quagmired meadow with a ridiculously off-camber upper dike and a quick upper loop section replete with: a) trucked-in heavy sand; b) scores of symmetrically placed pallets of garden peat lining the track; c) neatly arrayed concrete trucks and farm tractors; and d) a couple of awkward curbs and bridges, and you get the idea.

Pure bitch.

Just the way powerhouses Lars, Sven, Bart, and Erwin like it.

Hard.

Ground-and-pound.

This place. This race.

The heart of hearts. The marrow.

The race program always lists the sections of sand, grass, asphalt, in percentages. But it never breaks things down to what they really mean.

What this race reduces you to.

Niel 2007.

Six brutal laps. Between 9:00 minutes and 9:15 per lap.

Each lap: Two minutes on the bike. Riding. Asphalt, cobbles, cement.

Two minutes off the bike. Running. Because you can't ride. Over pitch, angle, shit.

Then, five minutes of something altogether else—

Engine room cycling.

Muscle it. Slog it. Get on top of it.

Sand. Side-hill. Bog.

40 rpm.

Average speed—19 kph.

Course width—eight meters across in places.

Pick a line, any line.

No matter. Sludge puddles a meter deep play no favorites.

"Hey, coach, I need a break. Sub me out."

"Sorry, son. No bench."

There are no domestiques. Or excuses. Or places to hide.

***

Arriving a bit late, I park in the only remaining team parking spot—essentially, someone's doorstep. Cars, campers, and buses cram a triangular hectare of city park. Weaving between unpacking mechanics and already woozy, bleary-eyed 'cross habitués, I spy two top riders in U.S. domestic 'cross: Euro rookie Chris Jones and privateer Jon Baker.

"You guys get signed in okay?"

"Yeah, registration's over in the bar," Jon says.

Concern in his voice, Chris cuts in, "I need a Campy derailleur. Snapped mine on the course warming up."

"Let's look around," I say.

We head over to a road-grimed Fidea van with the name "Petr Dlask" lettered on the side. All the big name riders have their names emblazoned on their campers.

"Hey, Peter. Long trip this time?" I ask.

"Not so bad. Eight hours on Thursday. But my family is there (in Czech Republic). And the mountains are there. I can't train here in Belgium. I know. I know … it's all in my head," he says.

"Good legs today," I say, offering up the well-worn cycling expression synonymous with "good luck." Pause. "You know anyone with Campy?"

"Not us. Try Landbouwkrediet," comes the voice of Peter's mechanic from around the side of the van.

"Dankuwel."

Chris moves on to locate the elusive Campy derailleur. I make some rounds.

Belgian rider Ben Berden gives me a friendly nod. Having served his 15-month suspension for using EPO, he's now enjoying racing again.

I find Sven covered in mud after his practice laps. Under the massive camper awning, he brushes up against son Thibau, side-swiping him with ooze. The huddled denizens, supporters with "Sven Nys" coats, roar with laughter. Cigarette smoke lofts in the open air.

Sven and I have a quick discussion about contracts and then there's just enough time for a chat with some of the droves of Erwin Vervecken supporters disgorging from fan buses. Erwin's wife, Liesbeth, in a navy-blue argyle sweater, sharply contrasts with the loud red of the fans' jackets, worn in honor of Erwin.

"Liesbeth, you're here," I greet her. "And the kids?"

"Ah, with the grandparents today."

I turn to some other supporters I recognize.

"Why are you here?" I joke with them.

"Where else would we go on a Saturday in winter?"

Then there's no more time for talk; the race will begin soon, and I'm helping Jon Baker in the pit. I head down with an extra set of wheels. Jon's father schleps his extra bike. The distance we have to travel is considerable. We detour through a carnival of merry-go-rounds and booths. Down to the straight at the start-finish line, into the bog—shin-deep in places—and over to a very tight double pit. A double pit area services both sides of a course and is very clearly defined in the UCI regulations. The double pit surface area, in total, is supposed to measure 70-by-15 meters to give some room to power hoses, pit lanes and mechanics standing ready to give and receive bikes to riders. The Niel pit, I muse, must be grandfathered in, because it seems about half the regulation size.

Already the hoses are busy. The familiar mist of high-pressure back-spray creates a shimmer on orange, black, blue, and yellow team jackets.

The fathers—of Lars Boom, Bart Wellens, and Erwin Vervecken—lean on saddles and philosophize about Rhino and Typhoon tire treads and the conditions. Silhouetted across the entire Rupel-dike above the pit—named for the dike that bisects the circuit—the hordes watch and wait. Multi-colored panels—ads for GVA, KBC, Primus, DiBO, Lotto, Nissan, Smeets—line the course as far as the eye can see. Unmistakable red-on-yellow letters signal where to buy *FRITUUR-SNACKS*. Tantalized spectators huddle ten-deep, waiting for their pre-race *fritjes*.

In garbled Flemish, the announcer says the crowd is 15,000 strong.

Time of day: 14:59.

The most compressed minute of anticipation in all of cyclocross.

Mechanics wedge feet into muddied position.

The calm before the maelstrom.

Then: smashmouthing time.

Three traffic lights above the start-finish line flash from yellow to green.

And forty-five of the world's best riders blast away. At the end of lap one, nearly every rider comes into the pit to change bikes. Forty guys in a line. That's forty mechanics fighting for one of the six pit hoses.

Organized chaos.

Bart runs. Lars marks (covers). The two forge ahead of the pack. A game of chess in a field of slop. Trading licks like some guitar work from an '80s Cult song.

Richard Groenendaal rides the tape, a dangerous technique where the cyclist, looking for any advantage, rides with his hand brushing the fencing tape along the course periphery.

Sven rifles his bike forward. One leg hammers down, then the other, and he shoots ahead.

Eventually, the climax.

Less than two laps to go.

Bart accelerates just before a steep sidewalk climb.

Lars—over-geared—looks cooked. His whole body looks to be in a paroxysm of pain and rage. He digs deep. Along the dike, Lars rides back up to his rival, Bart.

Bart runs a heavy sector of field, a picture of efficiency.

Richard has no energy left to hand his bike to his mechanic. He drops it like a bag of cement.

Across a vast open meadow of mud, Lars and Bart ride pedal for pedal.

Old school cyclocross.

Nails.

In a flash, over a hump, Lars gets a gap.

Just before the pavement, Bart, the darling of any Flemish crowd, seems to find something within. Something so powerful it forces a bystanding grandmother to go guttural.

"Komaan, Bartje!"

On the pavement now, Lars rides ahead.

Face miasmic. Mouth agape. A piece of meat.

And then, in a gesture that will become his trademark, his copyright, Lars, still on the bike, slaps his own face.

Right hand slaps right cheek. Left hand slaps left cheek.

Lars laps Chris Jones with one to go. Lars has 12 seconds on Bart. The black-and-yellow lion-of-Flanders flags seem to droop.

Sven—ever the tactician—uses a lapped rider's draft to take back a few seconds on Richard across the line, with one to go.

Bart's dad, Lucien, beckons for his son to come in to pit one. The move seems to pay off. A fresh bike seems to give Bart wings. But he falters, overshooting a slick-with-leaves corner.

Check for Lars.

But no checkmate. Across the dike for the last time, Lars punctures. He hides his frustration, while Bart senses blood in the water.

The assembly roars. Bart is the winner, his biggest win so far for the season. He attempts to wipe his jersey clean for the gallery. It's no use; it's soiled beyond recognition.

The fans can only guess at his debt. At his nearly six hours of training on a single day the week before.

Of his lifetime of debt. For moments like this.

Sven pulls back a few more seconds on Richard by not taking a bike—for the first time—in pit two. The subtle gain in time allows him to take his Dutch rival in the sprint for 3rd.

It's dusk now. Another race over.

I arrive back to the team area. Jon and Chris are upbeat despite the fact that Jon hit a post and bashed his leg. Chris needs to go to anti-doping, his number coming up randomly for urine testing after the race.

Jon says with a smile, "Tomorrow's another race."

"Keep at it guys. Way to go," I tell them. It's almost time for me to catch a train to the airport. Immersion over. I gotta get back home.

Before leaving the race area, I amble over to the flooded-with-humanity media tents. Lars is on his way to the podium.

"What was the deal with the head slap?" I ask.

"What?" he yells, as podium dignitaries summon him to hustle it up.

"The head slap. What was that all about?"

"Oh, that. I was totally toast there. I was thinking I could try to make pain in my face so I wouldn't feel the pain in my legs."

"Did it work?" I yell.

He has no time to answer.

Lars Boom, (Niel 2007)

The pit, (Niel 2007)

Bart Wellens, (Niel 2007)

PHOTOPRESS.BE

Sven Nys edges Richard Groenendaal at the line, (Niel 2007)   PHOTOPRESS.BE

26: THE RAVE

NOVEMBER 11, 2007

Wee hours. I take the first Izegem-to-Zaventem train to catch my flight home from Brussels.

I'm minding my own thoughts, half asleep, when we pull up to the station in Ghent, and suddenly there are thousands of kids, most of them high school or college age, packing the platform, trying to get on. The Belgian cops have no control and it's mayhem as the kids clamber aboard and pack all the seats, armrests, aisles, and doors.

I learn that they've just spent the last twelve hours raving at the biggest techno-fest in Europe. They're high on Ecstasy or speed, and a few of them start lighting up the morning doob.

It's 5:15 a.m. and I'm in the Land of the Lotus Eaters.

The guy who sits down next to me is, thankfully, older and full of info.

About 40,000 people from all over Europe made the weekend pilgrimage to a big factory building in Ghent, he tells me. Fifty euros a head.

Two kids plop down across from us. One—when he first gets on— shares a ham and cheese baguette with his mate. But no sooner do we pull away from the station than they're both slumped together, fast asleep.

With a half of a sandwich sticking out of their mouths.

The older guy next to me knows all about cyclocross, of course. He waxes almost lyrical about how Niels Albert didn't like the mud yesterday in Niel and how Sven is "too serious." He even plans to hit the afternoon telly for some action from the Pijnakker World Cup today.

Despite his disheveled state, his having been awake for a weekend, his hallucinogenic fog, the dude can still get his head around what's happening in the 'cross world.

Only in Flanders.

***

Brussels to JFK to Salt Lake City to Helena. It's a two-day hallucinogenic trip of a different sort to get from Belgium to Montana.

In the process, I learn from airport wi-fi that Lars Boom and America's beacon cyclocross performer, Katie Compton, win in Pijnakker's World Cup.

For Lars, it's confirmation. It's his first victory on the elite World Cup circuit.

For Katie, it's the third World Cup race of her career and her first win. I'm happy, but simultaneously regretful. I was there in 2002, in spongy Heerlen, Netherlands, when Alison Dunlap became the first American woman to win a European cyclocross race. And I was overjoyed to work with Gina Hall when she won an international cyclocross race during the first EuroCrossCamp in 2003, in Bakel, Netherlands. I'm bummed that I've missed this third American female triumph on European soil. But I know there will be more.

The Cult's "She Sells Sanctuary" gets me home.

Belgian cyclocross.

Something visceral.

Primal.

Pulchritudinous.

"The sparkle in your eyes

Keeps me alive

And the sparkle in your eyes

Keeps me alive, keeps me alive

The fire in your eyes

Keeps me alive, keeps me alive

I'm sure in her you'll find

The sanctuary.
I'm sure in her you'll find
Sanctuary.
Hey-yeah."

Photo: Tom Robertson

27: PLAYERS

Come mid-November, the international cyclocross season begins to batten down the hatches. In Belgium and the Netherlands, several big races come in rapid succession—Hasselt GVA, Asper-Gavere Superprestige, Koksijde World Cup, Gieten Superprestige, and the Igorre World Cup in Spain.

Across the pond, the U.S. selection races for the World Championships are underway, and America's top riders now bring their A-game to the USGP races in New Jersey and Portland.

Each incremental drop in degree air temperature signals a change in the riders' faces. Eyes narrow, mouths tighten, and cheeks chisel.

On a new circuit in Mercer, New Jersey, Ryan Trebon throttles the competition with two consecutive wins—Saturday in the dry, and Sunday in the mud. A few weeks later in Portland, never-to-be-discounted Tim Johnson wins on Saturday, setting up a winner-takes-the-series finale the next day. With drenching rain and howling winds literally uprooting trees during the Sunday men's elite race, Ryan emphatically rides away from the field to take his third national series title since 2004. The win sets the stage for one hell of a National Championship in Kansas City two weeks later.

I take a good long look around me in Portland (again as technical director)—and labor to dismantle some sopping course signage to help with the cleanup—when it occurs to me once again how different the American scene is from Belgium's.

At this final USGP series races in Portland, the start sheet lists—
Elite Men: 75
Elite Women: 41
Masters (aged 35+): 73
Juniors (aged 17-18): 23

And this doesn't even include hundreds of additional participants in the other categories: the B Women, Masters Women, C Women, B Men, C Men, Single Speeders, Masters 45+, Masters 55+, and Juniors 10-16.

It's no secret that Portland's weekly cyclocross series—the "Cross Crusade"—boasts the largest numbers anywhere on the planet. The series' all-time participant record is somewhere around 2,000 riders for a single day of racing.

In Belgium, the big races center solely on about forty top male riders. In the U.S., the big races encompass eight to ten different categories and levels, with far more racers as a result.

Danish cyclocross champion Joachim Parbo is a guy who has raced frequently on both sides of the pond, and thus has a fresh perspective. I remember the eloquent comments he shares about the U.S. after the USGP Colorado races in 2006:

"There are fewer spectators here, and people perceive that as lowering the worth of the races," he is quoted in *VeloNews*. "I would like to turn it around and say here you have so many more athletes. And that is surely positive. You have three, four times as many racers than in Europe. Because it's so competitive in Europe and so focused on the very best riders, there are much fewer people doing the sport than in the U.S.

"The crowd that goes to watch a 'cross in Belgium is like a football crowd here in the U.S.," he continues. "In Belgium, you're riding in a cloud of smoke coming from these fat men. Your pulse is 190, you're taking in all the air you can take, and you're breathing cigarette smoke. In that sense it is more athletic here. I really enjoy that."

Build it and they will come, the thinking goes. Build courses and athletes, then spectators, gate receipts, television. Supply. Demand.

It's all in its infancy in the U.S.

***

While his compatriots battle back home for American supremacy, Jonathan steams in the airtight cooker of European cyclocross. The pressure keeps building. Team management seems to foment trouble at every turn, and the urgency for results increases daily.

On Saturday, November 17, a Sunweb team doctor visits Jonathan's home to confirm whether he is indeed sick and unable to race in Hasselt.

On Sunday, November 18, the lid blows off at the Superprestige in Asper-Gavere, one of the most hallowed of all Belgian cyclocross races for its difficulty and tradition.

Despite exemplary pre-race television footage of Jonathan leading a kids' clinic, an altercation between Page and boss Mettepenningen after the race seems to throw Jonathan's whole Sunweb season into doubt. According to press reports and to Jonathan, the team management is claiming that he's still not achieving the expected results, not meeting his obligations, and should perhaps—although this is hard to imagine— be dismissed. Jonathan says he can't perform with such a negative atmosphere.

The whole drama plays out in a prime-time pre-race television interview, when Jonathan appears with the mayor of Asper-Gavere:

Jonathan: "I expect a lot out of myself also. I've felt a lot of negative pressure from the team management, to be honest. When that happens to me, I kind of shut down a little bit, and so for me it's not a good motivator."

(Footage of Jonathan talking to the mayor.)

Mayor: "You are very welcome here."

(Footage of Jonathan, Cori, and the kids.)

Cori: "We're used to American-style, where people are supportive, no matter what. Not like here where everybody puts expectations on you the whole time."

(Pan to Jonathan.)

"Winning is a little unrealistic right now, but a top ten would be fine for me, and that would be another step to the World Championships and the next part of my season."

The scenario is pure Belgium. Belgian television has created a handful of cyclocross superstars. Couple that with an average of 10,000 to 15,000 on-site paying spectators for the big Belgian races—broadcast live on Belgian networks Sporza and VT4— and you have a sport that everybody has an opinion about.

The economics of it are similarly intense. Eager for the chance to advertise their brand to thousands of passionate viewers, sponsors line up for the chance to be associated with races. Cyclocross is a part of the business plan. Riders who offer a return on a sponsor's investment are in high demand.

Disappointing riders bring disappointing profits. Page's Sunweb team management has a point, too.

Television and sponsors. Promoters and races. Spectators and TV and radio audiences. Support personnel and riders. Salaries and endorsements. The system is all very tightly connected.

And the interesting twist is called start money.

Remunerative. Yes.

Obligatory. Yes.

Equitable. No.

To get the best possible explanation of this, I phone John Van Den Akker, the manager—through his company, Cycling Service—for all cyclocross contracts for races in the Netherlands and for the top Dutch riders. He's not altogether happy with the apportioning of the pie.

"The problem," he relates, "starts with the popularity of cyclocross in Belgium." The overwhelming success drives the sport away from countries like the Netherlands. A big race in Belgium gets 17,000 spectators; a Superprestige like the Netherlands' St. Michielsgestel draws only 2,500. It's a downward spiral from there. The Dutch don't have live TV coverage of the races; they have smaller races, and fewer spectators paying entry fees, he says. As a result, the race organizers don't have enough money to pay riders the start money they've come to expect.

With start money, the fee paid upfront to riders just for appearing in a race, the superstars can expect to get as much as $7,000, no matter how well or how poorly they do on race day.

In 2007, the situation with start money is getting a lot of press in Belgium: Articles talk about the "greed" of Erwin Vervecken, Sven Nys, and Bart Wellens, who leave only the crumbs for the others.

"It even hurts riders like Lars Boom," says Van Den Akker, who represents Lars. "We find out that Niels Albert asks 3,000 euros per race, and Lars is only asking 2,500." Meanwhile, Sven and Erwin get 6,000 per race. "It gets out of control," Van Den Akker says. He is so troubled by the off-kilter economics that he has a bit of doom in his voice. "I'm afraid for the future of cyclocross for the moment," he says. "We're having a hard time here in Holland."

The dimension of earning power in international pro men's cyclocross suddenly hits me. The pay is not nearly as high as it is for professional road racing: Tour de France celebs and spring classics stars reportedly make as much as seven figures per year. Then again, pro cyclocross has an advantage over road racing because there are far fewer players at the top. If a second-tier European cyclocross rider finishes, say, between eighth and fifteenth at big European races; and if he can race thirty-five times for 1,000 euros per race—and earns a 45,000 euro base salary—then he can make in the neighborhood of $100,000 per year. Not many American mountain biking or domestic road pros currently bring in that kind of money.

And the big fish—Sven, Erwin, Bart?

Thirty-five races at 6,000 euros per start, plus a decent salary and endorsements, and they might be approaching $500,000. Maybe even as high as $750,000-plus per year.

Pretty solid.

Van Den Akker's comments are intriguing. But the finger-pointing, whomever it targets, does nothing to solve the bigger problem. With so much money going to so few riders, and with so little money getting funneled to the middle and lower ranks, up-and-comers and foreign riders have that much more difficulty making a living. If there's a set amount of money to be dispensed at any given Superprestige or GVA series race, and the top stars keep driving up their asking price, the trickle-down doesn't trickle down too far.

For top U.S.-based guys like Ryan Trebon and Jeremy Powers, who come over to do blocks of European races, the reality isn't pretty. They get 200 euros, or maybe 500, in start money. Roughly $300 to $600. Not much, considering their investment.

Things aren't a lot different in the U.S., where riders are only just beginning to receive start money.

America's best 'cross riders have yet to survive on domestic cyclocross alone. They must turn to other cycling disciplines—mountain biking, for one—to make a decent combined wage. Some try to spend a cyclocross season or partial season overseas, but the payoff can be nonexistent. European travel, housing, food, transport, and support costs—some borne by American sponsors, but some not—make the European proposition palatable to only a select few. Jonathan Page is the only American pro to have successfully made the jump to a European-sponsored pro contract with Sunweb. With a contract like this, an American can hope to make it.

And now even his situation is tenuous.

Game on   Photo: Tom Robertson

Sven Nys and Bart Wellens, (Igorre 2007)

PHOTOPRESS.BE

28: MALLORCA MAGIC

"A man perfects himself by working."

—Thomas Carlyle, *Past and Present*

For all the controversy in the Jonathan Page camp, there is nothing distracting for Sven—nothing but his own labor.

In fact, with his win the day before and then his thirteenth consecutive Superprestige victory in Asper, Sven initiates a period of domination virtually unheard of in modern sport.

November 17, Hasselt GVA: 1st

November 18, Asper-Gavere Superprestige: 1st

November 24, Koksijde World Cup: 1st

November 25, Gieten Superprestige: 2nd

December 2, Igorre World Cup: 1st

December 6, Ciclocross Internacional Asteasu: 1st

December 9, Veghel Superprestige: 1st

December 15, Essen GVA: 1st

It is a period of utter sangfroid. Regardless of conditions, distractions, exasperations, Sven manages to win seven of the eight races he starts over a span of four weeks. His win in Essen is his 202nd career victory.

From the outside, the most impressive aspect of this winning streak is his calculating victory in the sands of Koksijde. Slowed by a poor start and then by two uncharacteristic tumbles on the highest, deepest dune of the course, Sven never panics and rides into the final lap with only the pesky Fidea rider Klaas Vantornout for company.

What it must be like as a rival to know—with absolute clarity—that you're going to be destroyed by a rider stronger than you inside the final lap of a cyclocross race.

Approaching a bog-down section of sand, just before the same troubling high-point dune, Sven accelerates, and—in rapid succession—Vantornout bobbles.

Sven gets a gap.

Vantornout leverages his arms—long and extended—over the bars.

He looks like a praying mantis.

But it's game over.

A year ago in this venue's race, the win came in a riding attack by Sven on a sandy climb—that no one else could ride. This year, it's a simple, unmatchable pushing of the pedals at a critical moment.

What it must be like, to be the owner of the tool box with the most tools.

The only blemish in this period comes in Gieten. Perhaps it's the long trip to north Holland directly after the maximum effort in Koksijde. Or maybe it's because Niels Albert has never lost in Gieten in all his years in the younger categories. Most probably, it's that Albert didn't contest the elite race the day before, due to his desire to stay in the espoir category to secure the only title that has eluded him thus far in his young career—the U23 World Championship.

Fresh legs or no, it's essentially a day of mourning for the Sven faithful. Despite having won every Superprestige race dating back to December 24, 2005, Sven—impossibly—loses.

The winning streak? "It had to come to an end one day," Sven says in an interview with incisive Cyclingnews.com journalist Brecht Decaluwé.

From the inside, this period of sovereignty speaks to something deeper. I telephone Sven's trainer, Paul Van Den Bosch, to learn more about his training during this block.

"What's the secret, Paul?" I ask, allowing myself an understatement. "Sven's on a pretty good run."

"He's been in Mallorca," Paul replies. "Three weeks of training in the good weather. Flying back up to do the races. You know, it's a bit counterintuitive, but he's been doing only base training there. Four hours, five hours with some climbing. No intervals, no intensity; 120-150 kilometers just riding. It's impossible to keep him going with high intensity for the whole season—September, October, November, December, January, February—six months. You need some periods with just working on the aerobic endurance."

"But what about his training in January?" I ask, knowing that the World Championships at the end of January are what all other results are measured against.

"Well, then it's intensity again after the Belgian Championships in early January." At that point, there's only one race a week, he explains. "So in January, it's Monday recovery, Tuesday three hours endurance work, then Wednesday some specific intensity in the forest again—but not too high—followed by two hours in the afternoon behind the motorbike, then some tempo riding on Thursday, and Friday easy again. But 'easy' for Sven is always two hours. In fact, when he goes too easy the day before a race, like if he rides in an easy group ride, he says he always struggles in the first part of the race [the next day]."

The entire routine is posted on the website; I've read it and wondered how it's possible. "Are you ever afraid it's too much?"

"I do sometimes," Paul says. "But you know Sven. There's nobody like him. Nobody can do the work that Sven does. Nobody."

Who can explain this kind of commitment? Aside from the trainer, the only other link to what goes on within that deepness is—the soigneur.

***

I once asked my old friend U.S.A. National Development Team soigneur (now BMC soigneur) Chris De Vos to define the job. He had a hard time, the way everybody does when they try to describe a job that starts with giving massages but also involves being an aide of all kinds—a friend, confidante, trainer, assistant.

"The most important thing is to make sure the rider is comfortable," De Vos says. "You work with the rider's body through massage, getting him ready, helping him recover." With the massage, "you give him energy, you take away the bad energy, and you also help him to clear his mind. A soigneur is a small word for being a dad, a guy who helps the rider out with his problems between the rider and the manager, or the wife, or the kids, parents, coach, whatever the situation is. For sure, there's a lot of stuff going on between the table and the race."

For Sven, the guy "between the table and the race" is Rabobank Continental Team Soigneur Guy "Biste" Verbist, a Belgian who's one of the best in the business. With his attention to detail and caring hands, Biste is always in demand. He's the one you see on TV taking Sven's jacket before the race, whisking Sven away to the mobile home after a race, and carrying the ever-present podium bag. He's also the guy you don't see, behind closed doors, giving Sven a rubdown after a race or at a training camp. The title soigneur comes from the French verb "to care." But the term only begins to describe the role that Biste plays in the Sven machine.

For these three weeks in Mallorca, the two share a room. "There," Biste says, "we become like brothers. In Mallorca, it really is—how you say—a familyship. We are talking all the time about family, friends, his wife, his son, what we like to eat. We watch movies together. It's an important time. But during massage, it's something special. It's something not for words.

"These days in Mallorca," Biste continues, "Sven is doing four to five hours on the road. Yet his legs, when I'm massaging, they feel like they have only done an hour. That is how I know that Sven—this year—is really good."

"Does his energy transfer back to you?" I ask, carefully. "Is it mutual?"

"Again, there are no words to explain it—the connection between the soigneur and the rider. But I try. Okay, maybe I'm overstating it, and it's obviously a different kind of passion, but the feeling—it is said—is like having sex. By giving massage to Sven, it's like I'm helping him to go faster and he is giving me some sort of energy back. It's impossible to describe. I can only say that it is something like physical and mental therapy, but deeper, like something of the spiritual. Of the spirit."

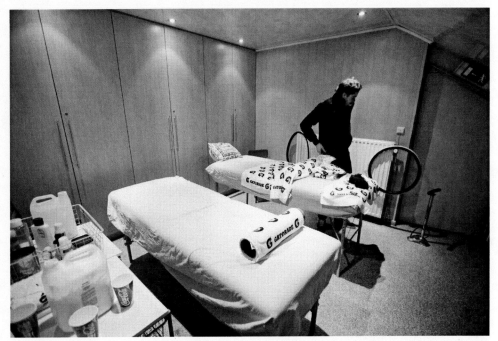

Post-massage, Danny Summerhill, EuroCrossCamp   Photo: Tom Robertson

29: KERSTPERIODE

And so it begins—the kerstperiode. Mario De Clercq once called this two-week block of nonstop racing his "mini Tour de France." Sven calls it his *rittenkoers*. His stage race.

A number of factors contribute to this being a fortnight of cyclocross celebration. First, Belgians love their holidays, and there's a keen sense of festivity in the air. Ornamental Saint Nicks can be seen climbing up little ropes outside countless house windows. From chocolate shops to lingerie boutiques, almost all the shops gussy up their displays for Christmas. People are out and about, home for the holidays, ready to party. Second, with school out and the working public largely on vacation between Christmas and New Year's, race organizers know they can get a crowd for any race, mid-week or otherwise. Third, the riders know this is the time to make money and build their form with an intense period of racing.

When I arrive for EuroCrossCamp V, it's with conflicting emotions. It's the fifth year in a row that I find myself in some frozen cornfield in rural Flanders directing a group of American cyclocross hopefuls. But I also find it difficult to be away from my family. Often, my wife and two kids are able to come to the camp. But this time they're back home in Montana. It's also challenging to be hard at it—on my own vacation—when I'll go straight back to my teaching duties after it's over.

Nonetheless, the camp's steadfast vision remains—international experience begets international results, which beget international recognition, which begets pro contracts for American riders. If Jonathan Page is the first American ever to be rewarded with a European pro cyclocross contract, I want one of my camp riders to become the second. And the third.

Also, being in Belgium during the kerstperiode, amid the grit and toil, is the best time to observe the top riders. The build-up to the World Championships begins to heighten now with these races, and in the same venues: Hofstade, Loenhout, Middelkerke, Diegem, Baal, St. Niklaas, year after year.

This particular camp group has me confident, but full of questions. How will they perform, how will they handle the stresses, both physical and mental? I'll certainly find out, since the camp involves nine races, fourteen days, thirty-six bikes, one director, one assistant director, six mechanics, three soigneurs, two chefs, seven vehicles, and eighteen riders aged 16 to 30 from the junior, Under 23, and elite categories.

A myriad of experiences.

Coming to race 'cross in Belgium encapsulates the central idea of Joseph Heller's *Catch-22*, a book I love to teach in my classes. There's something supremely rational yet simultaneously illogical in the fact that "you need to race here to get better, but you have to be better to race here."

In one of the camp's first races, a small one in Balegem, junior Gavin Mannion hits a tree in the middle of the course, smashes his helmet to bits, gets dizzily up, negotiates the off-camber, sketch-ball course, and finishes—dazedly—in the top ten. We monitor him closely for the rest of the camp. Another junior racer from Belgium isn't so lucky and gets carted away in a stretcher, with the race going on around him. He spends the night in the hospital, but is released the next day.

At another race, in the Netherlands at Zeddam (site of the 2006 World Championships), camp alumnus Jeremy Powers gives me goose bumps carving the muddy berms in a December sun made of slate—

Lars Boom, Vervecken, Groenendaal are there.

In the front group.

Jeremy, too.

It's huge.

As they say, you learn to ride your bike here.

After the Zeddam race, I notice Jeremy warming down on the rollers. With eighteen guys to transport to and from any given race, doing a proper post-race warm-down isn't so easy. Logistically, it takes too much time. It's more important to get on the road for the three-hour return trip. Jeremy is a camp graduate with his own set-up now—transport, mechanics, lodging. As it should be for an elite rider. But if you're still a developing rider, you can't always do your own U.S. routine. You have to adapt and do what's best for the group. It's how we roll.

While I give the riders quite a bit of freedom to explore training routes and Kortrijk coffee and waffle shops, I do want them to be punctual, neat, and have a routine to their day. Waking, eating, training, racing, massage, meal, and quiet times are all scheduled on a daily basis. This camp is about competition—not vacation.

It's always hard in the beginning with jet lag adjustments, but we usually hit our stride around the first Wednesday of the camp. For the entire domestic season, these guys have been dueling against each other. Now, the personal rivalries are put aside, on the playing field and in the kitchen where plenty of chores await.

In essence, we are a team of American cyclocross riders who have chosen to set the bar at the highest level, sacrificing the traditional home-for-the-holidays routine and the relaxation after the U.S. race season to prepare for the World Cyclocross Championships and learn how to race against the world's best. We go forward together, we demand the most of ourselves, and we help each other out. No other cyclocross national team functions with this kind of connection and performance level. The brotherhood and camaraderie make a lasting impact and resonate throughout the riders' cycling careers.

Danny Summerhill, 2007 World Junior silver medalist and veteran EuroCrossCamp member, describes it this way: "Every Christmas, a bond is formed, so we are almost like a band of brothers, with the very same people I do battle with throughout the road season months earlier. Once we get to Belgium, we march through the trenches together, helping each other get through the different challenges—missing our family back home, dealing with mechanical difficulties, learning how to employ different strategies to take with us into our next races.

"Without racing the CrossCamp," he continues, "I wouldn't know what racing 'all out' was like, because in Europe the standard of racing is so much higher than in the U.S., and you manage to push yourself to levels far greater than you have ever known before. I think racing 'cross in Europe makes you a stronger person, plain and simply because it forces you so far beyond the norm of what you are used to at home."

On Christmas day, I drive the hour to the managers' meeting in Hofstade on the eve of the World Cup. In the late day dinge—a kind of smog-cloud that obscures the downtown—there's no view of the historic Brussels cathedral as I turn onto the Ring, the motorway around the city.

Christmas afternoon. I shed some tears. Homesickness for my wife and kids.

Radio Donna offers "Fairytale of New York" by the Pogues.

"So happy Christmas,

I love you baby,

I can see a better time,

When all our dreams come true."

No dreams come true in Hofstade the next day. The sand just shreds our elite guys—Trebon, Powers, and newly-crowned national champ Tim Johnson (returning to Europe to race 'cross for the first time since 2002).

Only Jonathan Page finishes on the same lap. A creditable 17th. In front of 25,000 spectators.

It gets ugly on the blogs back home.

I have only one response.

Come on over. Today. Tomorrow. Come watch.

Better yet, come race.

Open invitation.

Have at it.

A reality check awaits.

At one point, mid-race, Sven Nys, Lars Boom, and Bart Wellens are blazing through the upper side of the double pit—a solid 200 meters of half-meter-deep sand, rideable to some, unrideable to most—while the chase group, racing for fourth place, is down on the beach passing through the lower pit. Erwin Vervecken and the other *achtervolgers* (chasers) are two minutes down.

Two minutes down.

Whoa.

Woe.

Sven hammers home another calculating win. Lars gets out-sprinted by Bart for second place. But it's the way Lars rides, the decisions he makes, that have me curious.

"Why did you change your bike on the lower beach pit?" I ask him afterward. "You were getting gapped there every time by Wellens."

"Bahh," Lars says, with his usual take-things-in-stride attitude. "You know I need to ride these races more. I need to learn the circuits better. But I didn't want to change in the upper pit because it takes everything I have to ride that deep sand and stay with Bart and Sven. But I'm happy. I'm not in top form yet, yet I'm still doing well. That's a good sign."

Indeed.

Some of our guys by comparison either DNF or finish as far back as two laps behind. But there will be other days.

That's the reassuring message I receive from friend Jean-Paul Van Poppel, who's at the race pitting for his son Boy. Boy was junior cyclocross world champion back in Zeddam in January 2006, but this is only his second 'cross race of this season. His dad has been sure to give him a good rest after the long road season riding for the Rabobank continental team. Today, Boy finishes 5th in the Under 23 race.

"Good results, they take time," Jean-Paul consoles me.

Head down, pretty dejected after the knackering our guys take in the elite race, I hump my way back to the van, encumbered with two bikes, a pump, and two sets of spare wheels. Passing the beer tent in ankle-deep sand, I'm suddenly broadsided by a scrum of six sauced-up slammers clamoring to clock each other with all the power they can muster. I can only guess at their argument.

Probably a fight over who's the best, Sven or Bart.

Knocked several feet and in a tangle of bikes, I scramble for higher ground and gaze forlornly as the boozed-up Belgian bruisers pummel each other. One guy has a hold of another guy's belt, of all things, and he's yanking, just yanking to cinch it tighter. The victim's face is a splotchy mess of blues and reds.

It's been awhile since I've seen real primal, animalistic, valorless violence.

Hooliganism, cyclocross style.

Welcome to my holiday.

***

DECEMBER 28, 2007

The mid-kerstperiode races seem to go better for the top Americans. The Azencross (literally, "cross for the Aces") in Loenhout is a race Ryan Trebon likes. He says it's a circuit that seems to find him a rhythm despite its ever-turning nature, its man-made bridge climbs, its serious whups. In 2005, he rode strongly in the main chase group—racing for 5th place—to finish 16th. This year, Ryan finally gets a result, finishing 21st. He seems to be showing signs of recovery from his ill-fated crash a few weeks earlier at the U.S. Nationals in Kansas City. (Due to poor course design, two different sections of the circuit came very close to each other. A crashing rider going in one direction drifted through the course tape and plowed into Ryan going in the opposite direction).

Jeremy Powers is 23rd in Loenhout, right behind Ryan. Not great results, but when you're hearing the Belgies poke fun at our American champ Tim Johnson, saying he can't ride 'cross as well as dabbling roadie Philippe Gilbert (who finishes 32nd in Loenhout), then you take what you can get. Up on the podium is the new guard—Lars Boom, Zdenek Stybar, and Niels Albert.

The showdown in Treviso is just four weeks away.

Next day, in Middelkerke, Jonathan Page finally gets the result he's been looking for, taking second place to Sven in the dunes and wind of the NoordzeeCross.

Frigid temps aside, the anticipation is feverish as we rendezvous (again, the very next day) at one of the oldest cyclocross races on the circuit—Diegem. This year it comes with a new twist: prime-time television coverage under the lights.

The atmosphere is electric. I make my rounds. The montage begins.

Outside the Sven Nys camper, a mass of fans ten-deep is crowding around the periphery of the awning, hoping for a glimpse of Sven on the trainer. I struggle through the wall of bodies to say hi to Isabelle and exchange gifts with the family, a Euro Christmas custom. Then I compare notes with trainer Paul. He has his own questions this time.

"Why was Page so good yesterday in Middelkerke?" he asks.

"I don't know," I say. "Maybe the stress is finally easing up."

"Ja, that's good, to be able to manage the stress," Paul says. "You see the stress of Fidea."

Paul gives me his accounting of the race tallies: Bart and Erwin have won two; Sven has won sixteen so far. All the biggest races.

"He could get twenty," Paul says.

"Maybe more."

We talk a bit about training and, before I leave, I ask Paul about Sven's plans for the Olympics. He's told me he might use a 'cross bike, even though it's a mountain bike race. Why would he do that?

"We hear the descents aren't so steep. It depends on the circuit. We see when we go do recon in Beijing in the spring," Paul says.

I thread my way back through the congregation, smiling to myself. Sven and Paul, with their quiet, revolutionary resolve. The ultimate irony.

If there's no cyclocross in the Olympics, the next best thing is for Sven to do well in the Beijing Olympic Mountain Bike event ...

... on a 'cross bike.

***

Erwin warms up on the trainer. His rotseason is officially in full swing: He's had only a couple of minor wins. Liesbeth tells me she just wants it to end. Erwin is used to winning, not losing, she says.

I know things are bad for them: My work in the racing world makes me privy to backroom talk about Erwin—*quantité negligible* is the term I've heard. French for something akin to "over the hill." It's a label he clearly doesn't deserve.

Seeing Erwin in the rainbow jersey, pistoning away on his rollers, it seems almost a sacrilege.

As I watch Erwin smoothly spinning away on his rollers in his warm-up, I want to relay some information to him. My two elite riders are sitting out this Diegem race tonight. With so many races, it's important to pick and choose which ones to go for and which ones to pass on and rest. So, after working the Junior and Under 23 races, I'm free to relax and enjoy the upcoming elite race.

"Erwin, my elite guys aren't racing tonight."

He doesn't quite understand me.

"I have no riders tonight," I repeat.

And, then, almost faintly, come his words—

"But you have me."

It's a forlorn moment for the reigning world champion.

I weave through the parking lot crammed with cars, campers, a carnival. To one side, the Diegem castle lights twinkle with approval. To the other, the church spire climbs up into the darkness. Out on course, nearly eighty television staffers with eighteen cameras are at the ready.

Five hundred meters away, overlooking the soccer field, there's a set of bleachers, a bar, and some changing rooms for the lesser-known riders without campers.

But the ritual is the same, whether you're royalty or a rookie.

Preparation for battle.

I pass by a small changing room; for a brief moment, I duck in.

It's the smell that first gets you.

The sweet, terebinthine scent hits your nostrils as soon you step in. Inside—away from winter rain that turns teeth to tin, calves to ice, toes to wood—the air hangs heavy, almost inert, with liniment and oil. It's quiet during the process—where a soigneur gives a pre-race leg rub using various pastes, creams, and oils collectively known as embrocation. Soigneurs knead gladiatorial sinew in preparation for the fray. With every pass of the hands, the soigneur sculpts, polishes, anoints. Lavender, rosemary, ginger, arnica, and menthol coax capillaries to their supple best. The soigneur's hands speak; the athlete's legs listen. We have kneaded and now we must sow. May your well-oiled pistons remain impervious to mud, slush, ice, and snow. Go forth, legs. Fulfill your destiny.

Then, the spell is broken. Cleated shoes ratchet up, rain capes sound a swishy knell, helmet straps click. The tenter-hooked crowd awaits its wheeled and weathered warriors. To fill them with embrocation of the soul.

Photo: Tom Robertson

EuroCrossCamp   Photo: Tom Robertson

EuroCrossCamp   Photo: Tom Robertson

Gavin Mannion and Noel Dejonckheere, EuroCrossCamp, (Laarne 2007)

US National Champion Tim Johnson, (Hofstade 2007)

Jeremy Powers giving the flick to Bart Aernouts, (Zeddam 2007)
PHOTOPRESS.BE

30: KARAKTER STUDY

DECEMBER 30, 2007

It's 7 p.m. in the pits at Diegem. All of my EuroCrossCamp riders have been transported back to Izegem to recover and get ready for the race in Baal in two days. I've stayed and found my way to the pit area to take in the elite race. The pits are often the best place to watch, for they offer an unobstructed view of the action.

Noise.

Mechanics on tiptoes, trying to pick out their rider from the pack. The oncoming peloton careens down a steep ramp, piercing the chill night air.

The pit marshall's whistle blares.

A jet overhead, landing in Zaventem, just a few kilometers away.

Screaming fans.

The announcer, in Flemish: *"De situatie … Hier is Sven Nys met Radomir Simunek."*

First riders through.

Cameras flashing everywhere.

Smooth hand ups, the bikes exchanged between mechanics and riders.

"Komaan, Sven," yells Sven's second mechanic.

"Hupp, hupp, JP," commands Jonathan Page's loyal mechanic, Franky.

Mechanics scurry with dirty bikes.

The roar of power washers in full action mode. Not enough hoses. Never enough power washers.

"The pit lane is way faster. Tell him next lap"—mechanic-speak in the background.

Sven's mechanics, reaching the same conclusion, move to a more strategic box where, if Sven utilizes the pit lane, he can take the little rise after the pit with more speed.

In the process, they discreetly switch his pit bike from Dugast Typhoon 34's to 32's.

Between industrial pressure hoses, the crowd din, and 747's on their final approach, the decibels deafen.

Another lap.

Gaps now.

Four to go. *Vier ronde.*

Sven and Simunek still together. Radomir Simunek Jr., 25-year-old son of multi-world champion Radomir Simonek (who would die in 2010, at age 48), rides for the cerulean jersey of the Palmans team. He's having a hell of a good race.

A few beats and the first chase group passes.

"Jonathan looks better," I shout to Franky.

"Yes, he's doing better now—racing in the first group," Franky says. "He switched trainers. From Mario to a new guy, Andre."

Andre Vergucht. A veteran trainer. I hadn't heard the news nor do I know this trainer. But, in my interior thoughts, I commend Jonathan for switching things up, trying to find the right formula.

"That's good," I say.

Lights blare.

Simunek falters. His dad-mechanic in the pit looks visibly disappointed.

As far as the eye can see, spectators teem over the circuit, yelling their hearts out. Pounding the fencing. Waving their arms. One inebriated soul actually bumps Sven on the head on the upper part of the course.

No matter.

Sven rides in alone.

Win number seventeen.

Simunek fights valiantly, but slips in a dark corner and has to settle for 2nd place, 20 seconds behind Sven. Jonathan rides strongly to finish 10th, backing up his strong 2nd place from the day before in Middelkerke.

The pit marshall, a local, maybe 70 years old, wears a bright red race staff jacket and stands proudly with his whistle around his neck. He says he loves working the races. "It's great, eh? The ambiance. Only one hour. Full on."

I ask if he's a volunteer or paid as a member of the race organization. He tells me he only gets 15 euros—$19— for working all day.

"Why do you do it?"

Looking at me, then through me, he says : "Bicycle race … Belgium … *karakter*." Using the Dutch word at the end. Forming a fist, then pumping it.

"Karakter."

***

Two days later, on New Year's Day, the Canibaal looks for another opportunity, this time on his home course in Baal.

Due to the notorious lack of parking, we prep our camp guys on the street, on one of only two roads in and out.

Three hours before the race, Sven drives past with his dad in the Pathfinder.

I remember our discussion from six months ago.

"The stairs," I ask him. "Did you raise them up again this year?"

Wink. Then another.

"For sure."

The elite men's race in Baal, defies—and nearly deifies—expectations. "Awe enables us to perceive in the world intimations of the divine," as Jewish scholar Abraham Joshua Heschel describes the sacred. Once in a while, when a competitor displays such awe-inspiring athleticism, it borders on the secular holy. New Year's Day 2008 is such a day.

Mud. Sweat. All comers, apart from Sven, in arrears.

Sven in his element.

Riding the stairs.

Those Empyrean stairs.

Riding the barriers.

Blasting the heavy course. Storied American road pro George Hincapie coined a phrase when a rider seems to be riding completely effortlessly. The phrase is apt on this day for Sven.

No chain.

I study each passing.

And with each lap, I begin to look beyond the schooling.

Beyond the utter efficiency. Beyond the sheer power.

Those are the visible things, put out for all to see.

There must be something deeper, something to do with the "in here."

Something to do with within-ness. And the only way to see it is to be here—in the present.

No race photo can pick it up. A photo is only a particle; it's static. Television can't discern it, because while footage is dynamic like a wave, it lacks total dimension.

To be at the course, within a meter of the 'crossman and his work, is to be a part of the field. Part of the multidimensional scene where every component is organized in relation to another. The place where it's possible to find a final clue.

The eyes have it.

Sven's eyes, as he pulverizes the circuit.

They're strabismic, askant, and dulled.

Due to the effort.

It's the look of utter giving.

Of utterly having given.

The result is total decimation.

Nose breathing the last lap, Sven approaches the finish line with almost a minute in hand.

I'm waiting, there on the line.

Just to make sure it's still there.

In the eyes.

***

Seventh place: Vervecken. Fourth: Boom. Third: Kevin Pauwels. Second: Stybar.

Niels Albert starts this New Year's Day race but, after a lap, gives it up. Bart Wellens is home in bed with fever. Are they biding their time for the big Belgian Championships on Sunday?

Jonathan Page and Ryan Trebon are sick at home, as well.

For Sven, meanwhile, there's been no cracking.

Not on this race day in his hometown.

The normally loquacious Michel Wuyts has only one word for it: "Magnificent."

The headline in the *Gazet Van Antwerpen*, the race sponsor, is "*Baas in Eigen Baal*," along with a full-page photo of Sven in his blue UCI skinsuit, arms aloft, fists clenched.

Boss in his own Baal. His own bundle, or bale, as the Dutch word *baal* translates. Shorthand for: Nobody beats you at home.

***

The next day, my campers and crew make the trip to St. Niklaas, Belgium, for the GP De Ster, the final race of EuroCrossCamp V. Sven's rittenkoers is almost complete. It's his sixth race in eight days. He's had four wins out of five.

St. Nik is always a good end-of-camp race because it's not part of a series, which makes it smaller and a bit mellower. Case in point: I spend some time with Sven at his motor home while my juniors are out on their pre-ride, and I ask him if he'd be willing to stop by to say hi to them if he has a chance. He says no problem. He wants to eat first and then he'll be over. At a bigger race, this would be an improbability given how many hundreds of onlookers stand outside his door. But at St. Niklaas, it's do-able, so I give word to the soigneurs to be on the lookout for *le patron*.

Unfortunately, by the time Sven comes over, I'm on my way to the pit—at this race, the pit is literally halfway around a big lake—and the juniors are headed to the start line. Noel has just arrived to the venue with our elite American riders and hasn't been informed of the plan, so he's pretty surprised when this guy in Rabobank kit comes pedaling across the infield of a dewy athletic track to where we we've set up camp. "What's Sven doing at our vans?" Noel is thinking. He and I have a good laugh about it later. Fortunately, some of our espoirs and elites are there to meet the greatest 'cross rider in history.

At the pit, meanwhile, the banter is fast and thick as usual. The mechanics' emotions roll high and low, depending on how the riders are doing.

I'm smiling early on, with Ryan leading the race. Maybe this is the day he will achieve what I've tried to cultivate in him for so long. Maybe this is the day he will embody one of my favorite Flemish expressions. Maybe this is the day Ryan will ride *met het mes tussen de tanden*. With a knife between his teeth.

Between laps, there's idle talk about the cold: Today, it's minus 2 C (28 degrees F).

Ex-world champ Radomir Simunek Sr. shrugs it off. After the race, he's got a big drive back to the Czech Republic for his son's battle with Stybar in the National Championships. (Each European nation has its National Championship on the first Sunday in January).

"It's minus 13 there," he says, stoically.

There's talk of tires. Talk of who's going well, who's going badly.

Then, there's the deflation.

My deflation.

I see Ryan and Jonathan get into a bit of a spat while jockeying for position in the sand about halfway through the race. I can't see exactly what happens, but after the race, Ryan claims that Jonathan sort of blocks his forward progress as they enter the beach section, while Jonathan maintains that Ryan takes a bad line and causes Jonathan to ride into the water as he tries to pass. Ryan finishes 12th and Jonathan DNF's. Neither says the incident has any outcome on the actual race, as both are coming back from illness. I'm not sure what to make of it, but I know that it's just another example of how much these two want nothing more than to be the strongest American in any race they enter.

Sven finishes 5th, preferring to take no risks.

The highlight of the day comes on the van ride home when I suggest to the guys that Sven took it easy to stay off the podium so he could get home in a timely fashion and rest up for Sunday's Belgian championship.

With his ever-at-the-ready wit, Under 23 EuroCrossCamp rider Brady Kappius deadpans—

"Yeah, that was my plan too. Ride just well enough to not make the podium."

That's Brady.

Bringing down the house.

Show time

Photo: Tom Robertson

Pit, Baal   Photo: Tom Robertson

The Stairs, Baal   Photo: Tom Robertson

31: THE SAND CASTLE

JANUARY 6, 2008

Given that the Belgians so thoroughly dominate cyclocross, common wisdom says that the Belgian Kampioenschap—the BK—is the most important 'cross race in the world. With the exception of a few strong riders from a few other countries, the very best riders today are Belgian. Hence, to win the BK is to win the virtual WK (World Championships). Sometimes you hear the expression, only half in jest, "the Belgian World Championships."

It's also one of the toughest races for Belgians, for psychological reasons. It's often more difficult, more stressful, to conquer one's peers—with virtually your entire country watching—than it is to succeed against relative strangers in other big races.

At this year's BK, because, again, the competitors are among the best in the world, the race has almost as much amplitude as the World Championships in Treviso in three weeks time.

And for a Belgian cyclocross racer to pull on the nation's tricolor is a profound honor in front of the people who matter most.

That said, the race itself—especially this 2008 Belgian Championship in the sand traps of Hofstade—acquires the connotational equivalence of a bunch of American kids playing sandlot baseball. Sven Nys, Bart Wellens, Erwin Vervecken, Niels Albert, Sven Vantourenhout, Klaas Vantornout—they've all been banging elbows in Belgian bike races since they were just out of training wheels.

The BK is both a replication of every other race in which they've battled each other and a consummation of all those years of staring each other down, squaring off, sparring with their sprockets.

It's just another race, but it's not just another race. And—only one bird can sing the strongest.

The race, which I'm watching live via the internet from Montana, starts with Fidea's Klaas Vantornout jumping the gun, but officials do not call for a re-start. The game is already on.

Early, Erwin is on fire, stringing out the group. By lap four of the nine-lap race, Niels Albert, the 20-year-old whiz kid, absolutely drills it and has Erwin, Sven, and Bart clamoring to keep pace.

The trademark sections of the Hofstade circuit (virtually the same as the World Cup course just two weeks before) are the sandy portions on the beach. Not only do riders need extremely good finesse to let the bike go where it needs to through the ankle-deep sand, but their upper bodies also have to be absolutely dynamic and flexible. Like water cascading down a mountain ravine.

Twenty-eight minutes in, disaster strikes for Albert. A front puncture. A long way from the pits. "Over and out" is all the commentator can muster.

Immediately Bart attacks and only Sven can follow.

Wellens and Nys.

Again.

One of the coolest aspects of Hofstade is how the television moto is able to capture the speed of the riders as they rocket through the sand toward pit two and the sandy run. On lap five, the moto flies along recording the battle royale and then, just before the run, Bart attacks to capitalize on his superior running speed. Sven is the first to get back to Bart and then, somehow, Erwin struggles to return to the front.

At the start of lap six, Albert is 27 seconds behind but, miraculously, by the end of the lap, he's back on terms with the leaders.

Vertical red-finned Nissan flags wave full in the wind as the strongest four riders in Belgium—maybe the world—race through a gauntlet of noise, cigarette smoke, and pain.

Along the beach, they ride just at the edge of the frigid lake water, rear wheel spray forming rooster tails behind their backs.

Lap eight and Albert puts in a big attack. Erwin is again dropped from the group but gradually manages to get back up.

For the fourth time in the race.

All four together to start lap nine.

Few final laps of a cyclocross race are as thrilling.

With a minute left to race—from the final pit to the line—it is the big four.

First, Erwin pits for his slicks (opting to put on tires he feels will be faster in the sprint once they hit the final paved section before the finish line).

No one else dares.

Albert lags behind Sven and Bart, obviously spent from his earlier efforts.

Then, in a moment we have almost come to expect, Nys attacks. With his superior technique, he transitions from the bike to the final set of stairs by taking the first step with his left foot, rather than taking another step with his right foot before starting the climb, as Bart does. Sven literally gets a leg up.

Wellens claws, scrambling up the five brick stairs, trying to answer Sven's final burst.

Sven's final bid.

Pale January late-afternoon light.

Sheen of sun mutes in low, washed angles.

Sand, forest trees, dirt, overcoats, buildings—suffuse in shades of brown.

No one can catch Sven. He crosses the line, both fists, in unison, shooting upwards in the air.

Bart crosses next. Then Albert comes around Erwin a few corners from the end to take the last step on the podium. Erwin has to settle for fourth.

Atop the podium, Sven pulls on the black, yellow, and red tunic. Belgian pro champion for the fifth time. King once more. Whether or not he wins again this season, Sven is sultan of this sandlot.

Vervecken chases Wellens and Nys, (Hofstade BK 2008)   PHOTOPRESS.BE

Laatste ronde—Vervecken, Nys, Wellens, Albert, (Hofstade BK 2008) PHOTOPRESS.BE

32: THE LONGEST TOES

JANUARY 26, 2008

It's the eve of the World Championships in Treviso, Italy, and Michel Wuyts and I are enjoying a post-dinner coffee in the empty press tent. Other than the odd TV technician, we have the space to ourselves. As is his manner, Michel starts in directly, wanting to share with me an age-old Flemish adage about toes. He relates that cyclocross is a sport that champions the rider with the longest toes. That it is a sport of such struggle, such scrutiny, such adversity, that the one who can take the most stepping on, the most abuse—from the training and racing, from the critics, from the self—has the best chance to become the winner.

Like so many other Flemishisms, this one seems particularly apropos for the pressure-cooker that is the final, frenzied, three-week build-up to the World Cyclocross Championships. Without the promise of an Olympic medal or the final yellow-shirted promenade down the Champs-Elysees reserved for the Tour de France winner, the World Championships of cyclocross are the pinnacle. To win the coveted rainbow jersey for being the best cyclocross rider on the planet and to don it in every race for the following calendar year is to be able to say—

I rule.

Present tense.

Michel and I begin our hour-long prognosticating about who will be on top at the end of the next day. Like so many of my interactions with members of the European cyclocross community—well, fraternity—my talk with Michel is never really an interview with questions and answers. Instead it is a conversation, full of enthusiasm, warmth, and respect. The teasing always seems mutual.

We start with the obvious favorite, Lars Boom. A week after winning his Dutch National Championship, he wins both World Cups in Liévin and Hoogerheide. The only other race he enters is the small mid-week race in Surhuisterveen. For training.

Having witnessed Lars winning the Worlds as a junior in Monopoli 2003 and as a U23 in Hooglede 2007, I know he has only one stone left to unturn—the elite world title. I've also been privy to Lars's training plans, compliments of his Rabobank trainer, Louis Delahaije, since 2005. After examining Lars's workouts—the precision, the control, the working of each zone and system—I believe he is completely physically primed for a big ride in Treviso. He even plays it coy with the media, saying he's new to the elite ranks; hence, he has reduced the pressure.

"Yes," Michel muses, "Lars will be very tough to beat. The only way is if the conditions are super technical or if Belgium rides completely as a team against Lars."

Michel and I both agree that such a tactic is highly unlikely given that every guy in Belgium's eight-man line-up could win on any given day. As a result, every Belgian will want to ride for himself rather than ride for the countryman who is the strongest.

Another player in the driver's seat is Bart Wellens, with his recent string of successes: 2nd in the Belgian champs; 2nd in Liévin; a win in Zonnebeke; and a day later, in the final race before Treviso, a 2nd in Hoogerheide. He's hardly won a race all year, but tomorrow could be the day to add a third world title.

"An up and down season," Michel sizes it up. "But no rider battles better than Bart. Look at his masterful tone with the press after Hoogerheide ... talking about how he's on schedule and that Boom will be 'beatable.'"

And what about Erwin? I have spoken to him several times in the past few weeks. He tells me he felt pretty strong at the Belgian Championships—a super start, some yoyo-ing and then in with a shout on the last lap, finally settling for fourth. A week later, a victory in Roubaix and, another week later, a third in Hoogerheide. All of his recent results have him positioned for an unfathomable fourth rainbow jersey. He tells me if it's dry in Treviso, he has a chance. Few riders can pick up the scent of victory in the late innings of the season as well as Erwin.

"For sure Erwin will be there tomorrow," Michel says. "I love how relaxed he is. He's had a tough season, but now, in the two weeks before Worlds, I like to say he is walking around in his pajamas. Living smoothly, calmly."

Privately, I wish I could say the same for our best American hope, Jonathan. He's had some good finishes of late, riding strongly to an 8th place in Hoogerheide. In fact, two days earlier, while out training with the U.S.A. juniors and Under 23's on the Montello climb north of Treviso, Jonathan cruises past, motorpacing behind the car. A blur of confidence and speed. Even at the team hotel, Jonathan seems relaxed, sharing his time with his accompanying family, his new sponsors, and the other American riders. Nevertheless, I'm worried that his difficult year with his team has left him sapped for the big show.

And then, as if to save the most perplexing for last, our conversation focuses on Sven. After his complete domination in Baal on New Year's Day, his calculating win a week later in the Belgian Championships, and his subsequent twentieth and twenty-first wins of the season in minor races in Otegem and Surhuisterveen, Sven seems to have lost the plot.

He's nowhere in the two final tune-up World Cups. Unable to battle, incapable of pushing himself any deeper, he looks completely empty. I ask Michel about Sven's seeming derailment.

"I've seen it coming, too," he concurs. "I knew it straight away two weeks ago, after Liévin. He was already exhausted, and then, on the Monday, the day after Liévin, because it was going to rain on Tuesday, the day he normally does his hard training, he went out and did four hours at 34 kph. And then, to see him unable to fight this past week, it's a shame. I can't understand why he pushes himself in those meaningless races, or why he has to continue to train so hard."

Having spent the previous six months exploring what drives Sven, I suggest to Michel that it isn't monetary greed that has driven him into the ground in this final preparation phase before Worlds. Maybe there is something to this aphorism about toes. Maybe Sven, as is his nature, has simply over extended, over reached, and now the elastic band has snapped.

"Quite possibly," Michel responds. "But let me end with another story."

I'm all ears.

"After losing last Sunday in Hoogerheide Sven did something very uncharacteristic for him, very against his nature," Michel tells me. "He phoned me and said that he hadn't eaten french fries in eight months and that he was going to have a whole plate of them that night for dinner, smothered in mayonnaise. Then, a half-hour later, he texted me with this message." Michel holds up his phone with the saved text message to display to me—

"I've eaten my fritjes, and now I'm going to train this week like a tourist and on Sunday, I'm going to race like a lion. I have nothing to lose and I'm gonna be quiet now, but on Sunday I will eat—like these fritjes—every rider in the World Championships."

Michel and I part. The air seems to hang heavy with chill, both in temperature and anticipation.

Tomorrow is the day.

Tomorrow is the day to see ...

... Who has the longest toes.

Belgian TV commentator Michel Wuyts

33: ORACLE OF TREVISO

SUNDAY, JANUARY 27, 2008

The day dawns clear in the industrial city of Treviso, 30 km north of Venice. Erwin has his wish. The white-gravelled start-finish straight shimmers in the Venetian sun and the frozen mud from the morning women's race has thawed to a dry sheen. As Belgian National Team Coach Rudy De Bie (the brother of Danny De Bie) predicts, the race will favor speed and tactics over brute strength and technical prowess.

Situated on the western shore of Le Bandie Lake, the 3.2 km circuit resembles a bow-tie configuration. On each of the bowed sections some grassed undulations look to take their toll on the riders over the nine-lap elite men's race. But as with all courses, one particular section has our U.S.A. staff and riders talking tactics and technique. Roughly a third of the way into the lap is the *rampa piscina*, a formidable climb of 50 meters at 25 percent. Such a steep, gravelled climb mandates a decision—try to ride it and risk sapping huge watts of power from the legs, or run it and perhaps be incrementally slower, but fresher in the end. We all agree it's a section where the leaders might not win the race, but where the race could be lost if the field bottlenecks and the front men ride away.

My coaching routine on race day is, foremost, to determine well in advance where I can stand on the circuit and relay snippets of advice to the our U.S. riders and convey any pertinent information via radio to our mechanics in the pits. In the biggest races in Belgium, a crowd-thin and, thus, quiet vantage point is unequivocally nonexistent. Here in Italy, however, even with an estimated 40,000 on hand, there's a fighting chance that I can find such a spot.

An hour before the start, with our team mechanics all set, our coaching radios re-checked, and the riders fully into their final warm-up (carefully watched over by our team soigneurs), I head out onto the course full of anticipation and reflection. How markedly different are the conditions from even a week before in muddy Hoogerheide? How counterintuitive might the race dynamics prove to be? Specifically, the faster a cyclocross race is in terms of average speed, the more likely that the lead group will be big in number, thus giving the interplay of tactics and teamwork more influence over the outcome. What will it take to gain that little extra edge on such a fast course, and where will it occur? Where will it come from? That one percent when every guy already has 100 percent? That extra scintilla of genius?

On this day.

On any day.

An entire season reflected; a whole career in a race.

My position is perfect—on a slight incline where the course tape wraps around a small tree, at the farthest point of the course from the finish line, just after the off-camber descent from the staired section. Not only can I get in my rider's ears here, but I also have an unobstructed view of both the giant television screen above me and the riders' faces as they shoulder-duck the tree to head back to the asphalt and on toward pit 2. The JumboTron will confirm what I want to know—rider position, time up, time down. But my vantage point, at arm's length from the riders' faces, will tell me what I need to know. Wherein lies the secret? A season, a lifetime of pursuit now coming home to roost.

This is the hour.

Thirty seconds before the start, the riders look anxious but amped. Bart, Sven, Erwin, resplendent in their light blue Belgian kits, all business in the front row. Lars looks pure boss in full Dutch orange. Zdenek Stybar—normally a Fidea teammate to Bart and Erwin, but now, as with all World Championships, a Czech—is inconspicuous on the far side, front row. Jonathan, with the navy U.S.A. emblazoned across his chest, stands ready just a row back. Ryan, nowhere to be seen, is already back in the U.S., his season never gaining any momentum after his crash at Nationals.

La strada bianca start/finish straight looms long and arduous with its atypical steady uphill grade. First in Italian, then English, then Dutch, the announcer's voice reverberates across the late afternoon scene.

Italian, Basque, and Lion of Flanders flags wave feverishly; spectators pound their fists on the fencing signage from one end of the straight to the other.

And the gun fires.

Lars rides the first half of the race like a torpedo, always in the first three. "I try a few times early on to get away," he tells me afterward, "but it is so crazy with so many guys in the lead group. My legs aren't super good in the beginning, but from all the motor pacing training, I have the speed. The only problem in the first half of the race is whether to ride or run the *rampa*. I ride it the first time up. Then I hear the calming advice from the side of the course"—long-time mentor Adri van der Poel—"telling me to run it, to save my legs. So, I just stay in the front and wait and wait."

Erwin, ever the protagonist in such big races, polices the lead group. "I feel good, but not as good as the last two World Championships. And, to have won three times before, I know what it takes to win. My sensations, this time around, are good, but not great."

The Frenchman, Francis Mourey, shows early, as do local hopes Marco Aurelio Fontana and Enrico Franzoi, as well as Belgian, Klaas Vantornout. Jonathan has his troubles, pitting several times to find the right tires but, as is his custom, he fights and stays in the first or second group.

At the halfway point, a group of fourteen hammers the front—one Swiss, one French, two Italians, two Czechs, three Dutch, and five Belgians.

But there's just nothing in it.

It's chess-match cyclocross. At 190 bpm. Television commentators bemoan the lack of a selection with cries of "peloton," unaccustomed to the mass of riders at the front.

Two laps later, there's still nothing in it.

Nothing sticks. The tension is unbearable. The pack throttles on. No one can snap the rubber band.

Full out, full tilt, à bloc—the athlete's nightmare.

How to break legs when no one's legs seem breakable?

The perplexity is written all over Sven's face. "I feel better than I've felt for many years in the World Championship race. But the hard thing is knowing when it's going to happen. Normally now, with my experience, I know where and when to go. But this time, everyone is so strong. My best chance is on the rampa."

With three to go, Stybar strings it out, but Lars is too vigilant and again the race comes together. Then, in the forty-eighth minute, a French rider momentarily loses concentration and crashes, forcing Bart into the fencing—the second year in a row that bad luck strikes Bart in the race. (In 2007, a television moto accidentally dislodges a pylon; Bart is unable to avoid it and crashes). The collective sigh of busloads of Belgians seems to hush the crowd on my side of the course. Somehow Bartje remounts and gets himself back to the lead group, disgruntled and battered.

Another lap and the tempo is relentless.

Still, nothing in it.

Until the moment to end all moments—

De laatste ronde. The last lap.

Fifty-eight minutes of poker, and now it's time to lay down the cards.

BAM—Dutchman Groenendaal lays it down for teammate Lars, a last act of sacrifice in his final world championship.

POW—Lars gives Stybar an elbow to start the last lap. "I'm here, this is *my* line," Lars seems to say.

BOOM—at 59:17, Lars drills it.

Éclat.

And, just like that, his wheel is gone.

Erwin has the cleanest shot to jump on, but Lars's acceleration leaves him having to close. ("If I only could have been in his wheel," he'll tell me.)

Sven has to come from seventh or eighth position, but is already on the limit when he gets up to the chasing Erwin. ("It's my one mistake in the race. I feel strong enough to win, but I can't react from my bad position and when you don't react, it's over.")

I watch the live footage on the screen from the other end of the course. I see the perfection of Lars's attack, the execution, the solo effort as he hammers toward me. The inevitable conflict, trade team versus national team, now plays its gray hand. In every other race of the season, Lars rides for the same team as Sven. Erwin rides for the rival trade team. But this is the championship. If Sven and Erwin can work together for Belgium, can they close the gap?

Lars rides with wings. Give the guy a gap on the last lap of a World Championship and it's, more than likely, game over.

In pursuit, Erwin pulls. And pulls.

Sven is on the rivet, on Erwin's wheel.

Lars runs the rampa. Both Erwin and Sven ride it. One final act of desperation.

Alas, for the two Belgians, there's nothing.

In it.

But for Lars?

There's something.

In it.

I'm sure.

I wait. I have to see. Because what I need to see is coming.

Lars scales the stairs, just in front of me, the legs of a gazelle, even after an hour. A remote-activated robotic TV camera (which has been zinging itself up a track adjacent to the stairs every time the riders pass) seems to almost burst its hinges during Lars's final ascent. Filming history.

Lars rounds the corner to my right, now headed for home. Full attack mode. This is the moment. I lock in on his glorious sunglassless eyes.

And there it is.

Since my first brush with this sport, back in that Lisbon apartment, I've somehow known that the secret to athletic excellence can only be conveyed through the eyes. Over the course of my twenty-year tutelage, I've come to discover its manifestation—oblique orbits of fiery color, slightly askant, seemingly dripping with lactate, cross-eyed with oxygen deprivation, all the while surrounded on the sides and bottom with vacant amounts of white.

The eyes of a madness.

I've seen the look time and time again in Sven, Erwin, Bart, but this time, singularly, in Lars. When I see it at the venue, on the course, I know that this is the rider who is going to kill it.

Only this time, with Lars's final passing, deep in the Tuscan hills, I now come to know it—this look in the eyes—by its elucidating name.

In Italian, they call it *grinta*.

Grit, determination, push, nerve, guts, will, heart, energy, verve, pluck—these English translations run close, but as with so much of cycling's lexicon, the endemic language always seems to go one better:

Faccia truce e arcigna: ha una grinta che spaventa.

Face grim and gruff: a fighting spirit that frightens.

This is what the eyes convey.

Indomitability.

And what the oracle imparts.

Grinta cannot be bought, injected, trained, or even willed. It comes from a deeper place, a place more mysterious and, ultimately, more human. It is something you can't predict because it presupposes calculation. It is something you have to discover within yourself. Each and every time. You know when you have it and you know when you have had it, but you never know when you will have it again, until you have it.

This—

"... mental capacity to break down not just one wall, but to go through four or five walls. The fire inside that pushes a rider to go through hell, to stay on the wheel." (Michel Wuyts)

"... fire in the eyes." (Erwin Vervecken)

"… mentality to push yourself beyond what your mind thinks it can do." (Sven Nys)

"… instinct within your character." (Lars Boom)

Look at any race of consequence. All things being equal—whether physical, scientific, financial, psychological, pharmaceutical—the guy who wants it the most will win.

Every time.

It's all in the fight. The spirit. The one truth we hold to be self-evident. The summoning is all.

Grinta—sine qua non.

Lars Boom training, (Treviso Worlds 2008)

The Attack, Lars Boom, (Treviso Worlds 2008) PHOTOPRESS.BE

Victory, Lars Boom, (Treviso Worlds 2008) PHOTOPRESS.BE

34: ENDINGS AND BEGINNINGS

MARCH 2008

In real time, on January 27, 2008, nine time zones to the west of the very moment Lars Boom achieves his apotheosis in Treviso, my brother-in-law, Mark Zylawy, dies in a car accident on his way to start another day as one of Portland, Oregon's finest police officers. Of all the people I have ever known, "Z-Man" (Mark's street name to those he serves) is the embodiment of determination, the quintessence of will, the exemplar of grinta.

Suddenly, I'm faced with the formidable hurdle of bereavement.

For many months, there is no hupp, hupp.

No resolve.

Gritless.

The words for this book or for any other pursuit do not come; they are swallowed up by the gravity of loss.

***

But—ever ever so slowly—the kernels of concommittance, of how cyclocross can mirror life, begin to come back. Suffering. Taking on wings. Bridging back up to the riders, their stories, their sport, our sport—

My volksong.

Lars's victory in Treviso represents the first win by a non-Belgian in the World Elite Cyclocross Championships since Dutch countryman Richard Groenendaal's win in 2000. Eight long years. But in Lars's end-of-season February races, he's far from his best. The parties, the media attention, the pressure of the last big races are all too much. His season ends inauspiciously.

On the phone in early March 2010, he's clearly got different goals on his mind. Although others predicted it could happen, Lars tells me he himself didn't imagine winning the world cyclocross title so soon—his first year as an elite. Now, with the Treviso rainbow jersey hanging in his closet, he says he will turn his full attention to the bigger frontier of road racing for the Rabobank Pro Tour team in 2010.

As much as I recognize what a loss this will be for elite cyclocross—that Lars presents just the right mixture of strength, agitation, and intrigue to combat the Belgian juggernaut—I know that I have no power to dissuade him. He has too much talent, too much investment, too much potential not to seek his fortune on the road.

So our conversation is sympatico, but with a hint of closure. Sure, I'll see him at races the next season. For sure, he'll try to defend the jersey at Worlds in his home country—in Hoogerheide—in January 2009. But, there's a shelf life in Lars's words. He's all about new challenges—Paris-Roubaix, Flanders, the Tour de France.

"My road training started yesterday, March 3, 2008. Just one-and-a-half hours. But it's the beginning, eh?"

Erwin readies for a vacation in Egypt, but with contract negotiations heavy on his mind. Better for him to negotiate now after his incredible 4th place in Treviso, while his stock is high, rather than wait until autumn. His team, Fidea, provides the best structure, equipment, winter program, summer training camps, and support of any out there. But with Stybar and Bart on the team, there are still too many chiefs. For Erwin to ride his own races, to try to win, he's better off on a new team. A new squad where he can be at ease with his own ambitions until he retires after the 2010 World Championships in Tabor, Czech Republic (on the same circuit where he first tasted World Championship glory back in 2001).

"In the team's eyes, Bart will always be the man for the people," he says. "When you go in a café or a village, they are for Bart. But I have my own audience as well. Fidea is an insurance company. The company world, say a board of directors, is where I have appeal."

Bart, meanwhile, is busy as ever, with his first book coming out and a wedding in August. After his disappointing crash and subsequent 15th place in Treviso, a strong end-of-season run has the man from Vorselaar in high spirits. I catch a glimpse, a byte of Bart's upcoming book, where he speaks of himself as the "nieuwe Bart" in reference to the races and forces that have changed him over his career. I'm bemused with anticipation. I wonder if in *Open Boek* we will see the new Bart speaking with the end of his tongue.

For our top American cyclocrossers, the paths taken after Treviso depend wholly on who is writing the paychecks. Jonathan, still the only real American specialist in international cyclocross, puts the Sunweb tension behind him and headlines a new American venture sponsored by Planet Bike.

"I'm looking forward to the chance to just race for a whole year without stress, without added bologna, without adversity. I have a great setup this coming year. It will end up being more money than I was making with Sunweb, and I won't have the hassles. My biggest objective is to be consistent next year and maybe win and stand on the podium in a few races." With his unremarkable 23rd place in Treviso in the rearview mirror, Jonathan also readies for the domestic spring/summer road season, riding for Battley Harley-Davidson.

Ryan preps for another year with sponsor Kona, splitting his time between the U.S. pro mountain bike circuit, the burgeoning domestic 'cross scene, and Europe. He'll again target cyclocross World Cups and bigger series races across the Atlantic. He still has a place and a name in the land of veldrijden. People remember some of his strong finishes. Race organizers still extend a decent start fee for the big man. Every opportunity I get, I encourage him to take it up.

American champion Tim Johnson's 26th and Jeremy Powers's 27th in Treviso bode well for the future of American cyclocross. Not that they can survive solely by being cyclocross pros just yet. In fact, Tim goes from Treviso straight into the road season, riding for Health Net-

Maxxis at America's biggest road event, the Tour of California in mid-February. Jeremy has a later start to his road season, but it's clear there's not much luxury for cyclocross focus among our top guys. Aside from Jonathan, the nation's best riders pursue cyclocross because they love it, not because they can earn a living at it. Yet.

Predictably, the immediate fallout from Treviso hangs heavy on Sven, despite his bronze medal. Critics in the media lambast Sven for putting trade team interests—Lars and Sven both ride for Rabobank—ahead of national pride (a Belgian not chasing down a Dutchman). But the finger-pointing—echoing the fallout after the 2000 World Championships in St. Michielsgestel, when Sven did not reel in the off-the-front Dutchman Groenendaal—rings empty with Sven this time around. Sven says he was on the limit, tapped out in Treviso when Lars attacked—a completely different dynamic than the chess match of St. Michielsgestel.

On the phone with Sven in late March, I'm moved by Sven's incredible consistency over the years. Take the aforementioned 2000. In that season, Sven is Belgian champion, World Cup champion, Superprestige champion, third in the World Championships, and ends with twenty-two victories. Similarly, in 2008, Sven duplicates all of the same results, plus ends the season ranked number one on the UCI list and takes the GVA Series to boot. It's his fifth GVA trophy and his eighth victory in the Superprestige series. Sven's track record of achievement in cyclocross's Grand Slam events is unmatched in the history of the sport.

And, as is typical, he never seems to rest on his laurels.

"It's true, I couldn't wait to start training again recently," he tells me. "I'm just back from Jamaica and skiing a week in the Alps, but I'm already totally focused on the Olympics in Beijing. Training in the chamber in Leuven, adjusting the settings to the atmospherics for Beijing: 33 degrees C, 70 percent humidity, power training at sea level."

Having come to know Sven, I now understand I have to push to get him beyond the numbers, to talk about the intangibles and the things he might change for the next cyclocross season.

Sven begins, "You know, for Lars, in the weeks leading up to Treviso, he had less pressure. Okay, I have no problem with Treviso because Lars was the best and, in the weeks before, he was very good also. But it's tougher for us Belgians—Bart, me, Erwin—racing these big series races, all the demands. This season, by the time I got to the Belgian Championships, I was over the top. After that, I wasn't at my best. It's hard because you don't feel it at the time, but I think I did two races too much in January. Next season, I will be more selective with the races I do."

Before I hang up, I share with him a theory I have about his style of winning and how it has changed over the years. In the early years, it was impossible not to admire the way that he won races—burning off riders with his sheer talent or out-riding opponents with his technical acumen. But more recently, he seems to bide his time more, mentally dissecting his rivals' weaknesses during the race and then exploiting those weaknesses on the last lap, with just the right attack at just the right time. I suggest to him that perhaps his elite mountain bike racing, with its longer durations, has helped him be more patient, more tactical in cyclocross.

Sven agrees, but, after a beat, says—

"Cyclocross is still about suffering, learning how to struggle, riding on character. You can't win every race. I'm only human after all."

Photo: Tom Robertson

Photo: Tom Robertson

EPILOGUE

"That's a hell of a story," I said.

"Ain't no story," he said. "It's what happened."

—Sherman Alexie, *The Toughest Indian in the World*

LATE JUNE. LATE AFTERNOON. 2012.

I'm in Baal again, and *again* have found my way to the indelible stairs on Sven Nys's home circuit. Sun-bleached and pocked, grass still growing between the steps, the stairs remain their inconspicuous, yet inimitable selves. But the dawn of five years before has now given way to the heat of the present. Cars are parking, men and women in suits are getting out, and whatever pastoral dulcitude I remember from past summer visits has given way to a sense of urgency and hubbub.

Turns out, these stairs, for all their specificity of purpose—serving as a formidable feature in Sven's self-designed New Year's Day race—provide a grander destination after all. Up the grassy slope, up past the actual race parcours, a stately brick home stands ready for a press conference announcing the creation of the Sven Nys Cycling Center. Provincial politicians, governmental sports dignitaries, various members of Sven's support team, numerous journalists, and Sven himself press upwards toward the appointed hour.

I join in the procession. On one side of me, Sven's team manager. On the other, Sven's new mental coach. I'm struck again by Sven's meticulous planning, this time for the life he will lead after he hangs up his cleats. In tandem with Golazo (the sports marketing company that represents Sven as well as other marquee athletes like road cycling superstar Philippe Gilbert and Belgian tennis great Kim Clijsters), Sven has teamed up to purchase the entire acreage to build a destination station for developing off-road cyclists. During the press conference, I learn that Sven will direct much of the cycling activities here, further immortalizing himself beyond his 1 World Championship, 7 World Cup overalls, 8 Belgian national titles, 8 GVA Trophies, 11 Superprestige titles, and now two Olympic mountain bike appearances.

The mythic stairs of the Balenberg do indeed lead somewhere after all.

***

Five years on.

The previous evening, I spend two hours with Erwin Vervecken, now retired, and a major player in Golazo's growing empire of Belgian sporting interests. Trim and fit, Erwin has managed the transition seamlessly and now devotes his work time to directing the UCI World Masters Tour, overseeing the cyclocross races that Golazo owns like Loenhout, Baal, and the Namur World Cup, and negotiating rider contracts for all Golazo cyclocross events.

Our meeting, held in a bar adjacent to the Diegem race circuit in suburban Brussels, proceeds with ease and a sense of catching up. A small scrum of bar patrons is obviously aware that they have a cyclocross god in their midst, but they leave us alone in a corner booth. Having known Erwin for over ten years now, there's a conversational comfort I appreciate deeply. At one point, I ask Erwin if he has any regrets about his career. His response is succinct but his example voluminous.

"No," he articulates. "Three World titles, Belgian national champion at every level, 22 major victories. I have no regrets. I feel like I made the most of what was in me."

Pure Erwin. A rider who always knew who he was.

But then, as our conversation winds down, he has one interjection.

"Regrets? No, or maybe only one. That day in Zolder. Worlds 2002. That's the best I ever felt in a race. If my derailleur hadn't snapped, I'm sure I would have four rainbow jerseys in my closet today. That day, it seems like yesterday. I could ride through walls that day."

While Erwin still lives in Herentals, his long-time teammate Bart Wellens has since moved from Vorselaar to Londerzeel, closer to Brussels. Still racing as one of Fidea's mainstays, Bart experienced some huge highs and lows this past season. During a heated battle in Essen just before the Christmas period, Sven snapped a derailleur and Bart's persistence paid off with a dramatic victory in one of the heaviest, slogging races of the season. But, later, just before the Belgian National Championships in Hooglede, Bart was struck down with a mysterious heart ailment and sudden fever and was unable to compete for the rest of the season. With months of rehab and recently cleared of any doping suspicions over the health incident, Bart is putting in his usual steady hours of road racing during the spring/summer as he readies for another cyclocross season in the fishbowl that is modern European cyclocross.

As for Treviso world champion, Lars Boom, after achieving so much in the discipline, he has left full-season cyclocross for a career on the road. Still with Rabobank, Lars showed the world what he could do with his cyclocross skills by riding majestically across the cobbles of Paris-Roubaix in April of 2012. In full pursuit of an off-the-front Tom Boonen, Lars flirted with a career-defining ride, only to succumb to the brutality in the waning kilometers of the biggest spring classic on earth. A regular tweeter of photos of his new child, Lars seems to be finding that all-important balance as a World Tour pro. But I miss seeing more of him on the cyclocross circuit, our last hello coming at the Namur World Cup back in December.

I do, however, manage to catch some of the 2012 Dutch National Road Championship on a Flanders hotel television. The eventual winner, Niki Terpstra, soloes forward through the pounding rain. But close behind is the irrepressible Lars, trying to bridge across on his own, hammering forward. Some things don't change. Bike racing is bike racing.

Likewise, after consecutive World Cyclocross Championships in Tabor (2010) and St. Wendel (2011), Zdenek Stybar has headed to perhaps greener pastures, with a jump to full-on road racing. This fall,

Styby is slated to ride his first Grand Tour with the Vuelta a España. Sadly, yet another cyclocross stalwart has shifted disciplines.

Blasting through to take up the vacancies at the top of the elite cyclocross pyramid are Belgians Niels Albert and Kevin Pauwels. In the case of Pauwels, the stoic 28 year-old currently sits atop the UCI rankings after winning the world cup overall title this past season. Not to be outdone, Niels Albert won his second World Cyclocross Championship in Koksijde before 68,500 rabid fans in late January 2012. Both Albert and Pauwels look set to take up the baton in the wake of the Nys-Vervecken-Wellens era.

As for the two Americans who feature so prominently in these pages, both Jonathan Page and Ryan Trebon are still hard at it, vying for cyclocross success on both shores. After years of being solely Belgium-based, Jonathan has recently bought a house in Utah to provide a half-year's dose of Americana for his wife and kids. Proud of what he has accomplished in the sport and yet still committed to another full season in the trenches of Belgian cyclocross, Jonathan maintains a remarkable position of being the only American to ever fully immerse in European cyclocross. Ironically, while he doesn't enjoy the commercial fruits that his American counterparts seem to be reaping, he abides by a certain ethos that, in the end, seems worthy and commendable: to commit to measuring oneself against the world's best is not so far from victory.

Ryan Trebon has his sights firmly set on riding another dominant U.S. season with his new signing to the powerful Cannondale-Cyclocrossworld.com team. He says he's hoping to travel to the important races in Europe, but it's clear that his cyclocross future lies predominantly on this side of the Atlantic. Teaming with the still hungry, multi-time national champion Tim Johnson and up-and-coming Jamey Driscoll, Ryan's biggest rival continues to be the emerging Jeremy Powers, now riding ever so strongly for the Rapha-Focus squad.

Just like Belgium, American cyclocross has its own stars and intrigue, and we have our riders, organizers, industry, clubs, sponsors, and media to thank for making it all happen.

And there will be no more telling example of this collective spirit than what goes down in Louisville on February 2-3, 2013. I'm not going to even try to convey the magnitude of this moment. To host the first World Cyclocross Championships outside of Europe in the history of the sport is borderline crack. As in cracker. If there's one thing I've hoped to convey in this book, it's that you have to see this sport.

To believe this sport.

Finally, on a personal level, both my work as a high school teacher and my involvement in cyclocross continue at a brisk pace. There's still so much work to be done. With the ambition of seeing our riders medal in Louisville, I will direct EuroCrossCamp 10 as well as a second summer U.S.A.C Cyclocross Development Camp here in Montana. In addition, through my position on the UCI Cyclocross Commission, I recently coached the first-ever UCI Cyclocross Development Camp in Aigle, Switzerland with former world junior cyclocross champion and fellow commission member, Beat Wabel. The energy generated by young riders from Turkey, Great Britain, Slovakia, Denmark, Czech Republic, and Italy reminded me of my earliest days in the sport.

Full-plate.

Full-stop.

***

After the Balenberg post-conference reception and a short meeting with various politicos, I tail Sven in my rental car to his new home with sprawling back yard, swimming pool, and BMX track for now ten-year-old son, Thibau. While we get situated by the pool, Sven's parents and Isabelle play finger soccer with Thibau on the kitchen table.

Our conversation continues along familiar lines—altitude chambers (Sven has just finished a two-week block of sleeping at altitude), the upcoming Olympics (a fascinating recounting of his tire issues in sloppy Moscow at the recent European Championships where he clinched his Olympic berth), and Mallorca (where he is set to go at week's end to continue his Olympic preparation).

Predictably, we spend some time discussing a thread that has become part of our common narrative: off-the-bike conditioning drills for cyclocross. I share some different trainings I'm doing with U.S.A.

cyclocross athletes and, in turn, he relays some exercises he's using with the younger guys on his Landbouwkrediet team during their training camps in April and September. I give him my flash drive and he fires up his laptop and we exchange footage of various workouts.

"Fifteen years as a pro and I'm still as crazy as ever for this sort of thing," he tells me. "That's something I'm really proud of. At the press conference this afternoon, I was talking about that. How, for fifteen years, I've lived the strict life of a pro. And the Balenberg Cycling Center project is my reward. It's a big part of my future."

At one point, Sven gets up to use the bathroom and a million and one things race through my mind. Snippets of a newspaper article I have saved and had been reviewing the night before seem to leap to the forefront of my temples. Sven's narration of his titanic battle with Stybar in Baal 2010:

"The battle of Balenberg: all about character.

Who would be the freshest cadaver?

Super hard lap. Slippery bikes, weighing thirty kilos.

Everybody at the limit.

In the race, we [Styby and me] could never close the tap.

[The faucet] always going full.

My spool of thread pretty much done.

Thank goodness I had a little bit of thread left."

Faucets running full. Diminishing spools of thread. The freshest cadaver.

This is the stuff of legend and I am sitting here with the king. By his throne. In his kingdom.

Then, another reverie. This time deriving from a recent David Brooks syndicated column about a Bruce Springsteen concert Brooks attended in Madrid:

"It makes you appreciate the tremendous power of particularity. If your identity is formed by hard boundaries, if you come from a specific place, if you embody a distinct [athletic] tradition, if your concerns are expressed through a specific paracosm, you are going to have more depth and definition than you are if you grew up in the far-flung networks of pluralism and eclecticism, surfing from one spot to the next, sampling one style then the next, your identity formed by soft boundaries, or none at all."

Had Brooks watched, as I had recently, the six-part nationally televised documentary entitled "De Flandriens van het Veld" highlighting all the Flemish cyclocross greats from 1966-2012, he might well have been writing about Sven. Certainly there's no better embodiment of Brooks's column-ending exhortations than the cycling career of Sven Nys: "Go deeper into your own tradition. Call upon the geography of your own past. Be distinct and credible. People will come."

Soft, solstitial light bathes the backyard and a sweet mugginess seems to heighten the realization that my time is almost up. Sven has had a long day and races on the road tomorrow in Oietingen. Just before he closes his laptop, he asks if I want to see a clip from a private filmmaker who captured the rarified moments directly after Sven's eighth National Championship in Hooglede-Gits, early January 2012.

Are you kidding me?

I'm thinking, no one's seen this. No one might ever see it.

Sven cues up the DVD and presses play.

In his grass-green colored Landbouwkrediet skinsuit, a muddied Sven rounds the final bend into the eye of the camera.

Arms aloft in victory.

Crowd harum-scarum with euphoria.

A mob scene at the finish.

Then into a small hallway. The camera follows directly behind an exultant Sven. But then, in one tumultuous moment, he can go no farther. Overcome with emotion, Sven slumps to a nearby bench.

Head buried in his hands, wracked by the effort, he sobs convulsively.

Biste, Sven's ever-loyal soigneur, places a comforting hand on his shoulder.

Runner-up Niels Albert, passing by on the way to the podium room, pauses in silent wonderment.

A beat.

Then Biste passes a beeping phone to Sven.

Sven waves it off. He can't even muster the effort to receive the congratulatory phone call from his wife, Isabelle.

He is in a place too deep.

A place from whence he has given his all. Where action and emotion, fitness and finesse, have merged in magical rarity.

A place of yoking.

A place of divination.

A place that lies *behind the stare.*

Sven Nys (Hooglede BK 2012)   PHOTOPRESS.BE

ACKNOWLEDGMENTS

TO ALL THOSE WHO HAVE HELPED ME ALONG THE WAY:

Amy Linn, Vicki Thomas, Nathan Phillips, Matthew Clark, Gert and Eric Matthys, Don Pogreba, Gretchen Edelen, Adam Ganz, Christi the Wordsmith, Brink Kuchenbrod, Jeff Caton, all athletes, students, and parents I've worked with—past, present and future, Peter Van Den Abeele, Keith Flory and all UCI staff, Noel Dejonckheere and Els Delaere, Frank Gonzalez, Scott Herzig, Michelle Richardson, John Gleaves, Patrick Burke, Elvira Ries-Roncalli, Rudy De Bie, Lyne Lamoureux, Steve Medcroft, Tom Robertson at tomrobertsonphoto.com, Peter Deconinck at photopress.be, Marc Gullickson, Ken Whelpdale, Jim Miller, Steve Johnson, Sean Petty, Benjamin Sharp, Kelli Lusk, Micah Rice and all U.S.A.C staff, Bruce Fina, Joan Hanscom, all EuroCrossCamp-Izegem staff and sponsors, all U.S.A. Cyclocross World Championship staff, all U.S.A.C and UCI Commissaires, Chris "Fox" De Vos, Louis Delahaije, Daniel Benson and *cyclingnews.com,* Brecht Decaluwé, Paul Van den Bosch, Nico Van Heste, Joe Sales, Jim Brown, Chris Grealish, Dan Seaton and Mindi Wisman, Peter Poelman, Beat Wabel, Hans Maessen, Charlie Wellenstein, John Fiore, Cary Larson, Carl Strong, Jason Van Marle, translational help from Marcel Van Garderen and Willem Visser, Didier Vanoverbeek, Bob, Jan, and Mark Babcock at Deeds Publishing, Isabelle Beel, Mario Vaerreware, Larry Colton, Helena School District #1, Stu Thorne, Brad Ross, Paul Boudreau, Adam Myerson, Richard Fries, Dave Towle, David and Christy Llewellynn, Charles Pelkey, Brook Watts, Tom McDaniel, Anthony Gallino, Toby Stanton, John Kemp, Bruce Kaiser, Richard Sachs, Lyle Fulkerson, Tom Stevens, Henrik Djernis, Adri Van der Poel, Sepp and Trudi Karrer, Thomas Hayles, Tom Clarke, Jonathan Vaughn, Jed Fox, Clark Natwick, Jiri Mainus,

Carl Ammons, Howard Hickingbotham, Simon Burney, Frankie Van Haesebroucke, Paul Schoening, Dag Selander, Donn Kellogg, Rosella Sidi, Paolo and Alessandro Guerciotti, Sara Ecclesine, Bill Marshall, Boone Lennon, Tim Rutledge, Andrew Yee and *Cyclocross Magazine*, Colt McElwaine and CyclingDirt, Brian Worthy, Juergen Eckmann, Neal Rogers and *VeloNews.com*, Ben Turner, Josh Liberles, Greg Keller, Pete Webber, Brandon Dwight, Richard Feldman, John Verheul, Jim Anderson, JD Bilodeau, Andy Taus, Dave Miller, Jeff Rowe and Focus Bikes, Jeremy Dunn, Dusty Labarr, Sam Smith, John Wilcockson, Marti Stephen, Patrick O'Grady, Graham Watson, Sue George, Bart Bowen, Dan Norton, Steve Tilford, Mark Legg, Sam Ames, John Behrens, Dale and Ann Knapp, Mark and Frank McCormack, Paul Curley, Jeff Linton/ ICW Bicycle Works, Emmett Purcell, Kevin Colville, Dave Hartman, Todd Anderson, Erik Tonkin, Shaun Radley, montanacyclocross.com, Joe Collins, Bill Elliston and all the other coaches I've worked with, and Big Sky Cyclery—thank you.

To those I've unintentionally omitted, I apologize.

ABOUT THE AUTHOR

Geoff Proctor has been involved in competitive cycling for over 25 years. He currently serves as National Junior/U23 Cyclocross Coach and, in conjunction, directs EuroCrossCamp. Proctor works closely on both programs with U.S.A.C's National Cyclocross and Mountain Bike director Marc Gullickson. In addition, in 2009, Proctor was appointed to a four-year term on the UCI Cyclocross Commission. This position provides the opportunity for North American cyclocross to have a voice on a global level as the Cyclocross Commission is responsible for international development, vision, calendar, and rules. Finally, Proctor leads a number of camps during the summer. In the past, he has directed the U.S.A.C 15-16 road camp in Belgium and currently coaches a U.S.A.C cyclocross development camp in Helena, Montana;

a U.S.A.C regional road camp in Oregon; and a UCI cyclocross camp for developing nations in Aigle, Switzerland.

Proctor and his family live in Helena, Montana where he teaches high school English, coaches his club's youth cyclists, and still races when he can.

APPENDICES

LARS BOOM'S TRAINING LOG

Day	Training
	Week 45: 5.11-11.11.2007 Phase: Preparation 2
Mo	Strength Training Phase 1 + Easy 2 hours
Tu	Normal Endur behind moto 3 hours
Wed	Training Nico Van Hest (with Ext. Interval) + Strength phase 1
Thu	Rest Day
Fri	Easy 1.30 hour with 6 (10sec.) sprint from standing position: 1 min.
Sat	Race Niel (1st)
Sun	Race Pijnacker (1st)
	Week 46: 12.11-18.11.2007 Phase: Preparation 2
Mo	Strength Training phase 1 + Easy 2 hours
Tu	Normal Endur behind moto 4 hours
Wed	Training Nico Van Hest (with Ext. Interval) + Strength phase 1
Thu	Rest Day
Fri	Easy 1.30 hour with 5 (15sec.) sprint from standing position:1 min.
Sat	Race Hasselt (5th)
Sun	Easy 3 hours + Strength Phase 1
	Week 47: 19.11-25.11.2007 Recovery Week
Mo	Strength Phase 1 + Easy 1.30 hours
Tu	Normal Endur behind moto 2 hours
Wed	Training Nico Van Hest (with Ext. Interval) Half program+ Strength phase 1
Thu	Rest Day
Fri	Easy 1.30 hours with 8 (5sec.) sprints from standing position:1 min.
Sat	Race Koksijde (3rd)
Sun	Race Gieten (3rd)
	Week 48: 26.11-2.12.2007 27-7 Dec. La Santa, Spain
Mo	Easy 1.30 hours
Tu	Ext. Endur 3 hours + Strength Training phase 1
Wed	Normal Endur 4.30 hours with 15 (5sec.) sprint from stand pos:1min.
Thu	Normal Endur 4 hours + Strength Training phase 1
Fri	Rest Day
Sat	Normal Endur 5 hours

	Strength Training	Easy/Loose	Ext. Endur.	Norm. Endur.	Tempo Endur.	Ext. Interval	Norm. Interval	Race CX	Sprint
	■		■						
				■					
	■					■			
		■							■
								■	
								■	
	■		■						
				■					
	■					■			
		■							■
								■	
	■	■							
	■		■						
				■					
	■					■			
		■							■
								■	
								■	
		■							
	■		■						
				■					■
	■			■					
	■								

Sun	Ext. Endur 4 hours with 6 (6min.) Tempo Endur uphill + Strength Train Phase 1
	Week 49: 3.12-9.12.2007
Mo	Easy 2 hours
Tu	Normal Endur 4 hours + Strength Training phase 1
Wed	Normal Endur 4 hours with 15(5sec.) sprint from stand pos:1min.
Thu	Normal Endur 4 hours + Strength Training phase 1
Fri	Rest Day-Travel Day
Sat	Easy 1.30 hours
Sun	Race Eerde Veghel (15th)
	Week 50: 10.12-16.12.2007 Recovery Week
Mo	Strength Training Phase 1 + Easy 1.30 hours
Tu	Normal Endur behind moto 2 hours
Wed	Training Nico Van Hest (with Ext. Interval) Half program+ Strength Phase 1
Thu	Rest Day
Fri	Easy 1.30 hours with 8 (5sec.) sprint from standing position:1min.
Sat	Race Essen (2nd)
Sun	Race Overijse (11th)
	Week 51: 17.12-23.12.2007 Phase: Race
Mo	Strength Training Phase 2 + Easy 2 hours
Tu	Normal Endur behind moto 3 hours
Wed	Training Nico Van Hest (hard) Half Program + Strength Phase 2
Thu	Normal Endur 3 hours + 10 (10sec.) flying sprint:1 min.
Fri	Rest Day
Sat	Easy 1.30 with 8 (5sec.) sprint from standing position:1min.
Sun	Race Zeddam (1st)
	Week 52: 24.12-30.12.2007 Phase: Race
Mo	Strength Phase 2 + Easy 2 hours
Tu	Normal Endur behind moto 2 hours
Wed	Race Hofstade (3rd)
Thu	Easy 2 hours

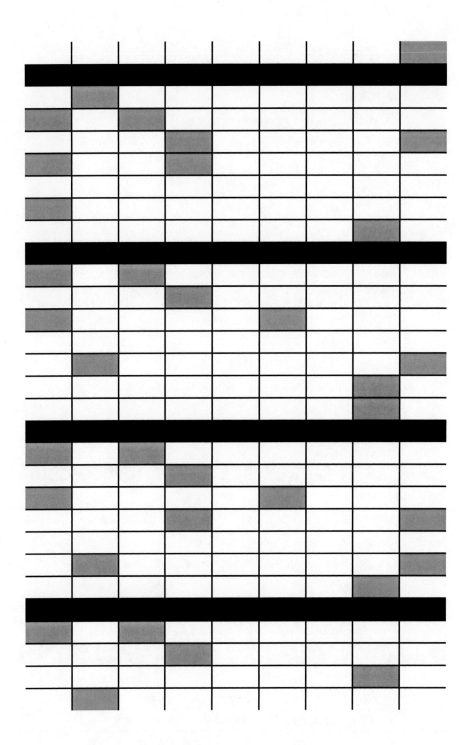

Fri	Race Loenhout (1st)
Sat	Strength Training Phase 2 + Easy 2 hours
Sun	Easy 1 hour

	Week 1: 31.12-06.01.2008 Phase: Race
Mo	Easy 1.30 hours with 6 (10sec.) sprint from standing position:1min.
Tu	Race Baal (4th)
Wed	Training Nico Van Hest (technique)
Thu	Testing Amsterdam
Fri	Rest Day
Sat	Easy 1.30 hours with 8 (5sec.) sprint from standing position:1min.
Sun	Race NK (National Champs) (1st)

	Week 2: 7.01-13.01.2008 Phase: Race
Mo	Strength Phase 2 + Easy 1 hour
Tu	Normal Endur behind moto 2 hours
Wed	Race Surhuisterveen (7th)
Thu	Normale Endur 2 hours + 10 (10sec.) flying sprint:1min.
Fri	Rest Day
Sat	Easy 1.30 hours with 8 (5sec.) sprint from standing position P:1min.
Sun	Race Lievin (1st)

	Week 3: 14.01-20.01.2008 Phase: Race
Mo	Strength Phase 2 + Easy 2 hours
Tu	Normal Endur behind moto 3:30 (not too hard by doing big pulls)
Wed	Training Nico Van Hest (Normal/not full on) + Strength Training Phase 2
Thu	Normale Endur 3 hours + 12 (10sec.) flying sprint: 1min.
Fri	Rest Day
Sat	Easy 1.30 hours with 8 (5sec.) sprint from standing position:1min.
Sun	Race Hoogerheide (1st)

	Week 4: 14.01-20.01.2008 Phase: Race
Mo	Easy 1.30 hours
Tu	Normal Endur behind moto 2 hours (not too hard by doing big pulls)
Wed	Training Nico Van Hest (Normal/not full on/half program)
Thu	Normal Endur 2 hours + 5 (10sec.) flying sprint:1min.

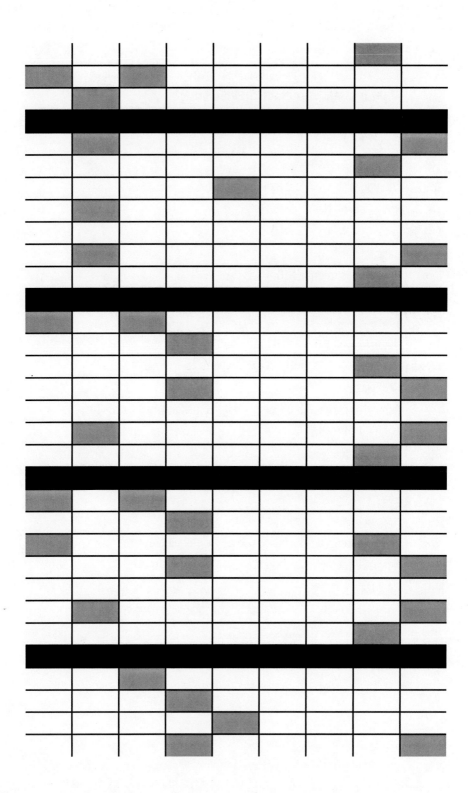

Fri	Rest Day
Sat	Easy 1-1.30 hours with 4 (15sec.) sprint from standing position:1min.
Sun	**WORLD CHAMPIONSHIPS TREVISO (1ST)**

	week5 28.01-04.02.2008
Mo	Easy 1 hour
Tu	Normal Endur 2.30 hour
Wed	Training Nico Van Hest (not too hard)
Thu	Race Hasselt Night Cross (1st)
Fri	Easy 1 hour
Sat	Race Lille (DNS)
Sun	Race Hoogstraten (DNS)

	Week 7: 04.02-10.02.2008
Mo	Easy 1.30 hours
Tu	Normal Endur behind moto 2:30 hours
Wed	Training Nico Van Hest (all Ext Interval)
Thu	Rest Day
Fri	Easy 1.30 hours with 8 (5sec.) sprint from standing position:1min.
Sat	Race Eeklo (15th)
Sun	Race Heerlen (2nd)

	Week 8: 11.02-17.02.2008
Mo	Easy 1.30 hours
Tu	Normal Endur behind moto 2 hours
Wed	Training Nico Van Hest (Normal/not full on/half program)
Thu	Normal Endur 2 hours + 5 (10sec.) flying sprint:1min.
Fri	Rest Day
Sat	Easy 1-1.30 with 4 (15sec.) sprint from standing position:1min.
Sun	Race Oostmalle (3rd)

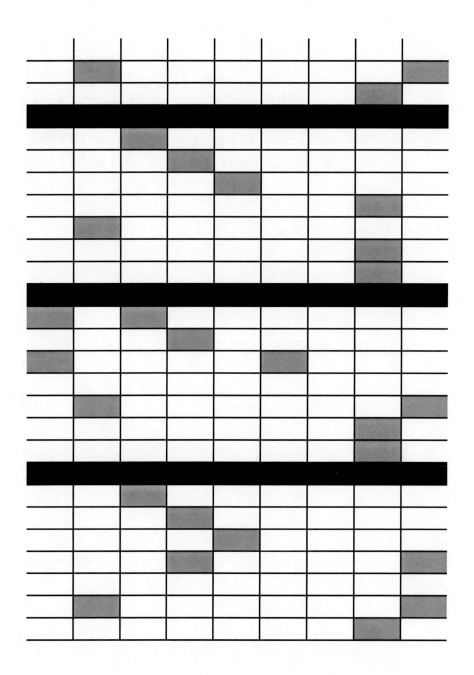

U.S.A. RESULTS AT CYCLOCROSS WORLD CHAMPIONSHIPS

1950 - 72

NO US PARTICIPATIION

1973

NO PRO TEAM

AMATEUR

48 Danny Nall
49 George Bannon
50 Steve Woznick
DNF Eckhart Reiger

1974

NO PRO TEAM

AMATEUR

44 George Bannon
46 Danny Nall
DNS Eckhart Reiger
DNS Mike Neel

1975

NO PRO TEAM

AMATEUR

46 Leroy Johnson
50 Fritz Liedl
52 Chuck Canepa
53 Jeff Saunders

1976

NO PRO TEAM

AMATEUR

42 Laurence Malone
43 Jim Gentes
DNF Danny Nall

1977

NO PRO TEAM

AMATEUR

32 Laurence Malone
40 Joe Ryan
45 Clark Natwick

1978

NO PRO TEAM

AMATEUR

29 Laurence Malone
35 Joe Ryan
DNF Clark Natwick

1979

NO PRO TEAM   AMATEUR

16 Joe Ryan
26 Laurence Malone
DNF Clark Natwick

1978

NO PRO TEAM   AMATEUR

29 Laurence Malone
35 Joe Ryan
DNF Clark Natwick

1979

NO PRO TEAM   AMATEUR   NO JUNIOR TEAM

16 Joe Ryan
26 Laurence Malone
DNF Clark Natwick

1980

NO PRO TEAM   AMATUERS   JUNIORS

18 Laurence Malone   17 Myron Lind
(ultimately disqualified for
not wearing his helmet
during the whole race)

38 Joe Ryan

1981 NO US PARTICIPATION

1982

NO PRO TEAM   AMATEUR   NO JUNIORS

39 Clark Natwick

DNF Myron Lind

DNS Joe Ryan

DNS Steve Tilford

1983

NO PRO TEAM   AMATEUR   NO JUNIORS

44 Clark Natwick

49 Paul Curley

DNS Steve Tilford

DNS Tim Rutledge

1984 NO US PARTICIPATION

1985

PRO	AMATEUR	NO JUNIORS
24 David Garfield	36 Steve Tilford	
	43 Paul Curley	
	DNF David McLaughlin	

1986

NO PRO TEAM	AMATEUR	JUNIORS
	33 Paul Curley	43 Frank Mc Cormack
	43 Casey Kunselman	

1987

NO PRO TEAM	AMATEUR	JUNIORS
	36 Paul Curley	39 Daryl Price
	46 Clark Natwick	

1988

NO PRO TEAM	AMATEUR	JUNIORS
	26 Don Myrah	34 Jonathan Vaughan
	39 Bob Reuther	42 Mark McCormack
	46 Clark Natwick	46 William Dolan
	47 Paul Curley	

1989

NO PRO TEAM	AMATEUR	JUNIORS
	42 Don Myrah	36 Jonathan Vaughan
	46 Casey Kunselman	46 William Dolan

1990

PRO	AMATEUR	JUNIORS
DNF Kent Johnston	42 Don Myrah	42 Paul Bonds

1991

PRO	AMATEUR	NO JUNIORS
DNF Kent Johnston	52 Jonathan Vaughan	
DNF Joe Parkin	DNS Don Myrah	

1992

NO PRO TEAM	AMATEUR	NO JUNIORS
	49 Jed Fox	

55 Thomas Hayles

DNF Thomas Clark

DNF Mark Blake

1993

PRO	AMATEUR	JUNIORS
DNS Daniel Fox	42 Thomas Clark	42 Justin Robinson
Frank McCormack	50 Mark Howe	
Steve Tilford	56 Thomas Hayles	
	58 Geoff Proctor	

1994

OPEN	JUNIORS
53 Jed Fox	42 Jim Savage
57 Don Myrah	62 Ryan Dahl
DNF Geoff Proctor	
DNF Thomas Clark	
DNF Peter Webber	

1995

OPEN	JUNIORS
37 Jed Fox	26 Jonathan Page
41 Thomas Clark	58 Justin Bartlett
55 Dale Knapp	
DNF Kevin S.Anderson	

1996

PRO	U23	JUNIORS
40 Leo Windlin	49 Jim Savage	58 Philip Breton
47 Jed Fox	56 Tim Johnson	
57 Thomas Clark	DNF Aaron Wilcher	
DNF Geoff Proctor	DNF Eric Drummer	
	DNF Alex Grabau	

1997

PRO	U23	JUNIORS
34 Jed Fox	47 Damon Kluck	41 Joshua Thornton
44 Dale Knapp	51 Justin Robinson	58 Narayan Mahon
49 Kevin Merrigan	54 Tim Johnson	
51 Jan Wiejak	DNF Johannes Huseby	

DNF Craig Undem

1998

PRO	U23	JUNIORS
29 Marc Gullickson	10 Tim Johnson	11 Matthew Kelly
39 Frank McCormack	53 Adam Krause	38 Narayan Mahon
42 Mark McCormack		
45 Dale Knapp		
DNF Thomas Clark		

1999

PRO	U23	JUNIORS
23 Dale Knapp	3 Tim Johnson	1 Matthew Kelly
DNF Marc Gullickson		5 William Frischkorn
		28 Walker Ferguson
		51 William Skinner

2000

PRO	U23	JUNIORS	WOMEN
29 Marc Gullickson	42 Jed Sheckler	2 Walker Ferguson	5 Alison Dunlap
32 Barton Bowen	43 Ben Jacques-Maynes	22 Toby Swanson	8 Carmen Richardson
37 Justin Robinson	50 Andy Jacques-Maynes	29 Justin Thompson	12 Ann Grande
38 Dale Knapp		31 Joshua Anthony	13 Ruth Matthes
DNF Alex Candelario		39 Alan Obye	24 Shari Kain

2001

PRO	U23	JUNIORS	WOMEN
13 Marc Gullickson	22 Alan Obye	17 Jeremy Powers	4 Ann Grande
29 Dale Knapp	43 Joshua Anthony	40 Aaron Bradford	9 Rachel Lloyd
		53 Aaron Menenberg	

2002

PRO	U23	JUNIORS	WOMEN
13 Tim Johnson	8 Adam Craig	22 Aaron Bradford	4 Alison Dunlap
22 Marc Gullickson	20 Jackson Stewart	33 Jesse Anthony	5 Ann Grande
23 Todd Wells	39 Alan Obye	39 Mike House	10 Carmen D'Aluisio

34 Jonathan Page	47 Joshua Anthony	40 Brent Bookwalter	13 Gina Hall
		49 Chris Hill	

2003

PRO	U23	JUNIORS	WOMEN
25 Marc Gullickson	30 Barry Wicks	16 Jesse Anthony	10 Ann Grande
37 Jonathan Page	37 Adam Craig	29 Konrad Lebas	11 Gina Hall
DNF Johannes Huseby	46 Ryan Trebon	44 Steven Cozza	13 Rachel Lloyd
DNF A.Jacques-Maynes	48 Alan Obye	48 Zak Grabowski	22 Carmen D'Aluisio
DNF Jackson Stewart	DNF Joshua Anthony	52 David Fleischauer	29 Christine Vardaros

2004

PRO	U23	JUNIORS	WOMEN
32 Jonathan Page	39 Jeremy Powers	22 Jamey Driscoll	4 Ann Knapp
33 A.Jacques-Maynes	40 Jesse Anthony	39 Konrad Lebas	5 Alison Dunlap
42 Jackson Stewart	41 Matthew White	46 Tucker Thomas	12 Gina Hall
	DNF Alan Obye	50 Adam Switters	14 Rachel Lloyd
	DNF Michael Cody	DNF Andy Brooks	17 Carmen D'Aluisio

2005

PRO	U23	JUNIORS	WOMEN
14 Jonathan Page	18 Jeremy Powers	49 Charles Marzot	7 Ann Knapp
15 Ryan Trebon	32 Jesse Anthony	56 Adam McGrath	19 Sarah Kerlin
30 Barry Wicks	33 Troy Wells	57 Bjorn Selander	24 Josie Beggs
45 Erik Tonkin	45 John Hanson	58 Mitchell Peterson	25 Rhonda Mazza
48 Ben Turner	DNF Matthew White	62 Brady Kappius	26 Barbara Howe

2006

PRO	U23	JUNIORS	WOMEN
10 Jonathan Page	41 Jesse Anthony	7 Bjorn Selander	9 Ann Knapp
33 Barry Wicks	44 Daniel Neyens	19 Danny Summerhill	24 Rhonda Mazza
36 Jeremy Powers	48 Brady Kappius	29 Chance Noble	25 Barbara Howe

48 Erik Tonkin	54 Adam McGrath	35 Alex Howes	33 Christine Vardaros
49 Jonathan Baker	55 Troy Wells	57 Ethan Gilmour	36 Maureen Bruno

2007

PRO	U23	JUNIORS	WOMEN
2 Jonathan Page	36 Jamey Driscoll	2 Danny Summerhill	2 Katie Compton
23 Ryan Trebon	39 Chance Noble	30 Nick Keough	11 Rhonda Mazza
43 Erik Tonkin	46 Daniel Neyens	33 Carson Miller	15 Kerry Barnholt
54 Barry Wicks	47 Charles Marzot	44 Jerome Townsend	32 Deirdre Winfield
57 Tristan Schouten		49 Sean Worsech	33 Christine Vardaros

2008

PRO	U23	JUNIORS	WOMEN
23 Jonathan Page	34 Jamey Driscoll	10 Luke Keough	9 Rachel Lloyd
26 Tim Johnson	43 Nicholas Weighall	32 Gavin Mannion	20 Kerry Barnholt
27 Jeremy Powers	44 Chance Noble	40 Steve Fisher	21 Amy Dombroski
	45 Carson Miller	42 Zach McDonald	22 Susan Butler
		53 Eric Emsky	DNF Katie Compton

2009

PRO	U23	JUNIORS	WOMEN
35 Jeremy Powers	27 Bjorn Selander	13 Luke Keough	3 Katie Compton
44 Matt Shriver	32 Danny Summerhill	19 Zach McDonald	11 Rachel Lloyd
49 Brian Matter	39 Nick Keough	28 Chris Wallace	13 Georgia Gould
52 Jonathan Page	42 William Dugan	30 Gavin Mannion	17 Susan Butler
DNF Ryan Trebon	49 Nicholas Weighall	38 Eric Emsky	19 Lauren Van Gilder

2010

PRO	U23	JUNIORS	WOMEN
14 Tim Johnson	26 Zach McDonald	33 Cody Kaiser	12 Meredith Miller
19 Jamey Driscoll	27 Daniel Summerhill	39 Chris Wallace	14 Amy Dombroski
30 Jonathan Page	32 David Hackworthy	44 Jeffrey Bahnson	23 Maureen Bruno-Roy

| 41 Jeremy Powers | 36 Jerome Townsend | 53 Skyler Trujillo | 31 Laura Van Gilder |
| 50 Ryan Trebon | 42 Luke Keough | 57 Matt Spinks | DNF Katie Compton |

2011

PRO	U23	JUNIORS	WOMEN
12 Jonathan Page	13 Daniel Summerhill	21 Andrew Dillman	2 Katie Compton
16 Jeremy Powers	23 Zach Mc Donald	25 Jeffrey Bahnson	26 Amy Dombroski
27 Jamey Driscoll	36 Cody Kaiser	50 Bjorn Fox	27 Meredith Miller
DNF Tim Johnson	39 Jerome Townsend		30 Kaitlin Antonneau
			DNF Susan Butler

2012

PRO	U23	JUNIORS	WOMEN
18 Ryan Trebon	12 Zach McDonald	14 Andrew Dillman	5 Katie Compton
26 Jeremy Powers	38 Cody Kaiser	17 Logan Owen	19 Nicole Duke
34 Tim Johnson		34 Curtis White	20 Meredith Miller
42 Jamey Driscoll		48 Tobin Ortenblad	23 Amy Dombroski
DNF Jonathan Page		55 Richard Cypress Gorry	26 Kaitlin Antonneau

WORLDKAMPIOENEN

YEAR	VENUE	OPEN/PRO	AMATEURS /ESPOIRS (U23)	JUNIORS	WOMEN
1950	Paris	Jean Robic	-	-	-
1951	Luxembourg	Roger Rondeaux	-	-	-
1952	Genève	Roger Rondeaux	-	-	-
1953	Onate	Roger Rondeaux	-	-	-

1954	Crenna	André Dufraisse	-	-	-
1955	Saarbrücken	André Dufraisse	-	-	-
1956	Luxembourg	André Dufraisse	-	-	-
1957	Edelare	André Dufraisse	-	-	-
1958	Limoges	André Dufraisse	-	-	-
1959	Genève	Renato Longo	-	-	-
1960	Tolosa	Rolf Wolfshohl	-	-	-
1961	Hannover	Rolf Wolfshohl	-	-	-
1962	Esch s. Alzette.	Renato Longo	-	-	-
1963	Calais	Rolf Wolfshohl	-	-	-
1964	Overboelare	Renato Longo	-	-	-
1965	Cavaria	Renato Longo	-	-	-
1966	Beasain	Erik De Vlaeminck	-	-	-
1967	Zürich	Renato Longo	Michel Pelchat	-	-
1968	Luxembourg	Erik De Vlaeminck	Roger De Vlaeminck	-	-
1969	Magstadt	Erik De Vlaeminck	René De Clercq	-	-
1970	Zolder	Erik De Vlaeminck	Robert Vermeire	-	-
1971	Apeldoorn	Erik De Vlaeminck	Robert Vermeire	-	-
1972	Prague	Erik De Vlaeminck	Norbert Dedeckere	-	-
1973	London	Erik De Vlaeminck	Klaus - Peter Thaler	-	-
1974	Vera de Bidasoa	Albert Van Damme	Robert Vermeire	-	-
1975	Melchnau	Roger De Vlaeminck	Robert Vermeire	-	-

1976	Chazay d'Azergues	Albert Zweifel	Klaus - Peter Thaler	-	-
1977	Hannover	Albert Zweifel	Robert Vermeire	-	-
1978	Amorebieta	Albert Zweifel	Roland Liboton	-	-
1979	Saccolongo	Albert Zweifel	Vito Di Tano	José - Inaki Vijandi (1)	-
1980	Wetzikon	Roland Liboton	Fritz Saladin	Radomir Simunek	-
1981	Tolosa	Hennie Stamsnijder	Milos Fisera	Rigobert Matt	-
1982	Lanarvily	Roland Liboton	Milos Fisera	Beat Schumacher	-
1983	Birmingham	Roland Liboton	Radomir Simunek	Roman Kreuziger	-
1984	Oss	Roland Liboton	Radomir Simunek	Ondrej Glajza	-
1985	Munich	Klaus - Peter Thaler	Mike Kluge	Beat Wabel	-
1986	Lembeek	Albert Zweifel	Vito Di Tano	Stuart Marshall	-
1987	Mlada Boleslav	Klaus - Peter Thaler	Mike Kluge	Marc Janssens	-
1988	Hägendorf	Pascal Richard	Karel Camrda	Thomas Frischknecht	-
1989	Pont - Château	Danny De Bie	Ondrej Glajza	Richard Groenendaal	
1990	Getxo	Henk Baars	Andy Büsser	Erik Boezewinkel	-
1991	Gieten	Radomir Simunek	Thomas Frischknecht	Ondrej Lukes	-
1992	Leeds	Mike Kluge	Daniele Pontoni	Roger Hammond	-
1993	Corva	Dominique Arnould	Henrik Djernis	Kamil Ausbuher	
1994	Koksijde	Paul Herygers	-	Gretienus Gommers	-
1995	Eschenbach	Dieter Runkel	Jiri Pospisil (EC)	Zdenek Mlynar	
1996	Montreuil	Adrie van der Poel	Miguel Martinez	Roman Peter	-
1997	Munich	Daniele Pontoni	Sven Nys	David Rusch	-

1998	Middelfart	Mario De Clercq	Sven Nys	Michi Baumgartner	-
1999	Poprad	Mario De Clercq	Bart Wellens	Matt Kelly	-
2000	St. Michiels-gestel	Richard Groenendaal	Bart Wellens	Bart Aernouts	Hanka Kupfernagel
2001	Tabor	Erwin Vervecken	Sven Van-thourenhout	Martin Bina	Hanka Kupfernagel
2002	Zolder	Mario De Clercq	Thijs Verhagen	Kevin Pauwels	Laurence Leboucher
2003	Monopoli	Bart Wellens	Enrico Franzoi	Lars Boom	Daphny v.d Brand
2004	Pont - Château	Bart Wellens	Kevin Pauwels	Niels Albert	Laurence Leboucher
2005	St. Wendel	Sven Nys	Zdenek Stybar	Davide Malacarne	Hanka Kupfernagel
2006	Zeddam	Erwin Vervecken	Zdenek Stybar	Boy van Poppel	Marianne Vos
2007	Hooglede	Erwin Vervecken	Lars Boom	Joeri Adams	Maryline Salvetat
2008	Treviso	Lars Boom	Niels Albert	Arnaud Jouffroy	Hanka Kupfernagel
2009	Hoogerheide	Niels Albert	Philipp Walsleben	Tijmen Eising	Marianne Vos
2010	Tabor	Zdenek Stybar	Arnaud Jouffroy (2)	Tomas Paprstka	Marianne Vos
2011	St. Wendel	Zdenek Stybar	Lars van der Haar	Clément Venturini	Marianne Vos
2012	Koksijde	Niels Albert	Lars van der Haar	Mathieu van der Poel	Marianne Vos

GLOSSARY

à bloc	French. Used to describe an "all out" effort.
barrier	A planked obstacle that is designed to make riders dismount. According to current UCI regulations, barriers can be up to 40 cm tall, and a set of two can be spaced 4-6 meters apart.
BK	Belgian National Championship.
DNF	Did not finish.
domestique	A cyclist who rides in such a way as to benefit a teammate. A domestique may be charged with fetching water bottles, pacing a teammate, and even giving up a wheel in the event of a flat tire. The role of domestique is more prevalent in road racing.
embrocation	Liniment, oil, or cream that is rubbed onto a cyclist's legs. Embrocations are often made up of ingredients such as capsaicin or menthol.
EPO (erythropoietin)	A banned blood-boosting drug.
espoir	A 19-22 year-old cyclist.
Flanders	The northern, Flemish-speaking part of Belgium containing Brussels, Bruges, Ghent, and Antwerp. Most of the important Belgian cyclocross races take place in Flanders.
Flemish	A dialect of Dutch spoken in Flanders.

flick	Noun and verb: to chop, cut off, close the door on, or take advantage of an opposing rider.
fritjes	Fried potato slices, similar to American French fries. In Flanders, there are generally served with mayonnaise. They are a popular snack food at 'cross races.
GVA	Gazet van Antwerpen, a Belgian newspaper and the title sponsor of the GVA Trophy race series, one of three professional cyclocross series in Europe.
helling	Dutch for "hill."
hematocrit	The percentage (by volume) of red blood cells in blood. Suspiciously high hematocrit levels can be a sign of performance enhancing drug use.
hypoxic chamber	A chamber in which athletes breathe reduced-oxygen air to simulate training at altitude.
Kerstperiode	A two-week block of races during the Christmas season. During the Kerstperiode, there is a race almost every day.
kit	A cyclist's uniform. Normally a kit is emblazoned with logos of the cyclist's team or sponsors.
laatse ronde	Flemish/Dutch for "last lap."

motor-pacing	Riding behind a motorized vehicle, normally a scooter, to simulate race speed and intensity. Believed to increase *souplesse* (suppleness).
nieuwelingen	Junior racers, ages 15-16.
off-camber (also adverse camber)	Used to describe a corner wherein the surface slopes away from the direction of the turn. Off-cambers become difficult to traverse when the surface is loose or slick.
palmarès	Victories.
pavé	Road that has been paved with setts or cobblestones.
pit	The area on a cyclocross course where a rider can receive mechanical assistance, change bikes, etc. Pits are generally staffed by the riders' mechanics who are charged with washing and repairing bikes as needed. The pit becomes a busy place during especially muddy races.
radquer	The German word for cyclocross.
rotseason	Literally "rotten season." A period during which a normally successful rider is unable to produce results.
rouleur	French. A rider who is capable of riding at a steady speed for a long time over varying terrain.
RPM	Revolutions per minute.

run-up	A section on a cyclocross course where most riders will be forced to dismount and carry their bike.
soigneur	French. A wearer of many hats, the soigneur may give massage, prepare food, drive riders to and from races, or do anything that a rider needs them to do.
souplesse	French for "suppleness." Used to describe legs that are capable of spinning a gear at a high RPM with a fluid stroke.
Sporza	The main TV sports network in Belgium.
SRM	Schoberer Rad Messtechnik, a crank-based power meter invented by Ulrich Schoberer that measures power output with strain gauges.
la strada biancha	Italian for "the white road" (usually white gravel in Italy).
Superprestige	One of the three professional cyclocross series in Europe.
tubular	A tire that is generally made by sewing a casing around a latex inner tube and then gluing a rubber tread onto the casing. In contrast to clincher tires, which are attached to the rim with a bead and air pressure, tubulars are attached to the rim with glue. The construction and attachment method allow tubulars to be run at lower pressures than clincher tires.
U23	Riders aged 19-22.

UCI	The International Cycling Union, the global governing body of cycling.
U.S.A.C	U.S.A. Cycling, the governing body of cycling in the U.S.A.
USGP	The United States Grand Prix, the top series in the United States.
veldrijden	Flemish/Dutch. Cyclocross.
Volk	Flemish/Dutch. People.
VT4 (now Vier)	A Flemish television channel. The home of *Wellens en Wee,* a reality show about Bart Wellens and Erwin Vervecken that covered three seasons from 2003-2006.
Wallonia	The Southern, French-speaking region of Belgium.
watts/wattage	A unit of power used to describe a cyclist's power output. With the rise of readily-available, lightweight power meters, power has largely replaced heart rate as a cyclist's main training metric.
Wereldkampioen	Flemish/Dutch. World Champion.
Wielrennen	Flemish/Dutch. Bicycle racing.
WK	World Championship.
World Cup	One of three professional cyclocross series in Europe. Run by the UCI, the World Cup is considered by many to be the most prestigious of all the series.

SOURCES

CHAPTER 2

- Csikszentmihalyi, Mihaly. *Flow: The Psychology of Optimal Experience.* New York: Harper & Row, 1990. Print.

- Nys, Sven, and Wendy Galicia. *Ik, Sven Nys.* Gent: Borgerhoff & Lamberigts, 2006. Print.

CHAPTER 3

- *Hell on Wheels.* Dir. Pepe Danquart and Werner Schweizer. Perf. Erik Zabel, Ralf Aldag. 2004. DVD.

- Fries, Richard. "Turning a New Page." *The Ride* Fall 2004: 24-29. Print.

CHAPTER 5

- Maertens, Philippe. *Wellens En Weetjes.* Gent: Borgerhoff & Lamberigts, 2007. Print.

- 5VT4. *Wellens en Wee.* 2003-2006. Television.

- Wellens, Bart. *Open Boek.* Gent: Borgerhoff & Lamberigts, 2008. Print.

CHAPTER 12

- Decaluwé, Brecht. "Ben Berden Finds New Sponsor." *Cyclingnews.com.* N.p., 17 Oct. 2007. Web.

- Jones, Jeff, ed. "HLN Reveals Landuyt Case Dossiers." *Cyclingnews.com.* N.p., 3 Oct. 2005.

- Delaney, Ben. "Q & A: Davis Phinney." *VeloNews* 11 June 2007: 22. Print.

- Whittle, Jeremy. *Bad Blood: The Secret Life of the Tour De France.* London: Yellow Jersey, 2008. Print.

- Alasdair, Fotheringham. "Looking After Number One." *Cycle Sport* Apr. 2002: 156-57. Print.

- "Rondetafel (deel 2): Startgelden." *CycloSprint* Nov. 2007: 10-13. Print.

CHAPTER 13

- Drake, Geoff. "More Running than Riding at CX Worlds." *Velo-news* 14 Mar. 1986: 1+. Print.

CHAPTER 15

- Bassez, Patrick. *Biomechanica Van Het Fietsen,.* Diss. Vlaamse Trainersschool, 1999-2000. N.p.: n.p., n.d. Print

CHAPTER 16

- "Malone Leaps to 32nd in World Championships." *Velo-news* 11 Feb. 1977: 1. Print.

CHAPTER 17

- Boyce, Barry. "The World of Cyclocross." *http://www.cyclingrevealed.com/cyclocross/Intro_CX.htm*. N.p., Jan. 2006. Web.

CHAPTER 20

- Emerson Young, Richard, Alton L. Becker, and Kenneth L Pike. *Rhetoric: Discovery and Change.* New York: Harcourt, Brace & World, 1970. Print.

CHAPTER 22

- Fournel, Paul. *Need for the Bike*. Lincoln: University of Nebraska, 2003. Print.

CHAPTER 24

- Decaluwé, Brecht. "Page Struggles under Sunweb-Projob Pressure." *Cyclingnews.com*. N.p., 19 Nov. 2007. Web.

CHAPTER 25

- Duffy, William. "She Sells Sanctuary." By Ian Astbury. Rec. 1985. Love. The Cult. 1985. Cassette.

CHAPTER 27

- "(Parbo Comments on USGP)." *VeloNews* Nov. 2006: n. pag. Print.

CHAPTER 29

- "Fairytale of New York." *If I Should Fall from Grace with God.* The Pogues. WEA/Rhino, 1987. CD

CHAPTER 30

- Heschel, Abraham Joshua. *God in Search of Man: A Philosophy of Judaism.* New York: Farrar, Straus, Giroux, 1955. Print.

EPILOGUE

- Brooks, David. "The Power of the Particular." *International Herald Tribune* 27 June 2012: n. pag. Print.

APPENDIX

- Delahaije, Louise. *Lars Boom Training Program.* N.p.: n.p., Winter 2007-2008. Excel.

- Vanoverbeek, Didier. *U.S.A. Results at Cyclocross World Championships.* N.p.: n.p., July 2012. Word.

- Vanoverbeek, Didier. *Worldkampioenen* N.p.: n.p., July 2012. Word.

- Babcock, Mark. *Glossary.* N.p.: n.p., Aug. 2012. docx.

- Babcock, Mark. *Map-Belgium.* N.p.: n.p., Aug. 2012. Adobe Illustrator File.